IMAGES of America

CARMEL
A HISTORY IN ARCHITECTURE

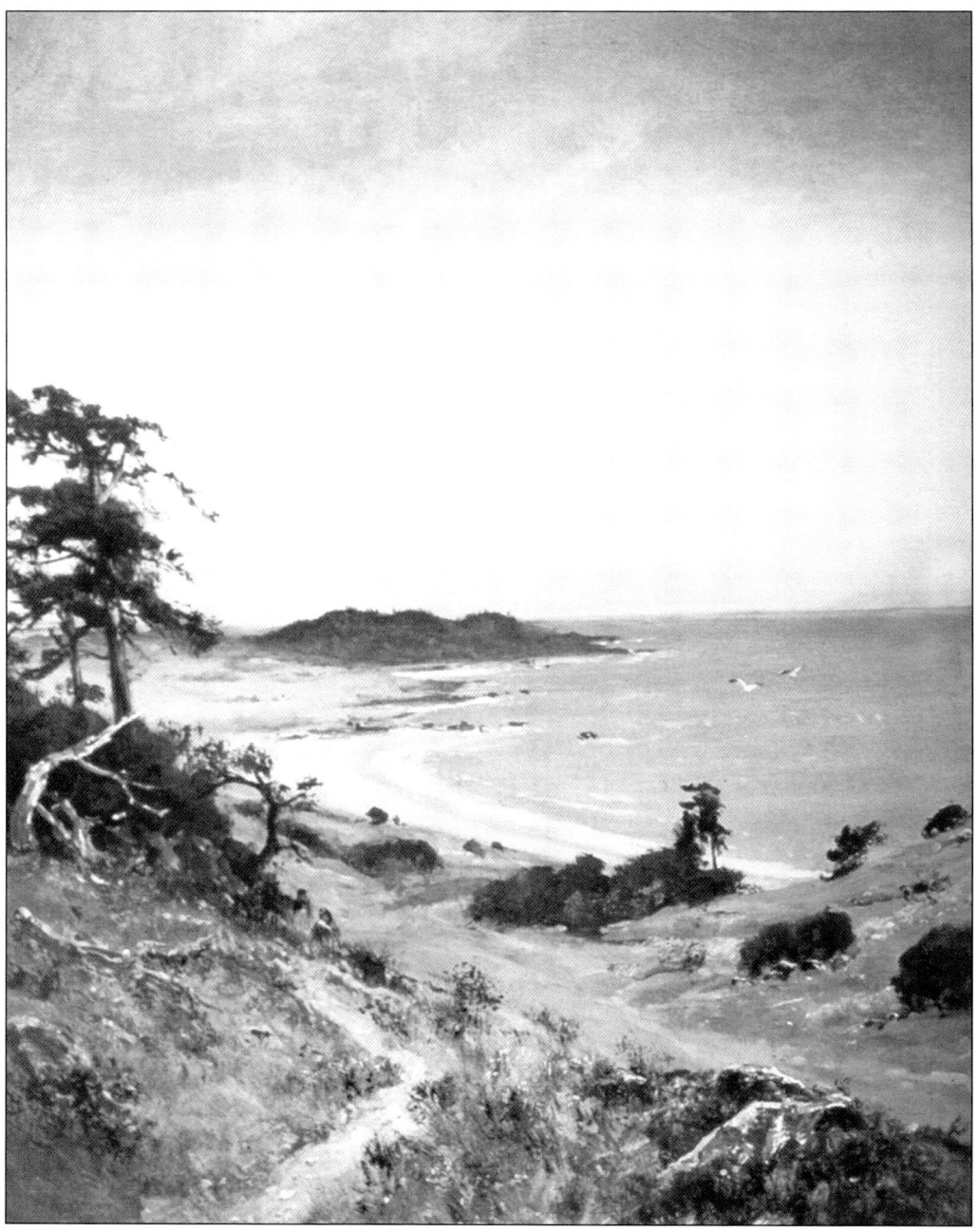

Noted California painter William Keith captured the essence of Carmel's early landscape setting in this bucolic 1893 view. The image was used for the frontispiece of writer Inez Haynes Irwin's book *The Californiacs*, published in San Francisco by A. M. Robertson in 1916. (Photograph from the author's collection.)

ON THE COVER: Contractor Edward Kuster and his wife Ruth check building plans in the Court of the Golden Bough c. 1925. (Photograph courtesy of Pat Hathaway, Historic California Views.)

IMAGES
of America

CARMEL
A HISTORY IN ARCHITECTURE

Kent Seavey

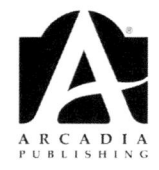

ARCADIA
PUBLISHING

Copyright © 2007 by Kent Seavey
ISBN 978-0-7385-4705-3

Published by Arcadia Publishing
Charleston, South Carolina

Printed in the United States of America

Library of Congress Catalog Card Number: 2006933250

For all general information contact Arcadia Publishing at:
Telephone 843-853-2070
Fax 843-853-0044
E-mail sales@arcadiapublishing.com
For customer service and orders:
Toll-Free 1-888-313-2665

Visit us on the Internet at www.arcadiapublishing.com

For Carmel "Cappy" Martin, friend, mentor, and one of Carmel's finest

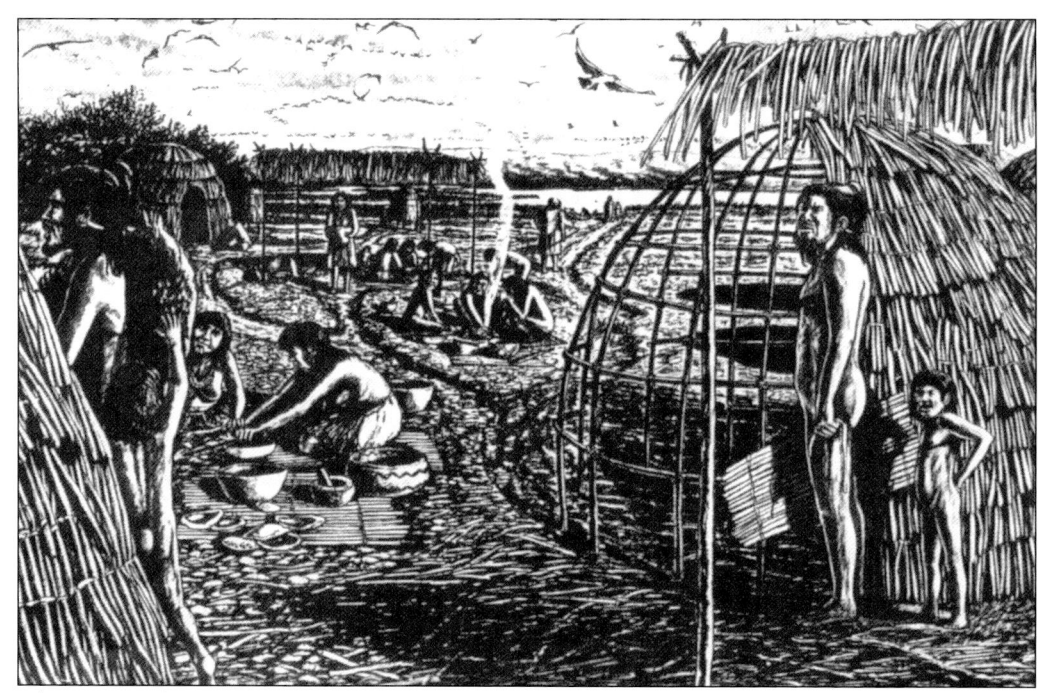

This image of Rumsien-Ohlone village life in California prior to Spanish occupation shows the construct of a typical dwelling. They were conical huts made of bent willow poles stuck in the earth and shaped by horizontal ribbing of the same material. Bundles of tule rush were used for the exterior wall cladding. These living units ranged from 6 to 20 feet in diameter, with a central fire pit. (Drawing by Michael Harney; courtesy of Malcolm Margolin.)

Contents

Acknowledgments		6
Introduction		7
1.	A Mission Establishment	9
2.	Pioneers Oh Pioneers	19
3.	Carmel City	27
4.	Carmel-by-the-Sea	37
5.	Seacoast of Bohemia	47
6.	The Court of the Golden Bough and Beyond	69
7.	In the Mediterranean Mode	97
8.	Carmel Modernism	113

Acknowledgments

The author wishes to express his sincere gratitude and appreciation for the courtesy and kindness afforded him by a number of institutions and individuals in making this small introduction to Carmel's architectural heritage possible. Thanks go first to fellow author Monica Hudson for establishing the context for Carmel's built environment in her Arcadia publication, *Carmel-by-the-Sea*. The Monterey Peninsula has rich repositories of visual information on its past, the best of these being Pat Hathaway's Historic California Views, a veritable cornucopia of local photographic history (www.caviews.com). The Henry Meade Williams Local History Department of the Harrison Memorial Library provided many images and sound professional assistance through two excellent archivists, Denise Sallee and Rose McLendon. Dennis Copeland, historian and archivist at the Monterey Public Library California History Room also provided significant photographs for the publication. Richard Janick, my colleague at Monterey Peninsula College, made available images from the institution's small collection of Morley Baer photographs. The Tor House and Gamble House Foundations also provided important material for the book. Many individuals, particularly those with long association and strong ties to Carmel, were generous in their assistance, as were the families of the architects and builders. Unfortunately space does not permit a full roster of those who provided information and photographs. Particular thanks go to the dream team of Dennis Copeland and Denise Sallee, who keep me honest, and Dr. John Castagna and Bruce Cates, who keep me electronically literate. Lastly I would like to thank the Monterey Bay Chapter of the American Institute of Architects (AIA) for their ongoing efforts to protect and preserve significant buildings in Carmel. Sins of commission and omission are mine alone and exist primarily due to available space.

Introduction

California's chain of Franciscan missions became the economic engine that allowed the Spanish/Mexican province first to survive, then to prosper. There were no architects in the province; the mission fathers became designers and builders. Skilled artisans had to be brought from Mexico both to build and to teach their craft. Master mason Manual Esteban Ruiz and journeyman builder Joaquin Rivera spent several years working on the mission church San Carlos de Borromeo.

The Mexican government secularized the Alta California missions in the 1830s, initiating their rapid decline. The stone church languished until 1884, when efforts began to protect the historic building. These activities continued intermittently until the early 1930s, when a San Francisco cabinetmaker named Harry Downie began restoring and reconstructing Mission San Carlos.

The California Gold Rush saw an influx of Americans and other nationalities to the Carmelo District that included dairymen, farmers, and shore whalers. They brought with them the traditional building practices of their places of origin and constructed their new homes in redwood, available at hand, and from dimensional lumber milled in San Francisco. As they prospered, they improved their properties to reflect their social status. Most design improvements came from builders' pattern books, available from lumberyards and planing mills that developed in Monterey in the late 1870s.

At that time, with impetus from the successes of the Hotel del Monte and the Pacific Grove Retreat, real estate entrepreneurs, expecting an extension of the Southern Pacific Railroad to the Carmel River, began mapping out and promoting "Carmel City" as a seaside resort for Catholics. They emphasized the presence of historic Mission San Carlos to draw interest. Many lots were sold, but few residences or commercial enterprises were established before the project suffered from the economic depression of the early 1890s.

In 1902, two very different men—Franklin Powers, a San Francisco attorney, and Franklin Devendorf, a professional real estate broker—joined forces in the Carmel Development Company, promoting the locale's physical beauty and salubrious climate and offering very reasonable rates for land purchase and payment. They encouraged "School Teachers and Brain Workers" as well as creative artists of all types to populate the newly named Carmel-by-the-Sea. A small group of Western false-fronted business houses were built on Ocean Avenue, establishing it as the commercial core of the fledgling community.

The 1906 San Francisco earthquake and fire kick-started the artists' colony. There was a rapid influx of creative and independent people. Many constructed their own homes, most in the woodsy arts and crafts mode. The style employed natural materials, expressing their structure and respect for the landscape setting. It used an open plan connecting the indoors and outdoors, which was perfectly suited to Carmel's physical setting. It became the style of choice well into the 1920s and beyond. Many of the builders were women.

By 1916, it was clear to Carmel's residents that Monterey County could not provide the necessary land-use controls to protect the emerging community's unique character and natural beauty. An election was held that year to establish a city government. Once formed, two political factions emerged, the art interests and the business interests. They continue to the present, as opposing forces in the ongoing development of the community. A product of this conflict was a 1929 zoning law, still in effect, stating that business development should forever be subordinate to the residential character of the community.

During the 1920s, the introduction of romantic revival Tudor and Spanish Eclectic architectural forms were embraced with equal enthusiasm by both the business and art interests in the village. The downtown today is most reflective of this period of picturesque development, which continues to account for much of Carmel's architectural character. This period of economic growth and expansion saw an influx of well-known California architects, whose professional designs and building methods were not lost on Carmel's builders. Local talent was abundant. Lee Gottfried reintroduced Carmel stone as an indigenous building material, and Hugh Comstock created his highly popular "Fairy Tale" cottages, which are still being emulated today.

The Depression slowed building in Carmel. However, civic improvements like the Sunset School and auditorium and a new fire station were constructed without any concession to the high standards of design quality the community had come to expect. William W. Wurster introduced the village to his "soft modernism," a generational extension of San Francisco Bay Area regionalism. Comstock and others worked in the Western ranch style. The 1930s and 1940s saw an influx of innovative young architects and building designers. All employed elements from both traditional European and American modernism to create primarily residential designs that continue to fit seamlessly into the Carmel landscape. American master Frank Lloyd Wright's Walker House at Carmel Point is the paradigm of this movement.

During the 1950s and 1960s, the Carmel offices of Robert Stanton and Robert Jones acted as conduits for yet another generation of the architects and designers who have left their mark on the evolving visual character of community. Fortunately a few more recent arrivals continue to learn from the past, helping to maintain the unique architectural expression that is Carmel-by-the-Sea.

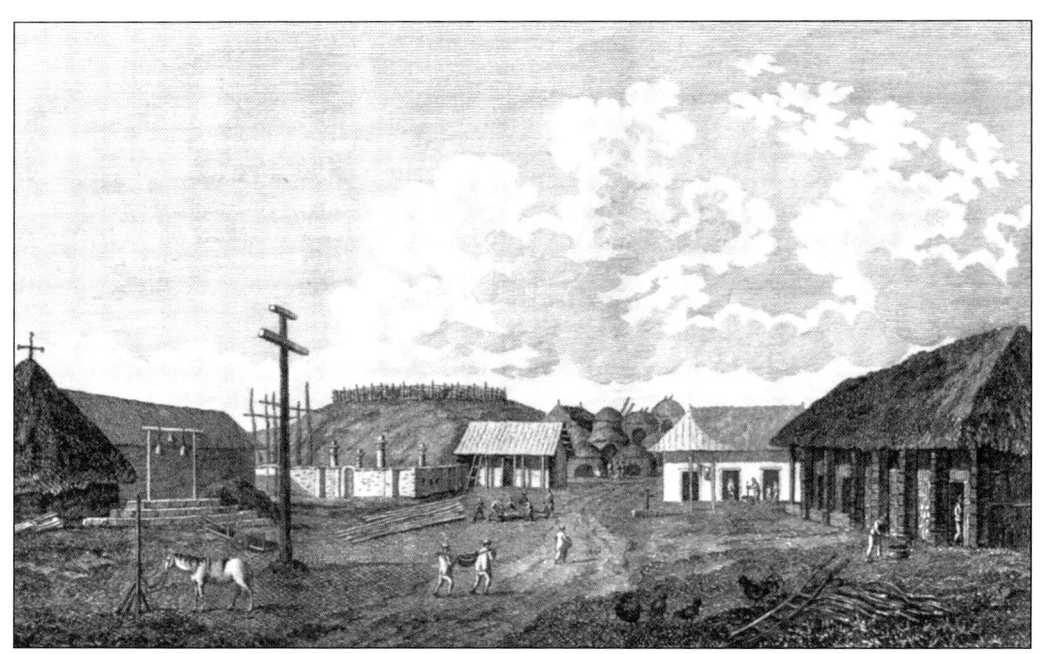

In 1794, artist John Sykes, with the British Vancouver expedition, provided the first view of the stone church in construction at Mission San Carlos. (Photograph courtesy of the Monterey Public Library, California History Room Archives.)

One

A Mission Establishment

Building a mission was not easy. At the outset, two priests and a few soldiers had to fabricate the initial structures with rude tools from the natural materials at hand. As native peoples were brought into the system, they required training before they could become an effective workforce. Skilled artisans were imported from Mexico for some of this work, as well as design and construction of the more significant buildings, particularly stone churches. Mission San Carlos was a work in progress from 1771 to 1815, when the quadrangle was finally enclosed. When secularization was imposed in the 1830s, the missions declined rapidly without the neophyte workforce needed to maintain them. Civil administrators sold the buildings not held by the church for salvage. Recognition of the missions as a significant cultural resource did not begin until the 1880s, and then only slowly. Rehabilitation and reconstruction of San Carlos was facilitated in the 1930s by an active fund-raising group and the skill and dedication of a lay Franciscan builder, Harry Downie, whose lifework became the preservation of California's earliest European buildings.

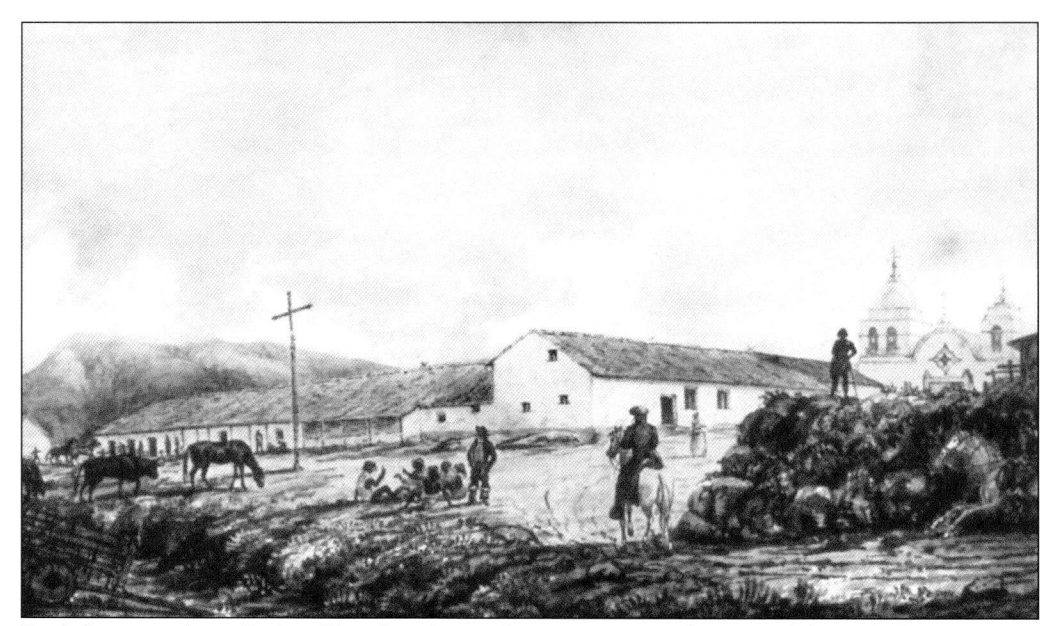

English watercolorist Richard Beechey depicted Mission San Carlos toward the end of its prosperity in 1827. The mission church, dedicated in 1797, is visible to the right. The priest's quarters, guest rooms, and guardhouse occupy the tile-roofed adobe buildings enclosing the quadrangle to the left. (Photograph courtesy of the Monterey Public Library, California History Room Archives.)

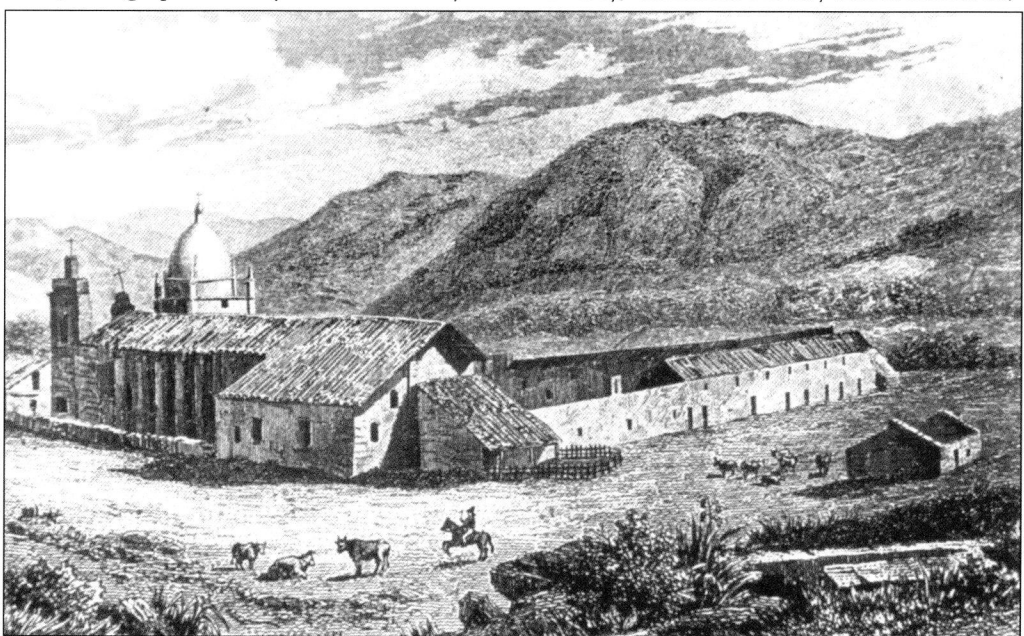

Secularization of the Alta California mission chain began in earnest toward the mid-1830s. Mission San Carlos was one of the first turned over to civilian administration. The rapid decline of the mission can readily be seen in this engraving of an 1839 watercolor by Francois Edmund Paris, artist with the French Laplace expedition. (Photograph courtesy of the Monterey Public Library, California History Room Archives.)

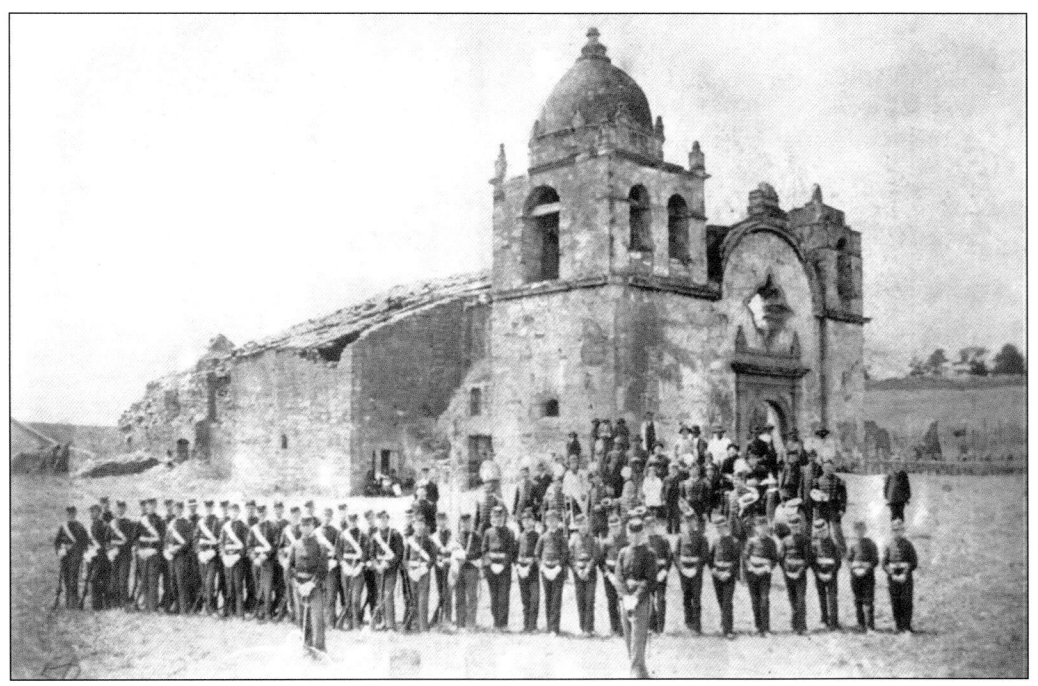

Members of San Francisco's St. Patrick's Cadets form an honor guard at the opening of Fr. Junipero Serra's grave on July 3, 1882. The parish priest, Fr. Angel Casanova, raised enough funds to clear the sanctuary floor and reinter the remains of the Franciscan founders of San Carlos. This was the first step in the physical rehabilitation of the mission. (Photograph by C. W. J. Johnson; courtesy of the Monterey Public Library, California History Room Archives.)

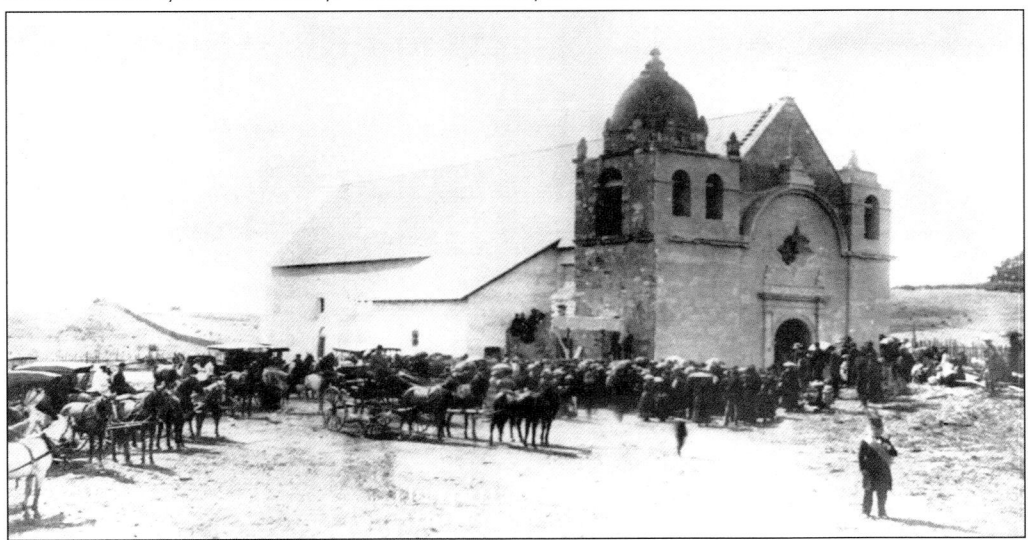

Fr. Angel Casanova spent the year seeking funds for the full restoration of the mission church. It is seen during its rededication on August 28, 1884, the 100th anniversary of Father Serra's death. Unfortunately the new wood-shingled roof was almost 20 feet higher than the tiled original, considerably compromising the building's historic character. (Photograph by C. W. J. Johnson; courtesy of the Monterey Public Library, California History Room Archives.)

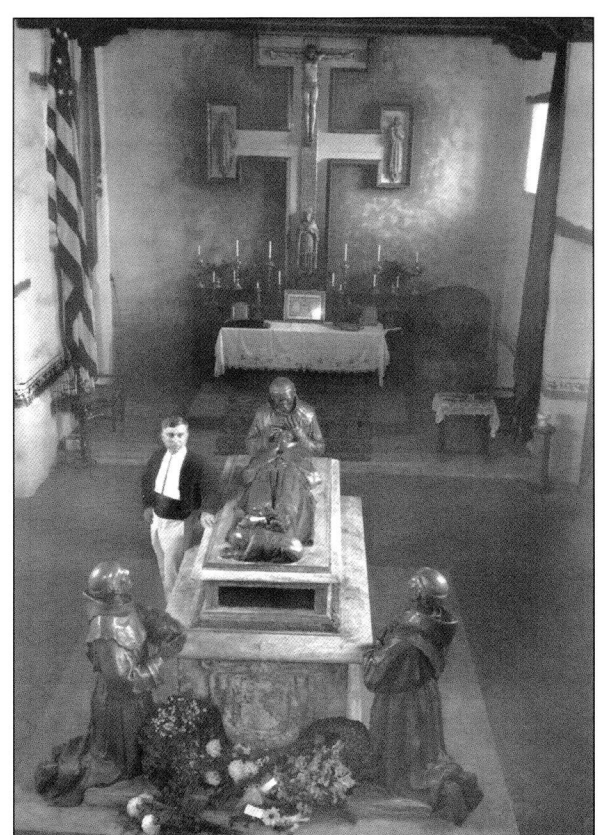

In 1924, artist-architect Jo Mora poses beside his recently completed bronze-and-travertine memorial cenotaph for Fr. Junipero Serra in the small chapel he designed on the south side of the mission church facade. The artist also created the large wooden cross behind the altar. Mora designed a small building on the north side of the church as a residence for priests. (Photograph by Lewis Josselyn; courtesy of Pat Hathaway, Historic California Views.)

Seen here c. 1936, Henry J. Downie was a cabinetmaker with the firm of A. T. Hunt in San Francisco specializing in reproduction Spanish furniture. In 1931, the cabinetmaker began repairing religious statues for the Catholic diocese in Monterey. Downie continued this work at the Carmel Mission, where he remained for nearly 30 years, becoming a preeminent authority on the restoration of California's missions. (Photograph by T. C. Smith; courtesy of Pat Hathaway, Historic California Views.)

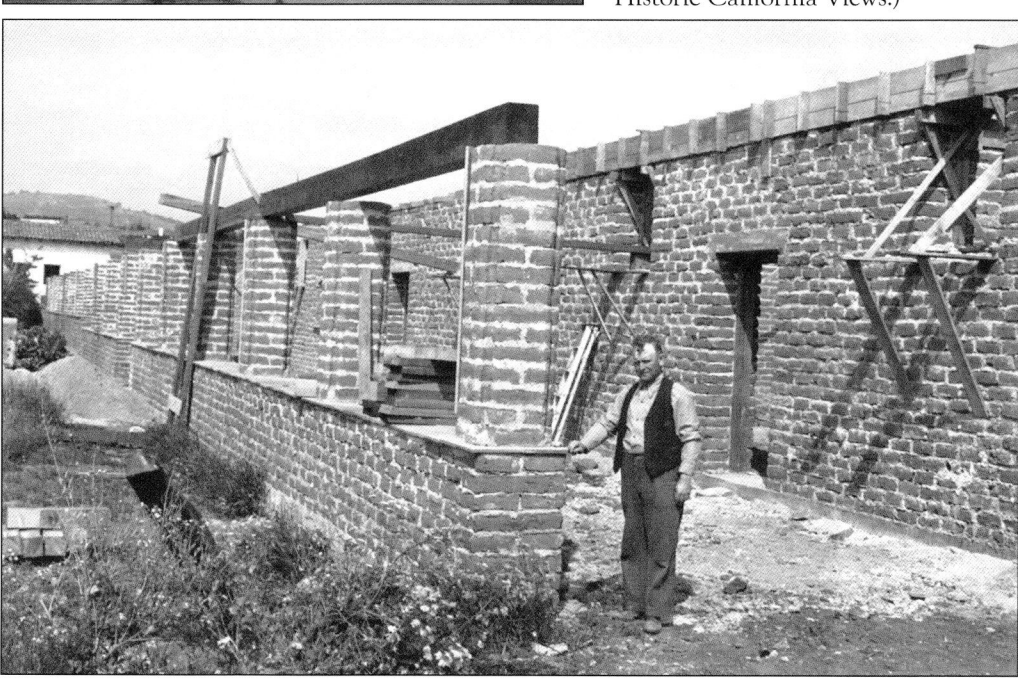

One of the first jobs of the Carmel Restoration Committee when established in 1935 was to raise funds for rebuilding the church roof. Father Casanova's steep 1884 gable was pulling away from the roof structure. Workers, seen above in 1936, are erecting scaffolding in preparation for new wooden ceiling arches approximating the original 1790s design. (Photograph by Lewis Josselyn; courtesy of Pat Hathaway, Historic California Views.)

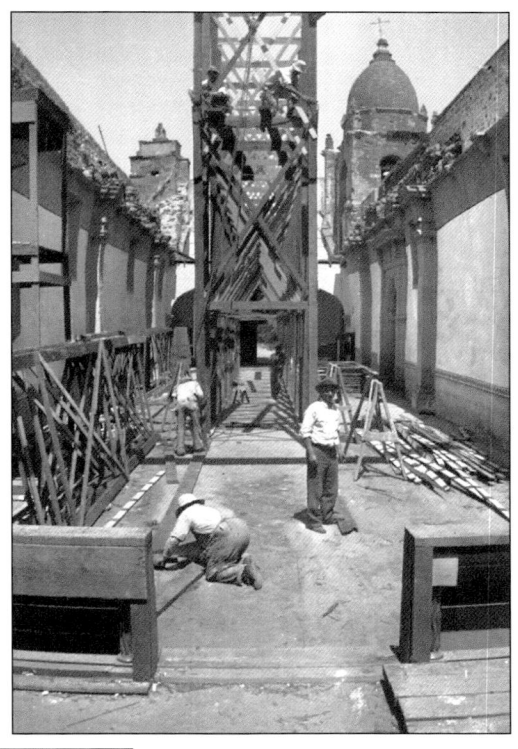

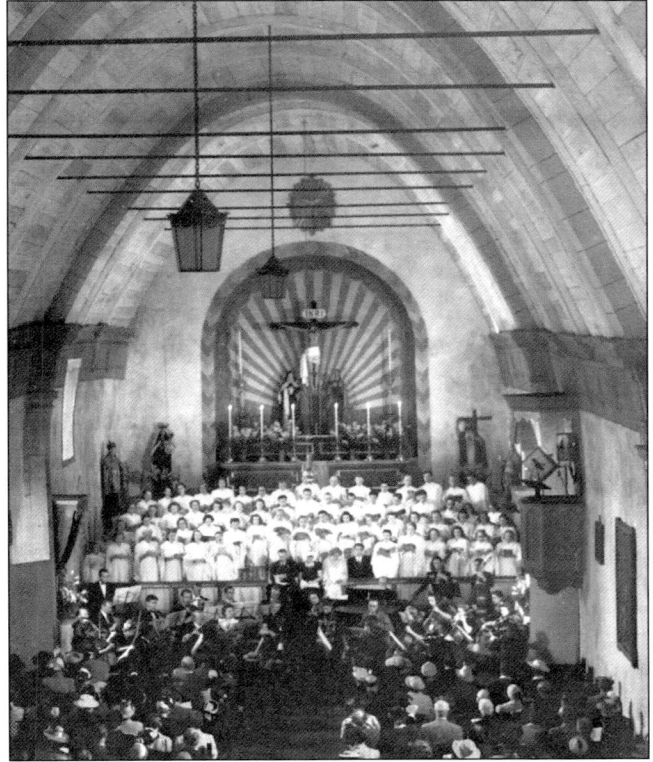

Members of the Bach Festival Orchestra and Chorus rehearse before a live audience in 1954 under the restored catenary arched ceiling of redwood planking resting on wooden arches. The roof system is held in tension by steel tie rods. In 1957, Sir Harry Downie replaced the painted altar screen seen at left with a carved and polychromed reredos he fabricated in the style of the one found at Mission Dolores in San Francisco. (Photograph courtesy of the Harrison Memorial Library Collection.)

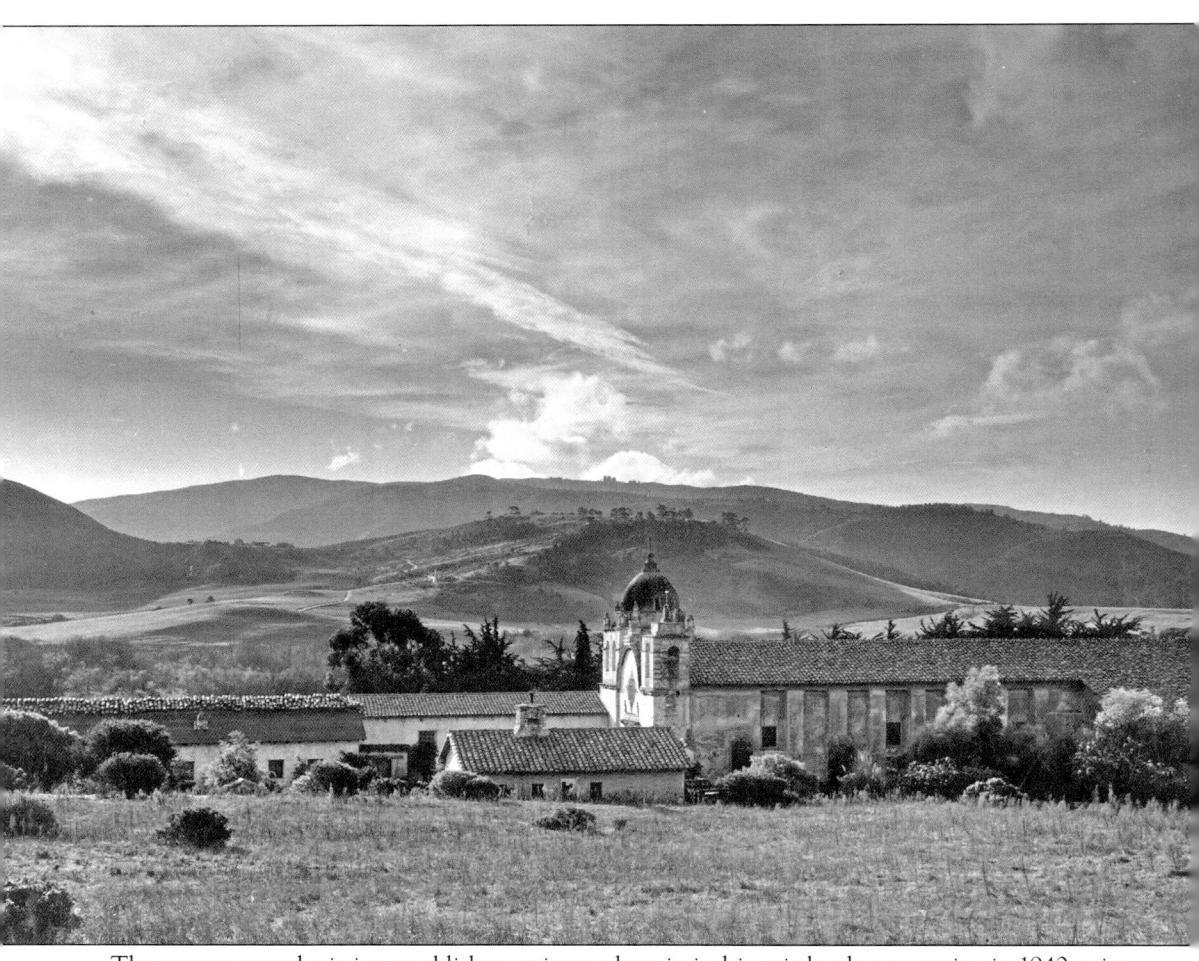

The reconstructed mission establishment is seen here in its historic landscape setting in 1940, prior to encroachment by residential development. California author Helen Hunt Jackson encouraged the preservation of the missions in her 1902 book, *Glimpses of California and the Missions*. In it she noted that San Carlos "was perhaps the most beautiful, though not the grandest of the mission churches. . . . The fine yellow tint of the stone, the grand unique contour of the arches, the beautiful star-shaped window in the front, the simple yet effective lines of carving on pilaster and pillar and doorway, the symmetrical Moorish tower and dome, the worn steps leading up to the belfry—all make a picture whose beauty, apart from hallowing associations, is enough to hold one spell-bound." (Photograph by Sybil Anekeyev; courtesy of the Monterey Public Library, California History Room Archives.)

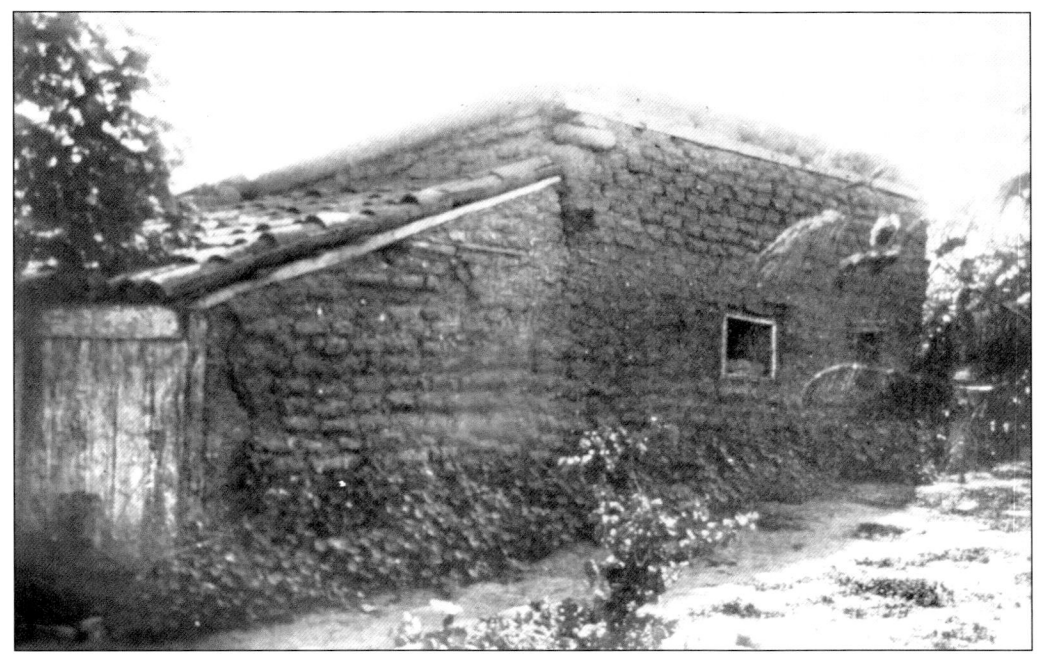

Fr. Francisco Palou planted an orchard and kitchen garden between the mission and the Carmel River in 1774, enclosing it with an adobe wall. An adobe lean-to was incorporated into the wall to house the orchardist. The building was modified in the 1870s and expanded in 1920 and again by Sir Harry Downie in the 1940s. Still occupied as a residence, the home is the oldest residential dwelling house in California. (Photograph courtesy of the Thomas Fordham Collection.)

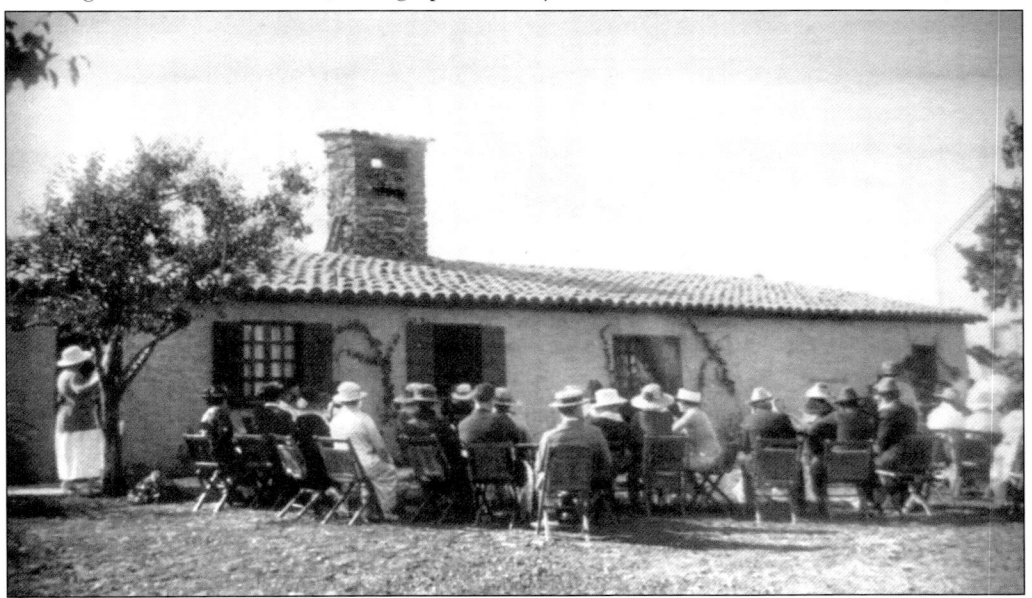

In 1920, Claribel Haydock Zuck rehabilitated and expanded the Pear Orchard House for commercial use. The following year, Monterey stonemason Juan Martoral added the fieldstone chimney. The refurbished building soon became a favorite dining spot, the Mission Tea House. (Photograph by L. S. Slevin; courtesy of Pat Hathaway, Historic California Views.)

MISSION TEA HOUSE

Near Mission Carmelo

Luncheon
12:30 to 2

Tea
3 to 5

Chicken Dinner
6 to 8

Dancing   Phone 907 W-4

Special Spanish Dinner served by appointment

In 1924, Clarabel Haydock Zuck and Mary M. Smith convinced Fr. Raymond Mestres to sell them the newly refurbished Pear Orchard House for restaurant use. Their Mission Tea House is still remembered by early Carmelites for its enchilada dinners and weekend tea dances. The popular dining spot fell on hard times at the onset of the Great Depression and had to be sold. (Advertisement from the *Carmel Pine Cone*, September 27, 1924.)

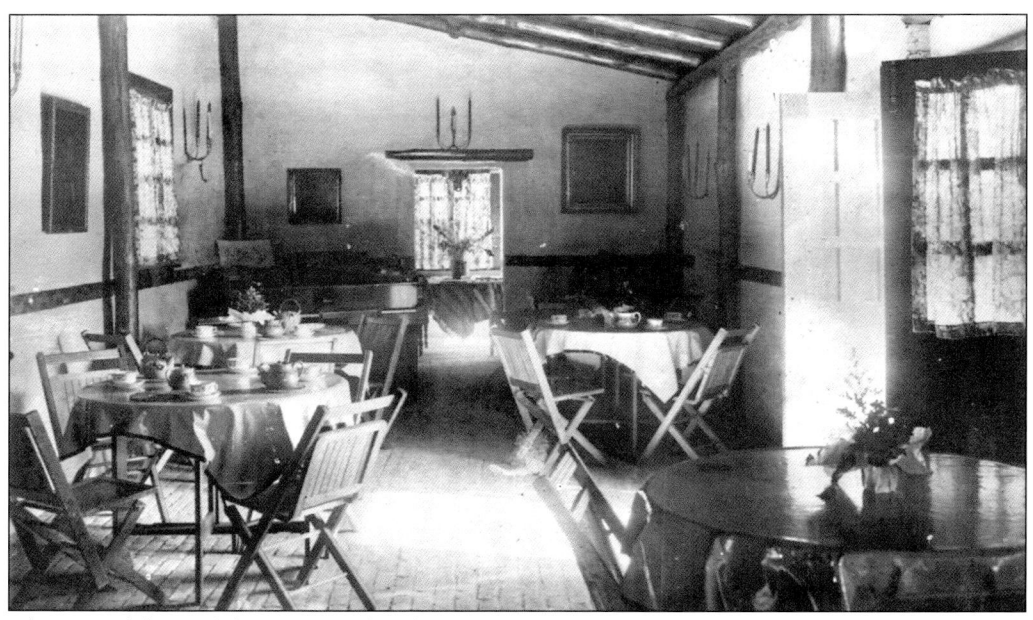

The remodeling of the Pear Orchard House c. 1921 included, in addition to the large stone fireplace, repair and replacement of the existing roof supports and tiles, a new brick floor, access doors for the garden patio, and replastering. Candlelight from simple wall sconces illuminated the interior. The kitchen and public bathroom were in the adjacent Machado House. (Photograph by L. S. Slevin; courtesy of Pat Hathaway, Historic California Views.)

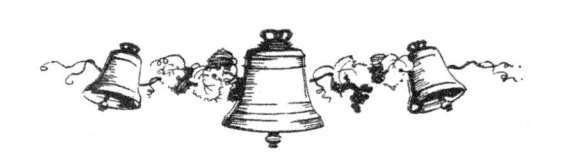

Portuguese-born shore whaler Christiano Machado served as the mission caretaker and orchardist from the 1870s to 1907, adding 200 new trees to the orchard during his tenure. He and his family lived in the Pear Orchard House until 1881, when the adjacent two-story, wood-frame house was completed. He is seen in 1909 next to the church bell tower holding the mission keys. (Photograph courtesy of Pat Hathaway, Historic California Views.)

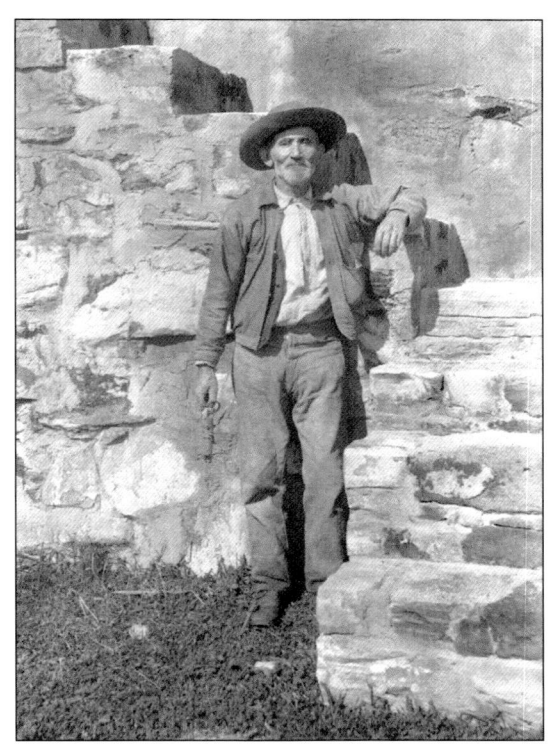

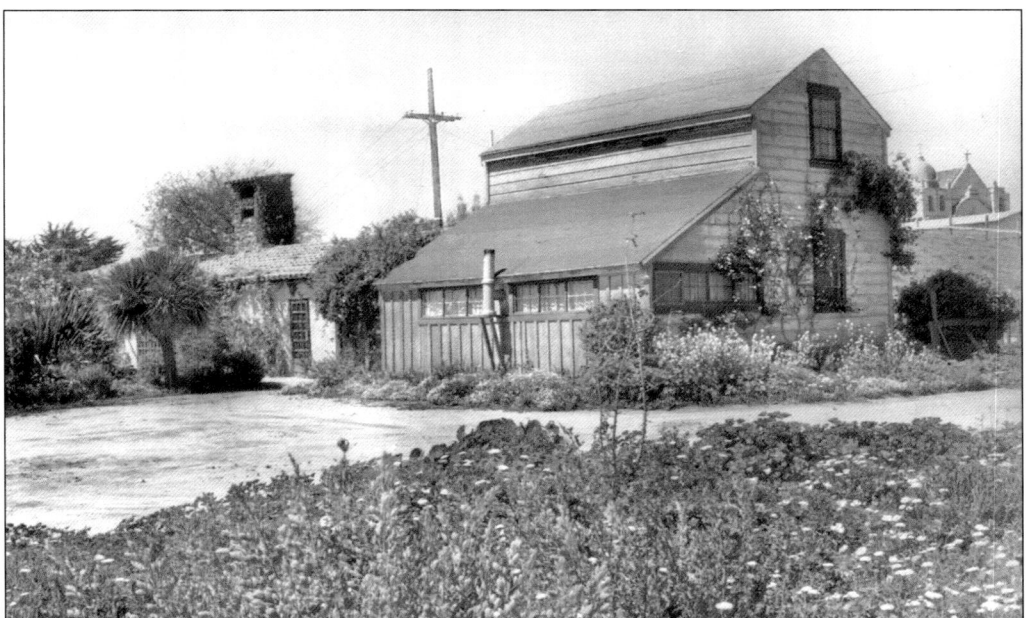

Known as the Machado-Tevis House, two Portuguese whalers from the Point Lobos shore whaling station, Christiano Machado and Antoine Victorine, built this barnlike vernacular residence in 1881. The redwood construction material had to be dropped overboard and floated ashore from a lumber ship off Carmel Beach. Machado and his family farmed the place for nearly 40 years. (Photograph by Lewis Josselyn; courtesy of Pat Hathaway, Historic California Views.)

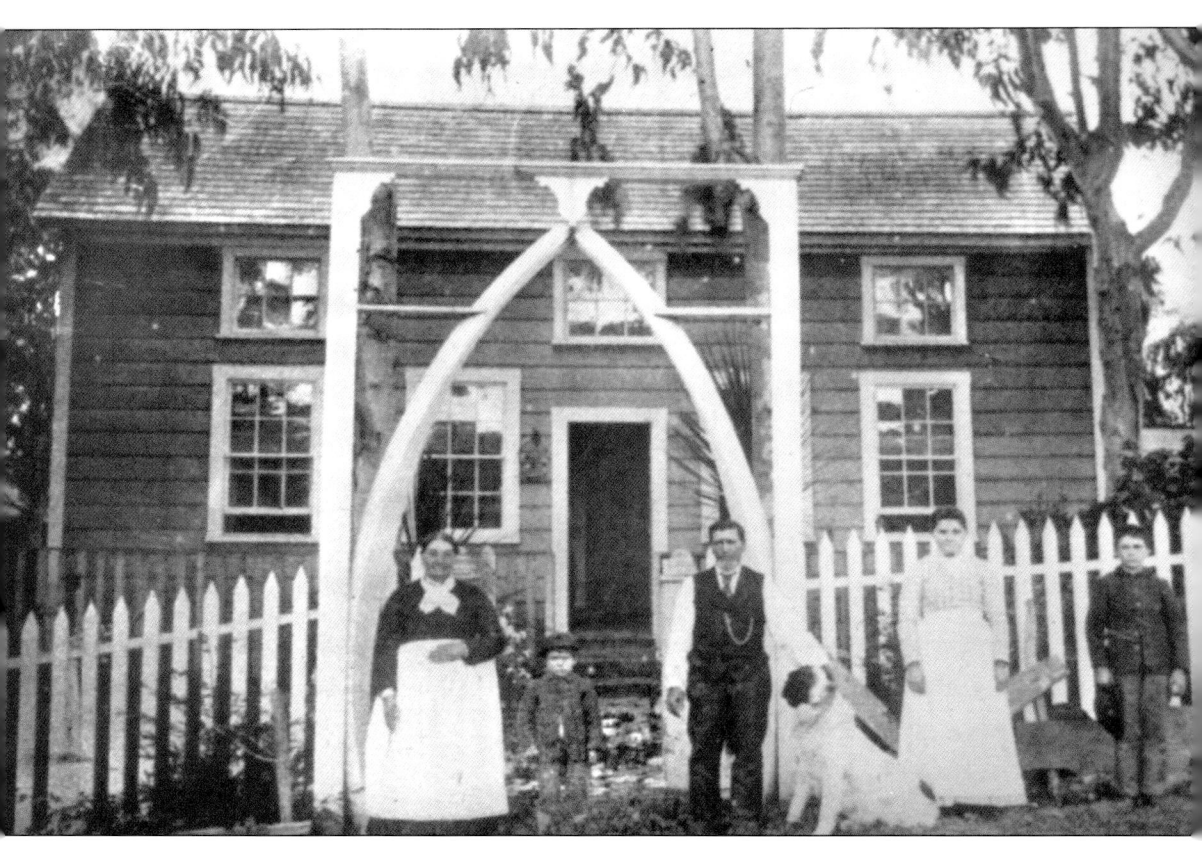

Antoine Victorine, his wife Maria, and their family are framed by the unique whalebone gate and white-picket fence fronting their New England saltbox–style house at San Jose Creek in the Carmelo District. Victorine built the wood-framed residence in 1879. A blue-water whaler from the Azores, Victorine was a member of the Carmel Whaling Company at Point Lobos. He ran his dairy operation in the off-season. (Photograph courtesy of Walter Victorine.)

Two
Pioneers Oh Pioneers

Building construction in Carmel in the post–Gold Rush era saw an immediate transition from the use of masonry to wood. This came first in the form of locally hewn log structures, like Matthew Murphy's cow barn. Building design was based on necessity and regionally remembered house forms. Some early lumber was shipped from San Francisco, like that used in the Machado home near Mission Carmelo. This lumber had to be off-loaded from a coastal steamer beyond the surf line and allowed to drift ashore. By the late 1870s, Lambert and Snively's Lumber Yard in Monterey was able to provide plenty of dimensional lumber for the John Martin, William Hatton, and Antoine Victorine dairy farms.

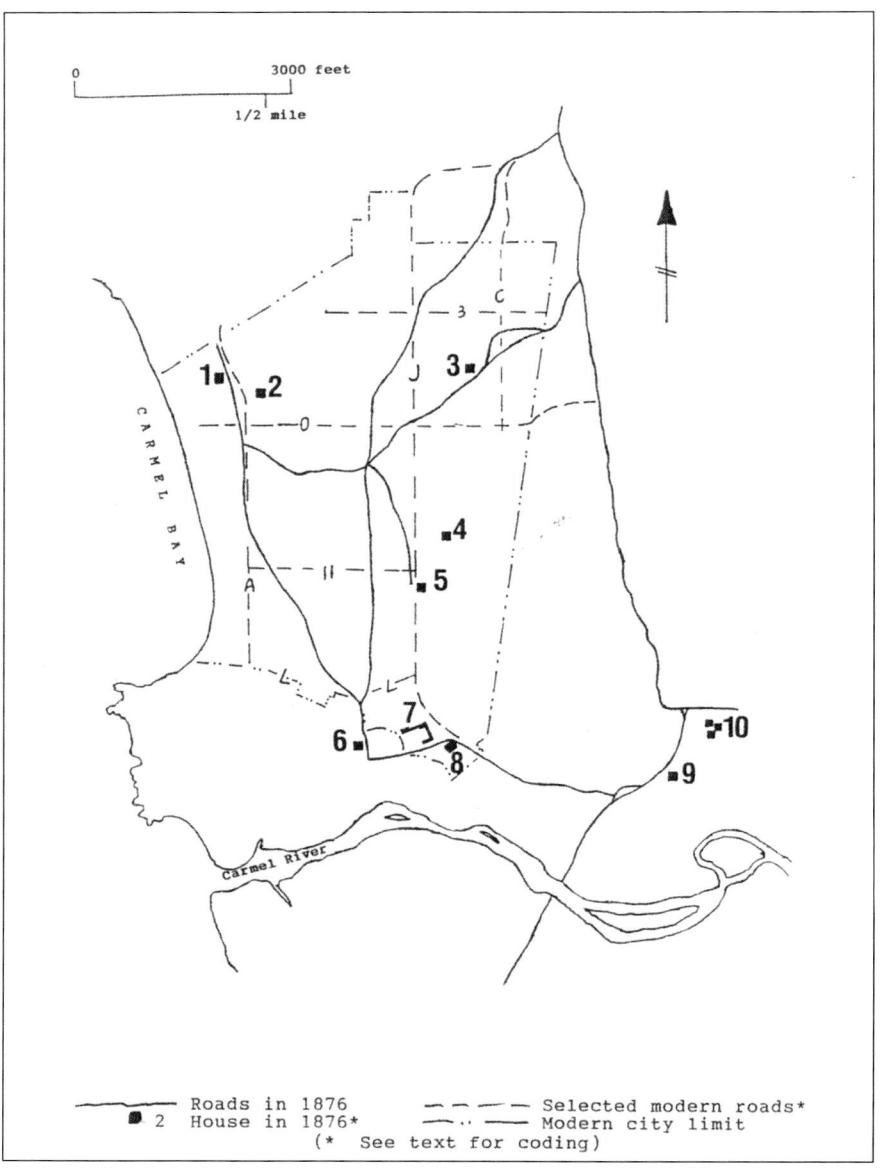

Geologist John Logan created this map of early Carmel in the 1980s. House No. 1 was built by Matthew M. Murphy, a Boston sea captain, c. 1849; No. 2 was owned by another Irishman, Patrick H. Sheridan, who came to California c. 1863; No. 3 was the cabin of Honore Escolle, a Frenchman who settled in Monterey in 1852 and later purchased the Las Manzanitas rancho; No. 4 is the house of John Foreman; No. 5 is unidentified: No. 6 belonged to Scottish-born John and Robert Martin, who established their Mission Ranch in 1859; No. 7 is Mission San Carlos, founded by Junipero Serra in 1771; No. 8 is Portuguese whaler Christiano Machado's house, built in 1881; No. 9 is the residence of Dominga Doni de Atherton, wife of Faxon D. Atherton, built in 1869; No. 10 is Irishman William Hatton's dairy, leased from Dominga Atherton in 1888 and purchased in 1892. Not shown are the homes of Virginia-born farmer Joseph W. Gregg and Portuguese whalers John V. Silva and Antoine Victorine just south of the Carmel River. (Map courtesy of the Logan family.)

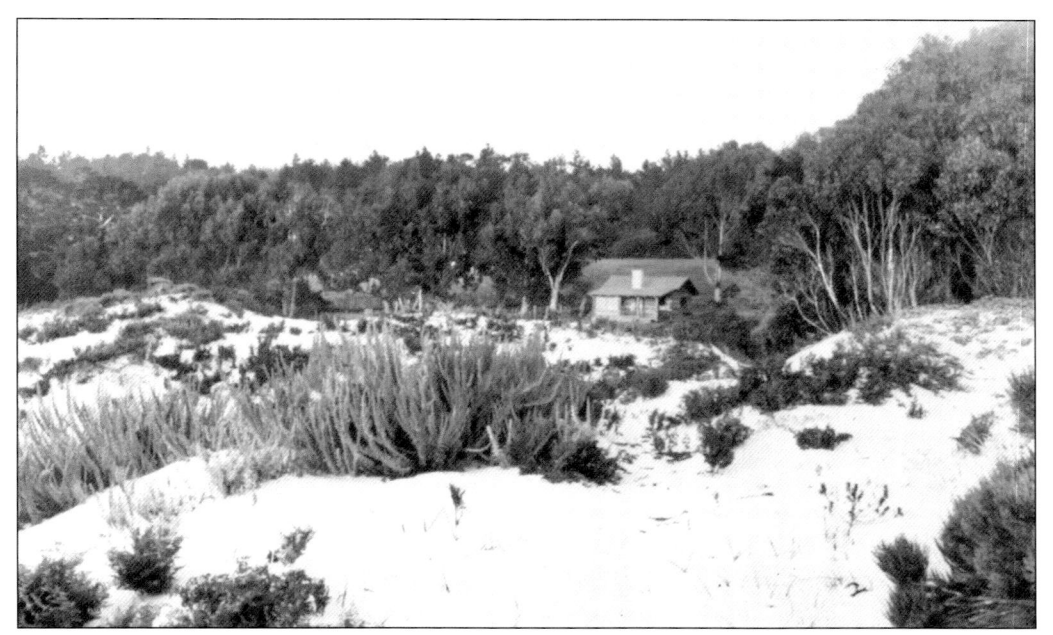

Seen c. 1905, Matthew M. Murphy constructed this single-pen, hewn-V-notch log barn in the sand dunes above Carmel Beach about 1846. The pioneer settler was a sea captain from Boston. His nephew John Monroe Murphy and John's wife, Ann, ran a dairy from the place in the late 1860s. Ann leased the property for sand mining in 1901. Frank Powers, one of the founding developers of Carmel-by-the-Sea purchased the 9.2-acre site in 1904. (Photograph courtesy of the Fassett family archives.)

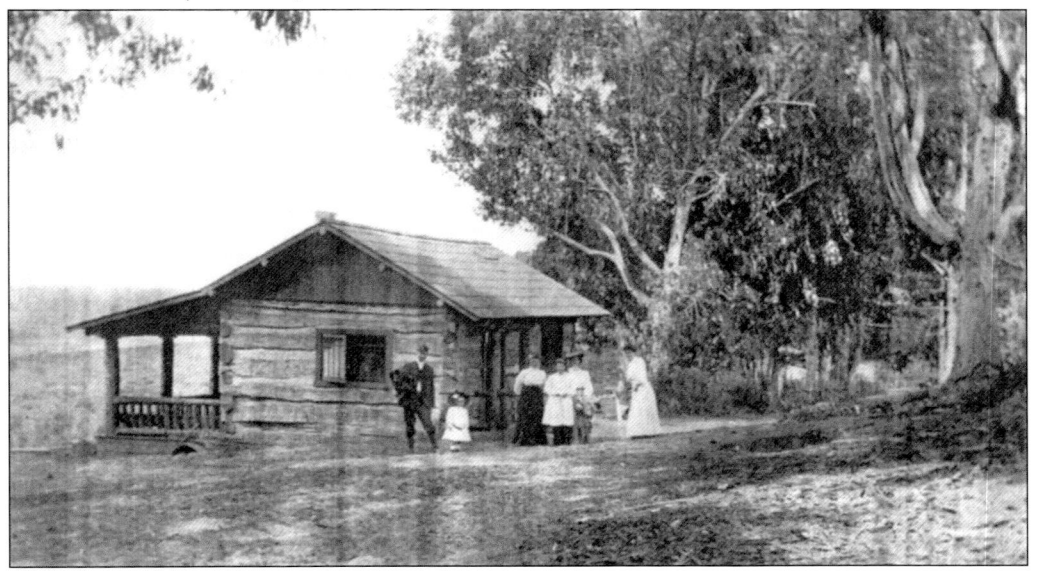

Frank Power's wife, Jane Gallatin Powers (far right), was a European-trained fine artist. She transformed the Murphy log barn into a painting studio and salon, where she entertained her many friends from San Francisco's bohemian art community. She was a strong influence in the promotion of Carmel as a colony for artists and helped establish the sense of individualism and creativity associated with the village. (Photograph courtesy of the Fassett family archives.)

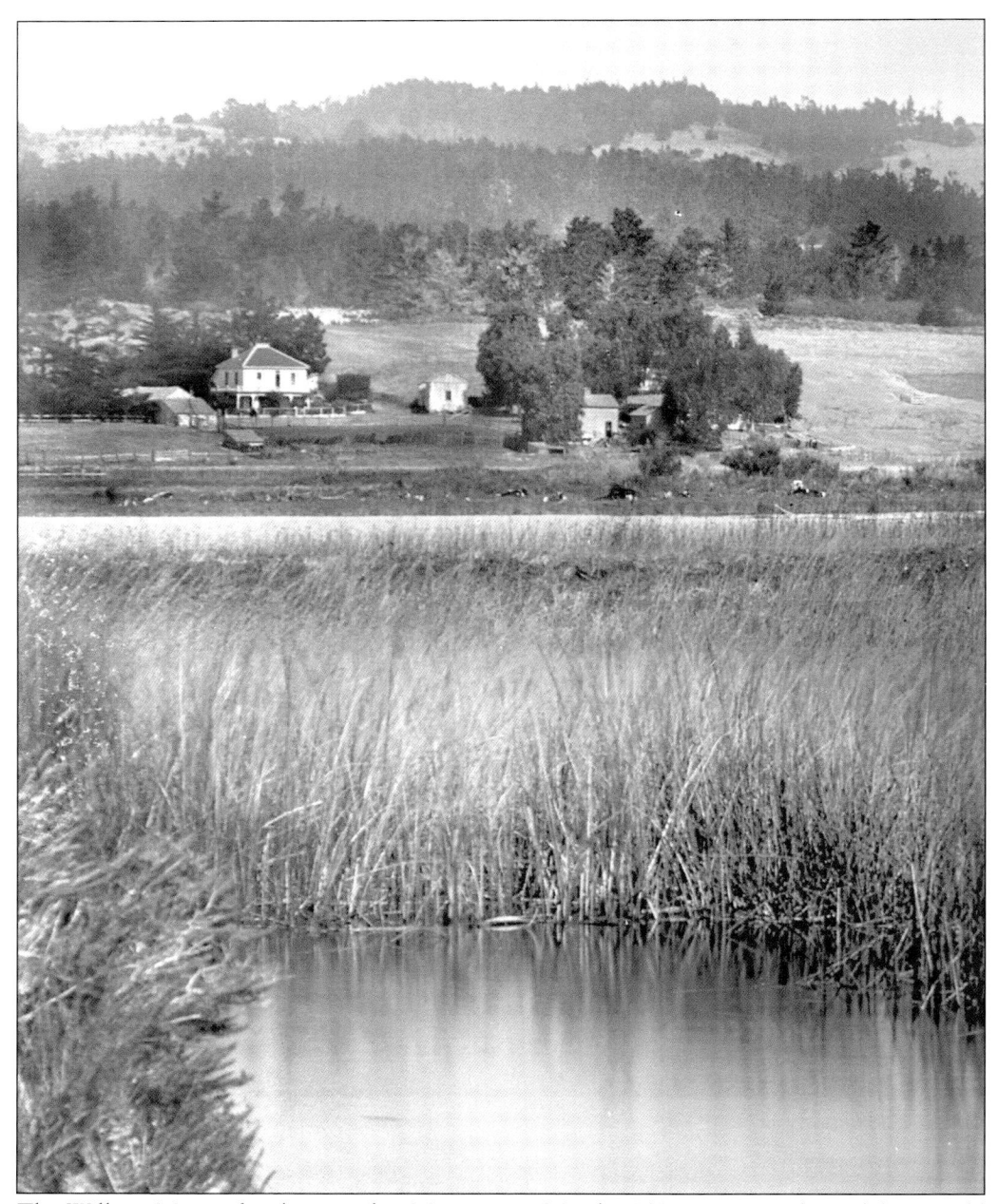

The William Martin family arrived in Monterey in March 1856 en route to the California gold fields. The elder Martin and his five sons liked what they saw and remained. First leasing, then buying the fertile land around the mouths of the Pajaro, Salinas, and, Carmel Rivers, the family struck gold in growing potatoes for the Sierra miners. John Martin, the eldest son and a trained cabinetmaker, purchased the land at the mouth of the Carmel River in 1859. John built up the Mission Ranch, seen here c. 1900, as a dairy and dry-farming operation in the 1860s. (Photograph by Lewis Josslyn; courtesy of Pat Hathaway, Historic California Views.)

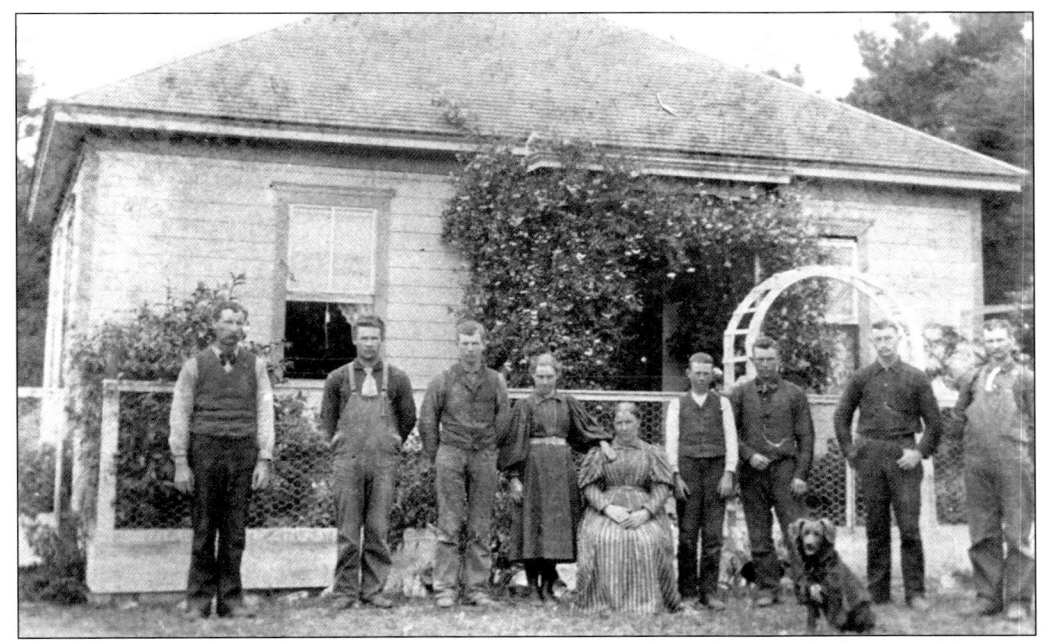

John Martin built this vernacular hipped-roof cottage in the early 1870s for his wife, Elizabeth Stewart (seated), and her three sons. They operated a dairy and raised potatoes and barley. The ranch consisted of barns, a bunkhouse, and several outbuildings. The Martin and Stewart surnames are closely associated with a number of Carmel Valley place-names. (Photograph courtesy of the Mission Ranch Resort.)

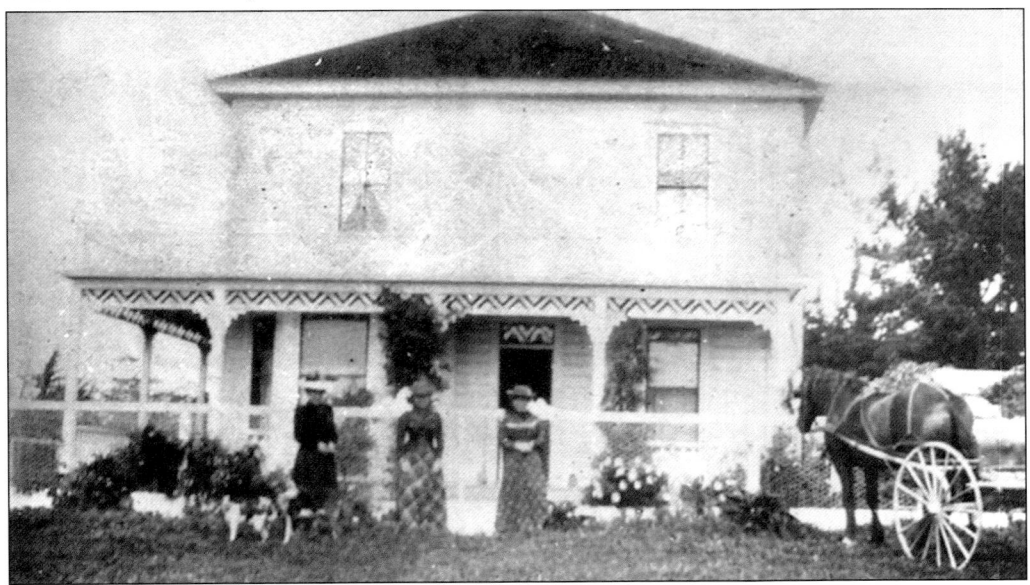

An expedient method for providing more living space was to simply raise an existing residence and frame in new rooms under it. The addition of an open veranda with sawn decorative trim was an indicator of increased prosperity. This farmhouse, seen c. 1896, is still present and is used for visitor accommodation at Clint Eastwood's Mission Ranch Resort. (Photograph courtesy of Marsha DeVoe.)

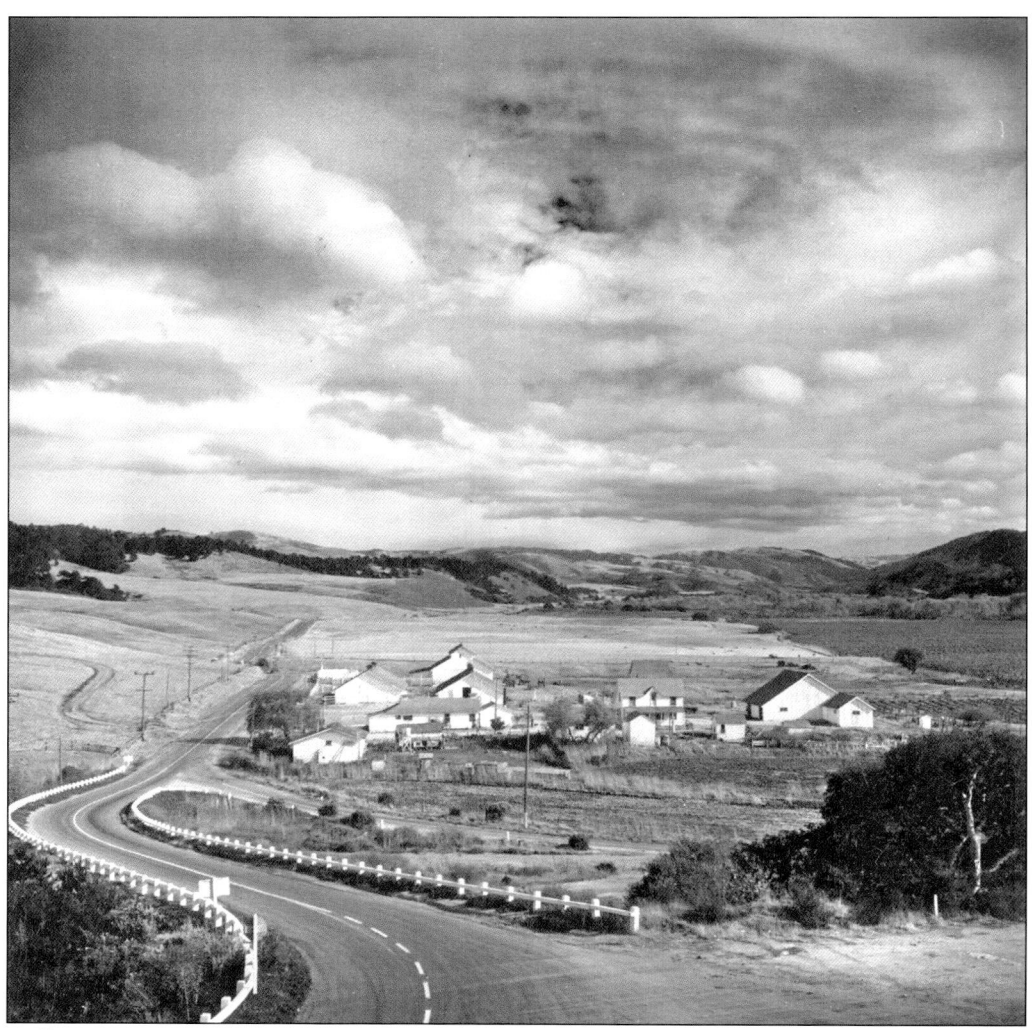

William Hatton's Lower Dairy was located east of Highway 1 and Carmel Valley Road on land that was once part of Lazaro Soto's Rancho Canada de la Segunda, granted by the Mexican government in 1839. After several ownerships, the property was purchased in 1869 by Dominga Doni de Atherton, wife of California pioneer Faxon Dean Atherton. In 1888, Dominga Atherton hired Hatton, who had other dairy operations in Carmel Valley, to manage her holdings. In 1892, the enterprising dairyman purchased the ranch. Hatton had earlier introduced Durham cattle into the existing Holstein stock and built a laboratory to improve the butterfat content in milk. The dairy was a model of efficiency and produced quality products for its clientele. (Photograph by George Seideneck; courtesy of the Monterey Public Library, California History Room Archives.)

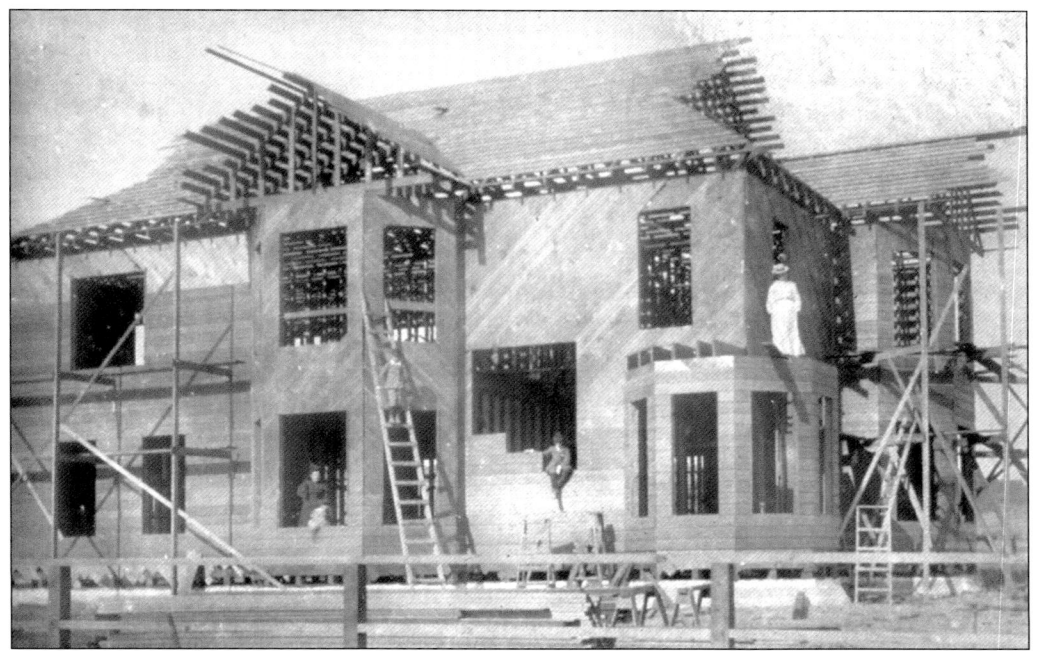

Hatton family members pose in the unfinished shell of their 1895 eighteen-room Queen Anne–style house on the southern slope of Carmel Knolls, at the mouth of Carmel Valley. The balloon-frame construction denotes the availability of dimensional lumber, while the skin of the residence exhibits diagonal sheathing—used for strengthening against wind loads—and finish horizontal board siding. (Photograph courtesy of Marcia DeVoe, Harrison Memorial Library Collection.)

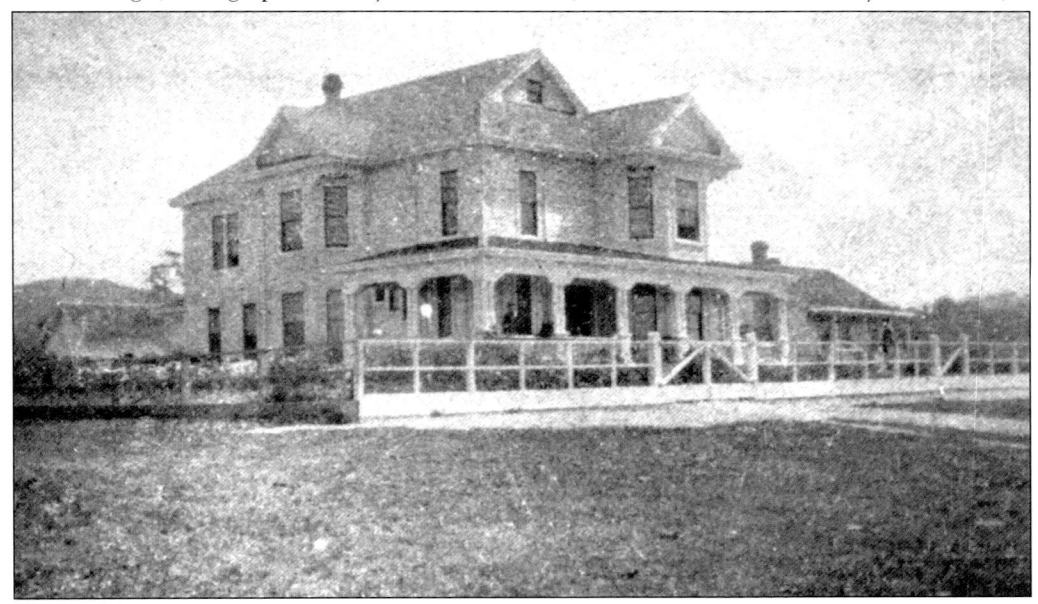

The Hatton family's home was the largest and most fashionable in the Carmel area when it was completed in 1895. It was also the first to be designed by an architect, C. D. Cooper of San Francisco. Douglas Knox Frasier, builder of Monterey's Oak Grove neighborhood, was the contractor. (Photograph courtesy of Tamsin Hatton McAulay.)

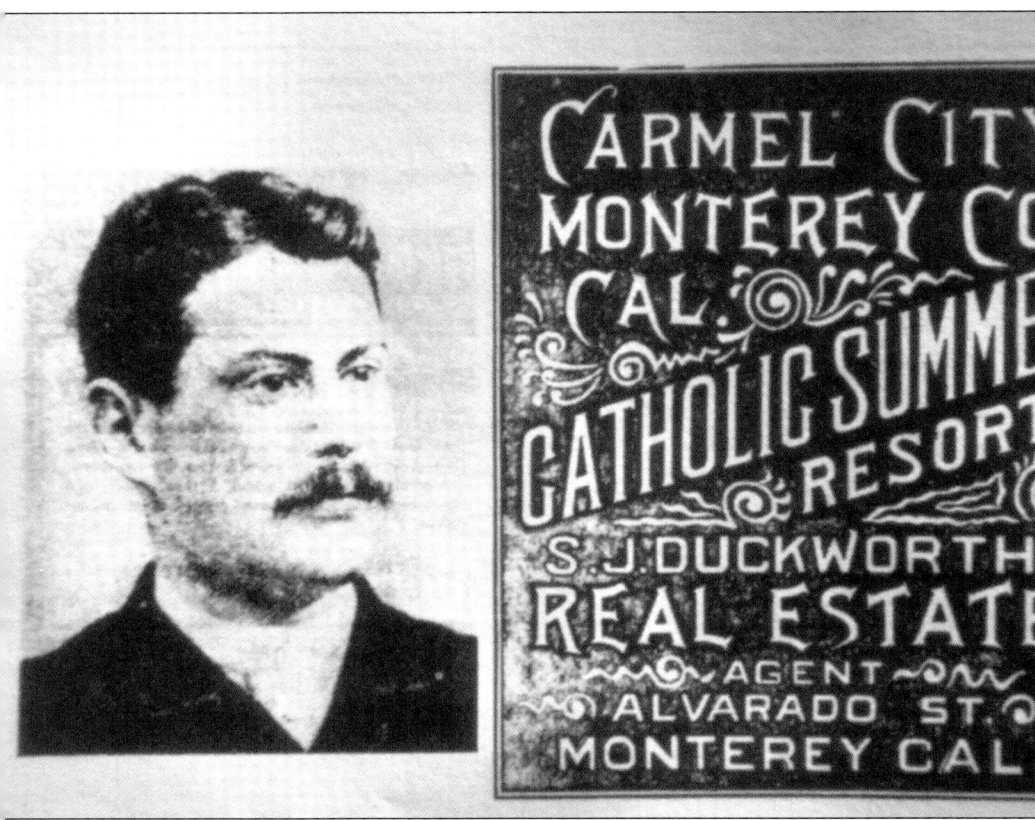

Santiago J. Duckworth is seen in an advertisement for his Carmel City development. In February 1888, Monterey realtors Santiago and Belisario Duckworth entered into a bonded agreement with local merchant and landowner Honore Escolle for the subdivision of 324 acres of his Las Manzanitas Rancho into town lots. The Las Manzanitas was located in rolling woodlands just north of John Martin's Mission Ranch and west of Will Hatton's dairy land. Based on the success of the Pacific Grove Methodist Seaside Retreat, Carmel City was intended to become the first Catholic summer colony in California. (Photograph courtesy of the Harrison Memorial Library Collection.)

Three

CARMEL CITY

The proposal to create Carmel City had strong support from the Young Men's Institute of California, an influential Catholic organization that envisioned a theological seminary as part of the resort community. Between 1889 and 1892, the Duckworths developed the initial infrastructure, including an 18-room hotel and some residential units, and sold over 200 lots. Of the original 700 parcels platted, about 200 were sold by 1892 at prices ranging from $40 to $55 dollars for 40-by-100-foot building lots. By 1892, Abbie Jane Hunter, founder of the San Francisco based Women's Real Estate Investment Company, had joined forces with the Duckworth interests and had a large community bathhouse constructed on Carmel's beach. The mid-1890s saw a national recession that greatly slowed Carmel's growth.

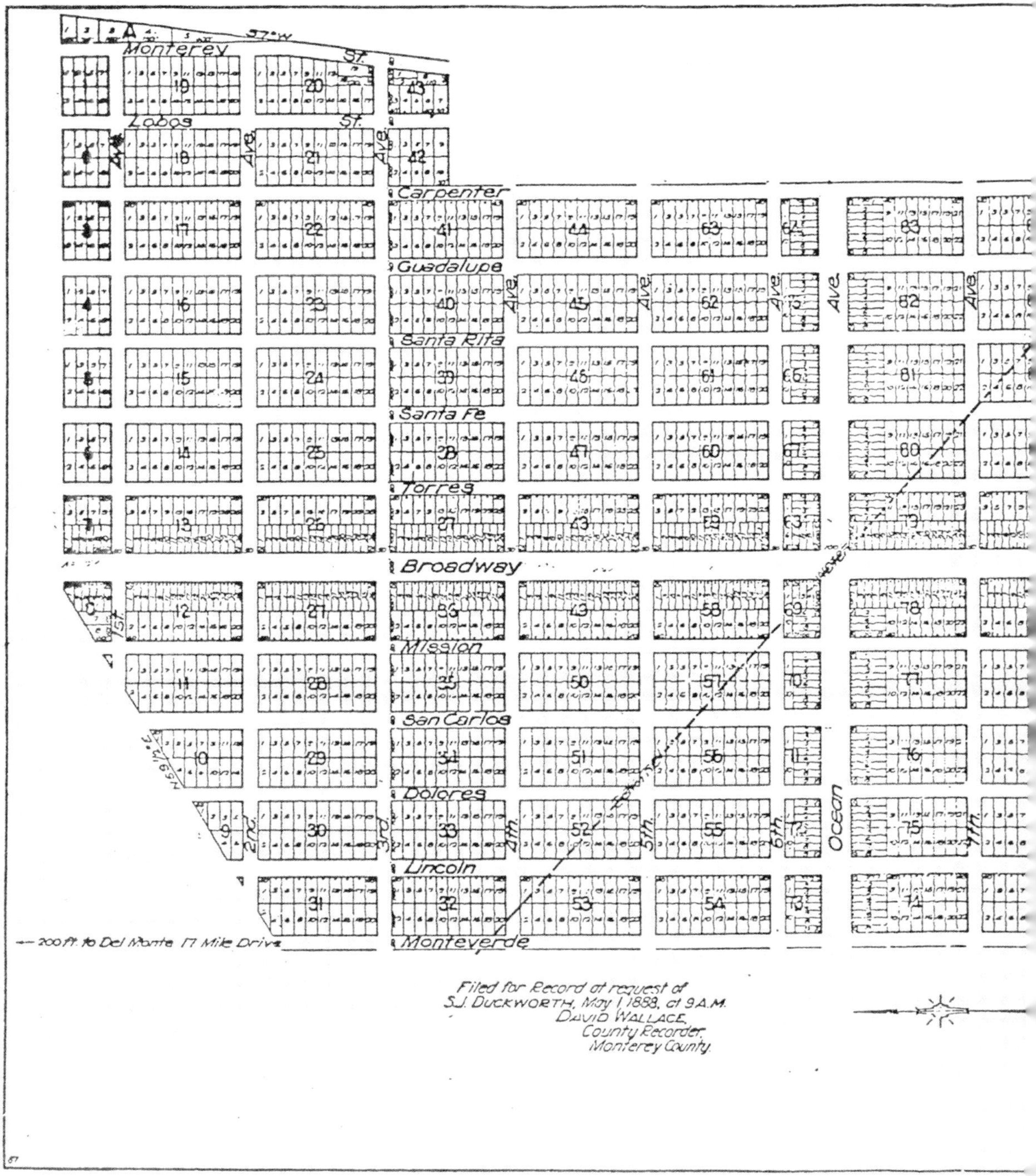
Monterey St.
Lobos St.
Carpenter
Guadalupe
Santa Rita
Santa Fe
Torres
Broadway
Mission
San Carlos
Dolores
Lincoln
Monteverde
2nd.
3rd.
4th.
5th.
6th.
Ocean
Ave.
← 200 ft. to Del Monte 17 Mile Drive
Filed for Record at request of
S.J. DUCKWORTH, May 1 1888, at 9 A.M.
DAVID WALLACE,
County Recorder,
Monterey County.

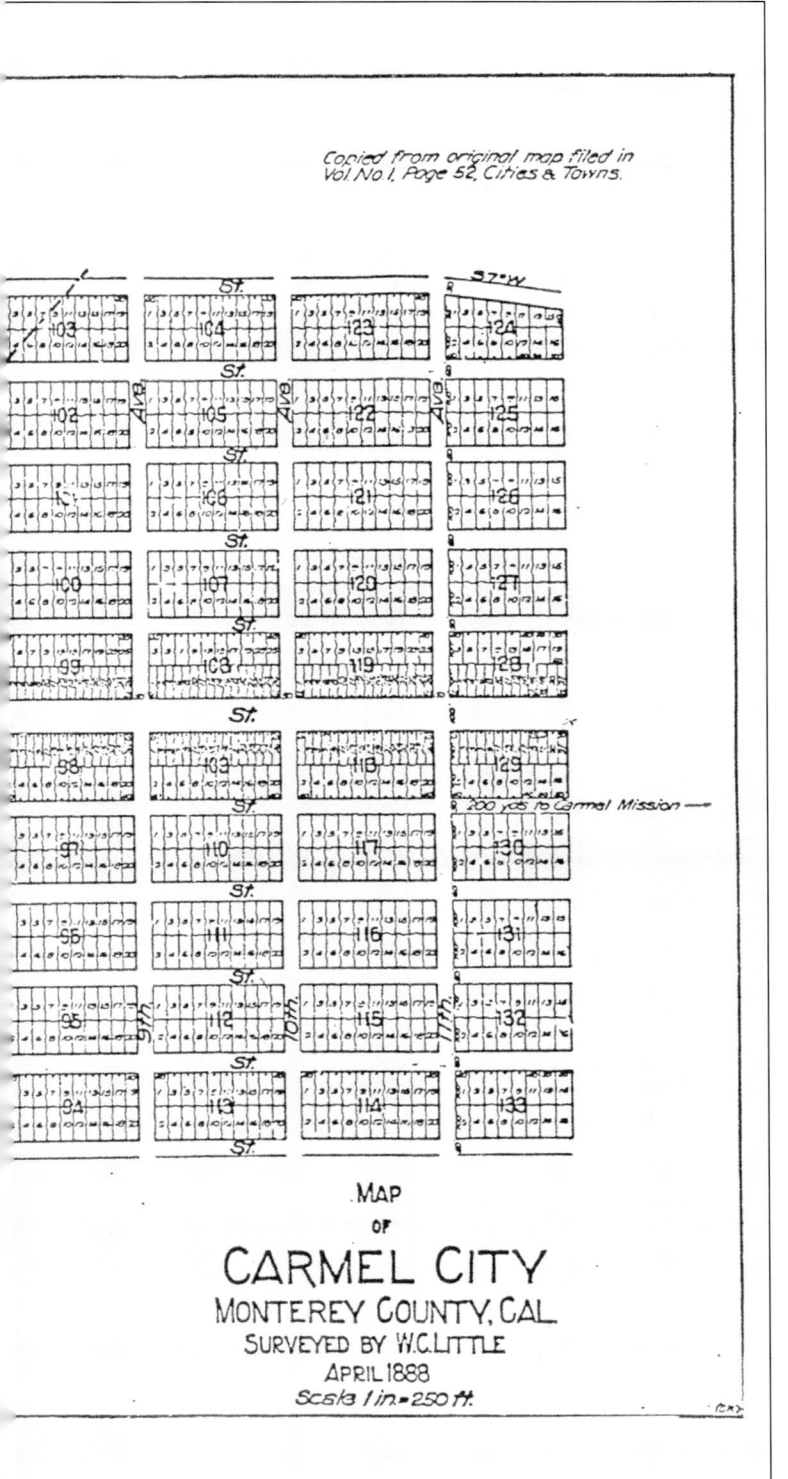

MAP
OF
CARMEL CITY
MONTEREY COUNTY, CAL.
SURVEYED BY W.C. LITTLE
APRIL 1888
Scale 1 in. = 250 ft.

The Duckworth brothers hired land surveyor Walter Colton Little of Monterey to plat the Carmel City tract. Little's assistant, Davenport Bromfield, did most of the legwork. Bromfield proceeded to lay out the paper town by imposing a standard American grid pattern on the hilly terrain. One hundred thirteen residential and commercial blocks were platted between what is now Valley Way to the north and Twelfth Avenue to the south. Monterey and Carpenter Streets marked the eastern boundary, with Monte Verde Street as the western boundary. Two wide thoroughfares, Broadway and Ocean Avenue, bisected the subdivision into four general sections. Broadway is now Junipero Street, and Ocean Avenue runs through Carmel's principal business district. (Map courtesy of the Monterey County Recorder's Office.)

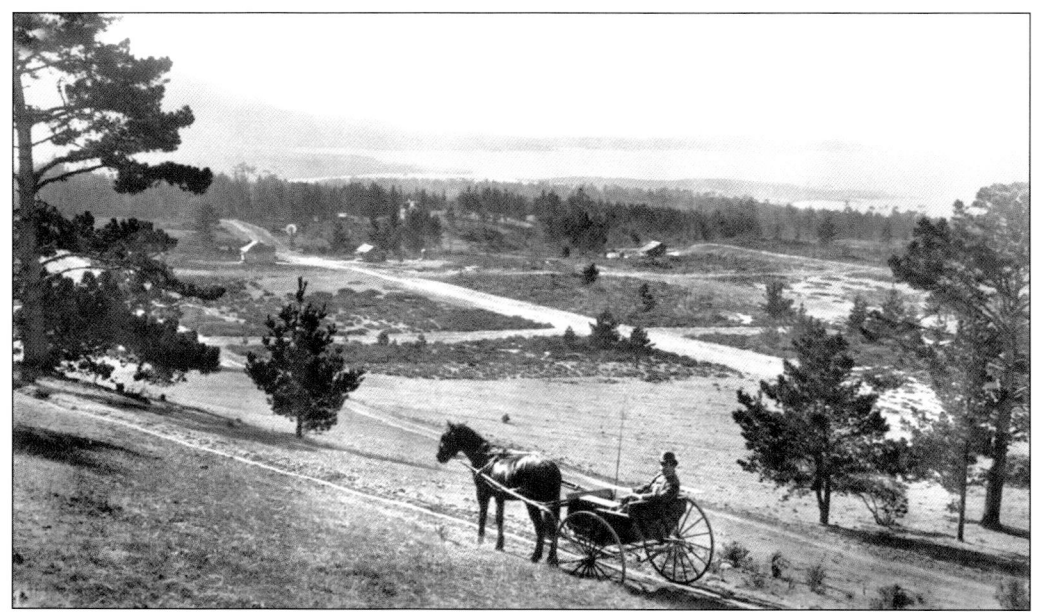

This promotional photograph shows Santiago Duckworth c. 1890 in his sporting rig above the recently graded Carpenter Street. Note Point Lobos in the background. The residence above the tree to the left may be that of surveyor Davenport Bromfield. The house to the right of Bromfield's was built by carpenter Delos Goldsmith for Duckworth. (Photograph by C. W. J. Johnson; courtesy of the Harrison Memorial Library Collection.)

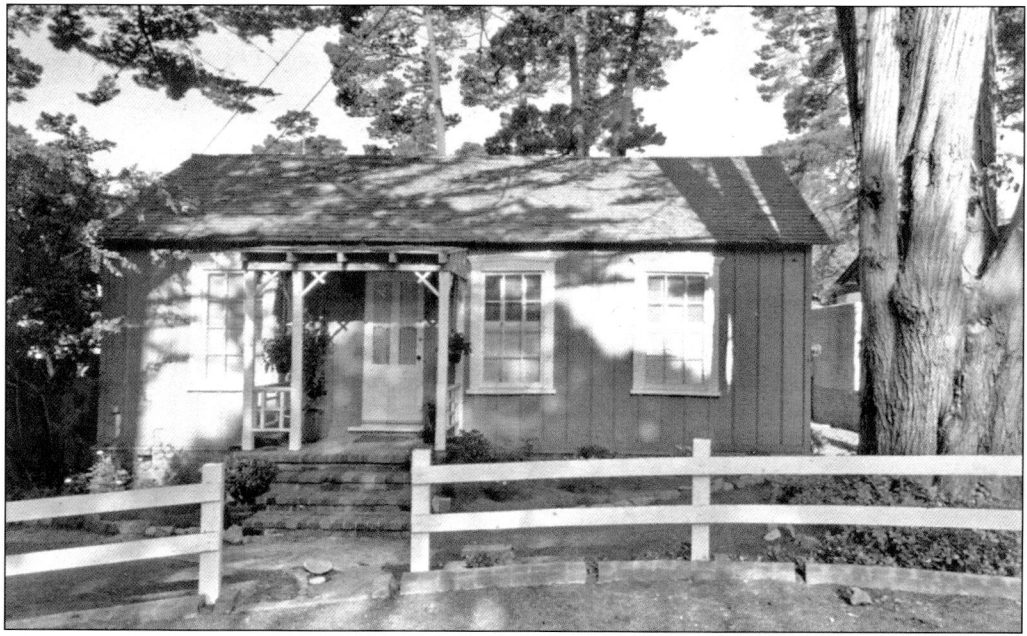

This vernacular side-gabled redwood board-and-batten residence was built in 1888 by carpenter Delos Goldsmith for Santiago J. Duckworth. The pedimented window casings and stick-like bracketing on the porch posts are its only concessions to decoration. (Photograph by Morley Baer; courtesy of Monterey Peninsula College.)

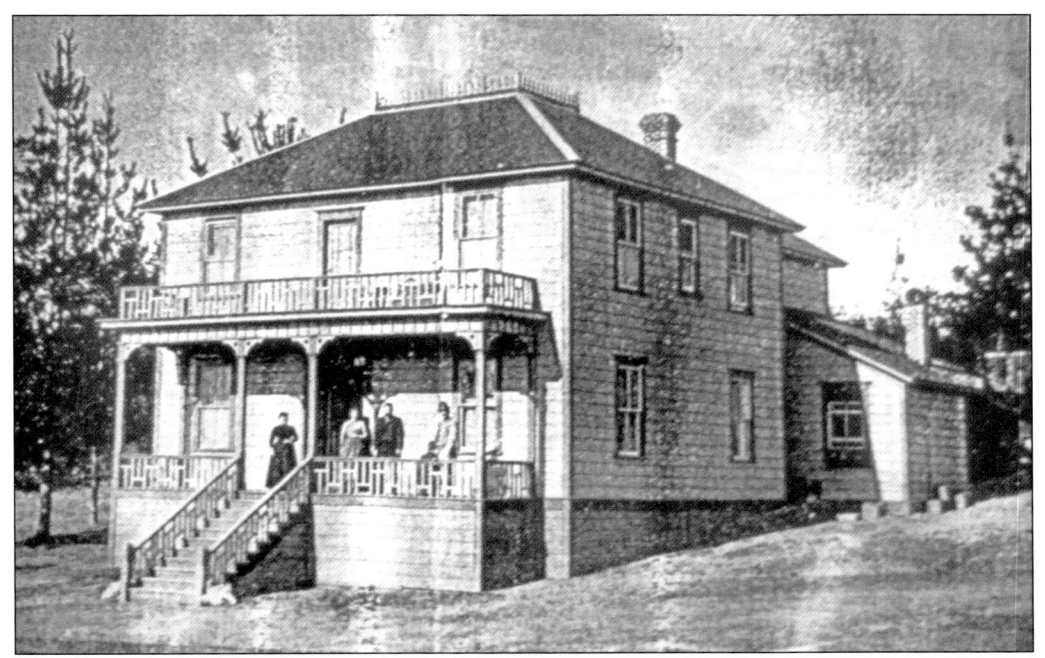

The El Carmelo Hotel was described in an 1889 issue of the *Monterey Cypress* "as pretty and commodious a little hotel as one would want to see. The hotel is an 18-room house, besides a bath-room, patent closets, and every convenience imaginable, with accommodations for about 40 persons." The building was designed by Douglas Knox Frasier. (Photograph by C. W. J. Johnson; courtesy of the Harrison Memorial Library Collection.)

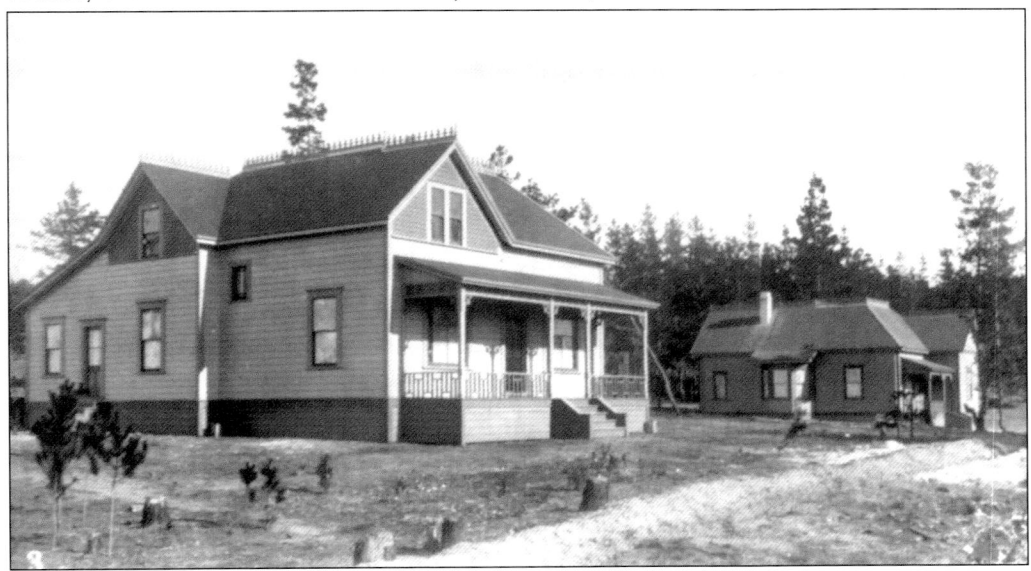

Designed by contractor Douglas Knox Fraiser c. 1888, these two Queen Anne–style cottages were built by Delos Goldsmith. Goldsmith was an uncle of Wesley R. Hunter, son of promoter Abbie Jane Hunter. Augusta Robertson, another Goldsmith relative, lived in the house on the left at the northwest corner of Fourth Avenue and Guadalupe Street. (Photograph by C. W. J. Johnson; courtesy of the Harrison Memorial Library Collection.)

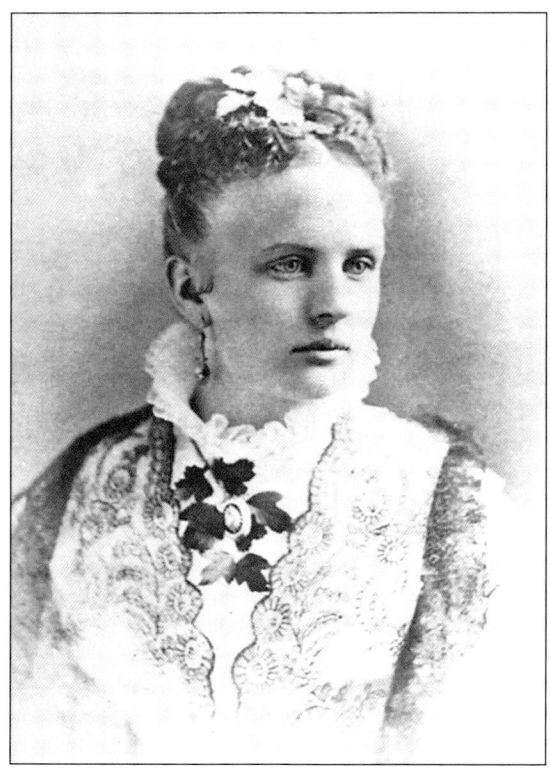

Abbie Jane Hunter was the first woman developer/builder in Carmel. In 1892, her Women's Real Estate Investment Company acquired 164 acres of the Carmel City Tract. She sold about 300 lots, mainly to teachers, professors, and writers, who had dubbed the place their "Haven of Rest." Hunter's efforts could not overcome a nationwide depression, and she had to sell her interests in 1898. (Photograph courtesy of the Harrison Memorial Library Collection.)

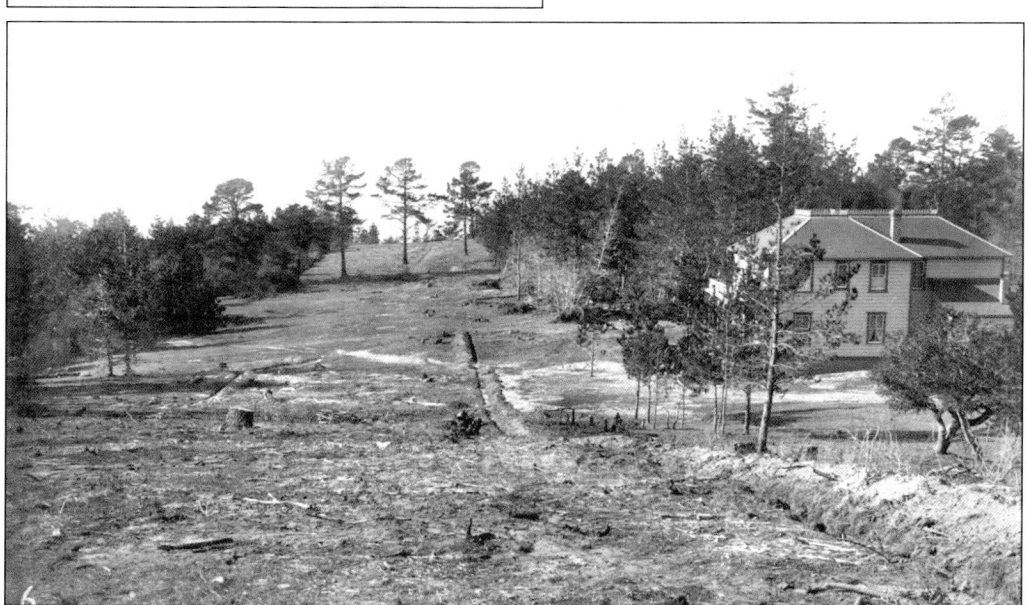

This c. 1888 view down Ocean Avenue looks west toward Carmel Beach. The Hotel Carmelo is on the right, at the northeast corner of Junipero Street. Access to the beach bathhouse was no easy matter. Victorian decorum required full street dress for both men and women. The distance from the hotel was about 10 city blocks. (Photograph by C. W. J. Johnson; courtesy of the Harrison Memorial Library Collection.)

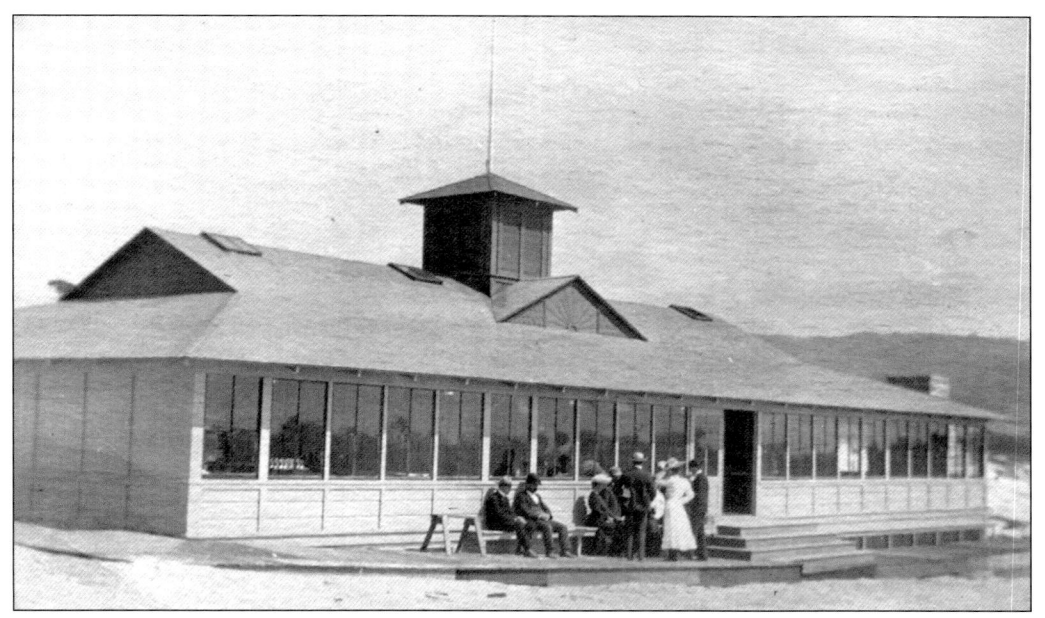

Real estate investor Abbie Jane Hunter, with Delos Goldsmith as builder, was responsible for the construction of a community bathhouse on Carmel Beach in 1889. The rental cost of a dressing room, bathing attire, and a towel was 25¢. It is seen here c. 1905. (Photograph by E. A. Cohen; courtesy of Pat Hathaway, Historic California Views.)

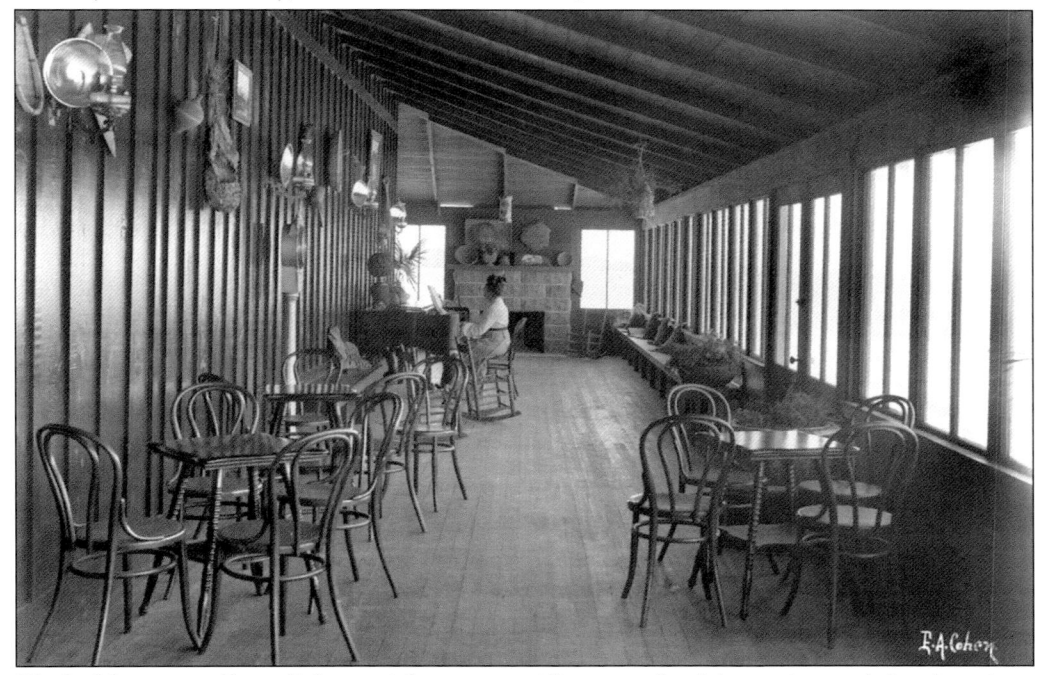

The bathhouse was Carmel's first social center, providing space for club meetings and church outings, as well as serving peanuts, popcorn, candy, sandwiches, and lemonade. It was a favorite spot for residents to observe winter storms. In 1929, the commodious public building was sold and dismantled. (Photograph by E. A. Cohen; courtesy of Pat Hathaway, Historic California Views.)

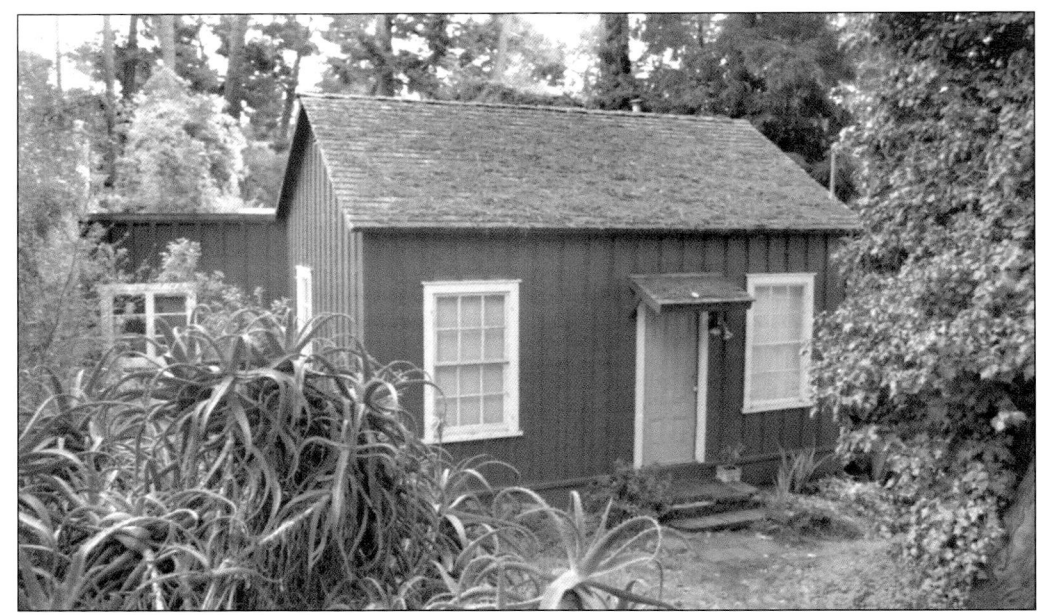

Stage driver Alfonso Ramirez was the owner/builder of this c. 1888 board-and-batten cabin on Santa Rita Street northeast of Second Avenue. A direct descendant of Rumsien people from the Carmel Mission, Ramirez was a driver for the Monterey-Carmel Stage Line. He had a corral for his horses behind the cabin. There was a stage stop near Second Avenue and Carpenter Street before the beginning of the 20th century. (Photograph by the author.)

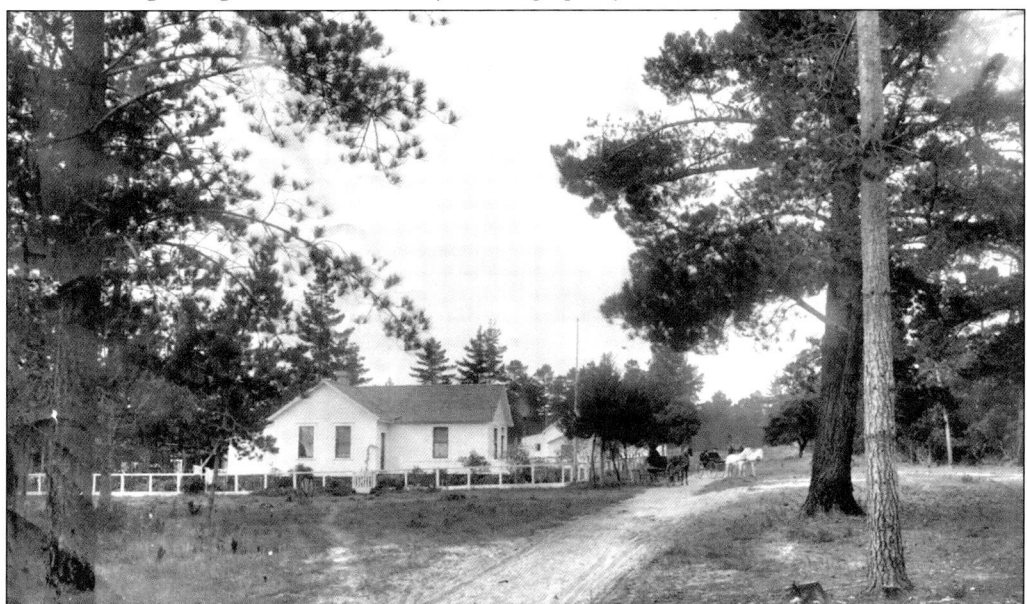

John P. Cogle built this small gable-and-wing house on San Carlos Street between Fifth and Sixth Avenues at the beginning of the 20th century. Cogle worked for developer Frank Devendorf as a crew foreman clearing timber for Carmel's streets. Carmel's housing at this time was basically wood-framed, working-class vernacular, reflecting the tastes and budgets of its owner/builders. (Photograph courtesy of the Harrison Memorial Library Collection.)

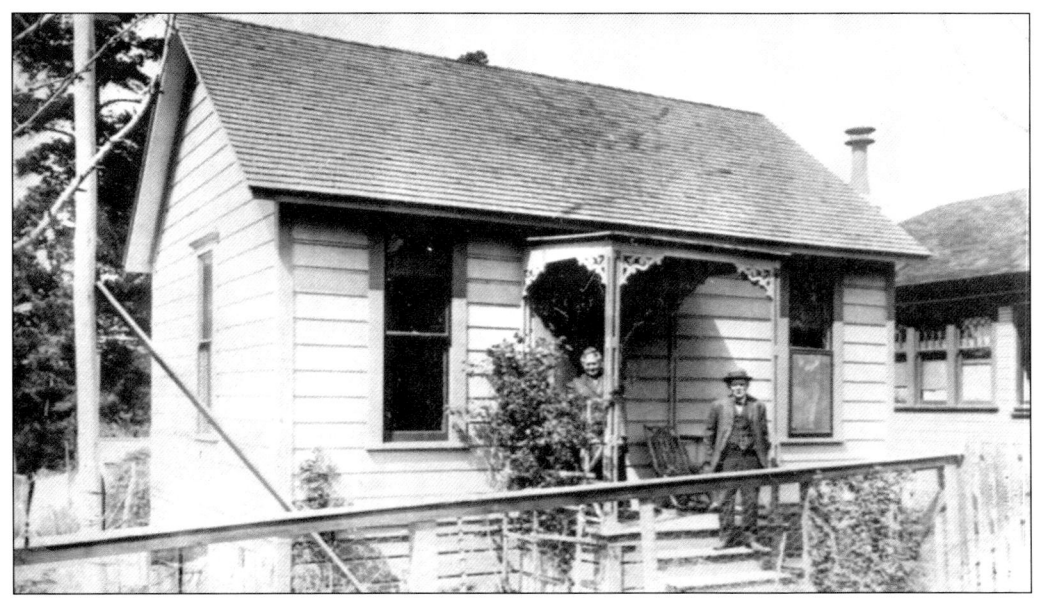

Alfred Horn, next-door neighbor to John Cogle, was a trolley turntable operator in San Francisco. He built this side-gabled redwood cottage in 1894 as a vacation getaway. Displaced by the 1906 San Francisco earthquake, he moved his family to Carmel, where Horn drove stages, delivered mail, and rented a room to developer Frank Devendorf. (Photograph courtesy of the Harrison Memorial Library Collection.)

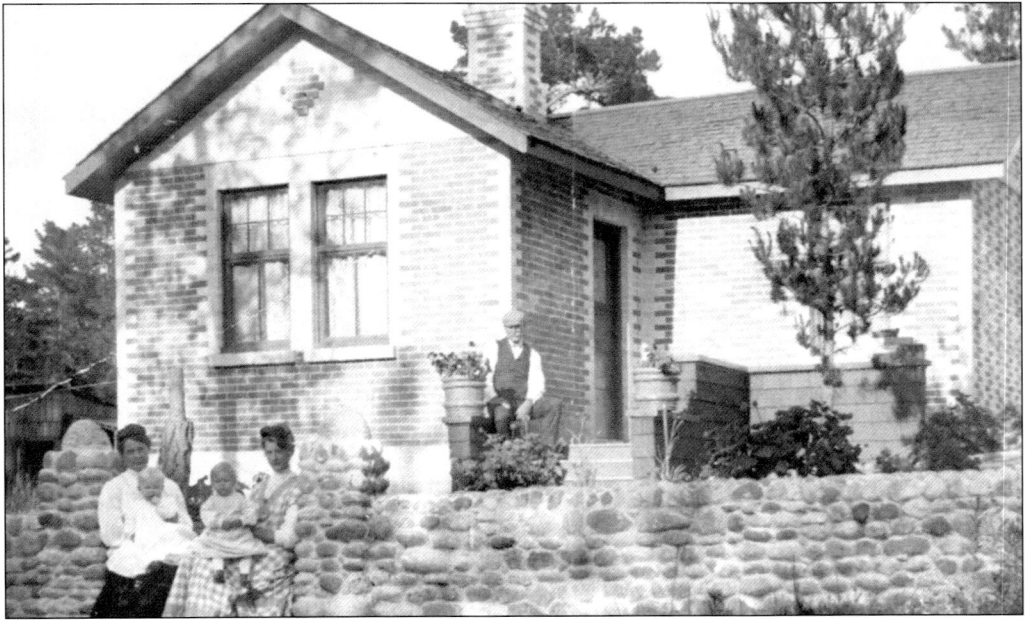

English master mason Benjamin Turner constructed the first brick house in Carmel City in 1898. Located near the southeast corner of Monte Verde Street and Fifth Avenue, the small gable-and-wing residence was a showcase for the mason's skills. Turner employed decorative quoining at the corners and at door and window surrounds. His son Harry joined the business in 1915. (Photograph courtesy of the Harrison Memorial Library Collection.)

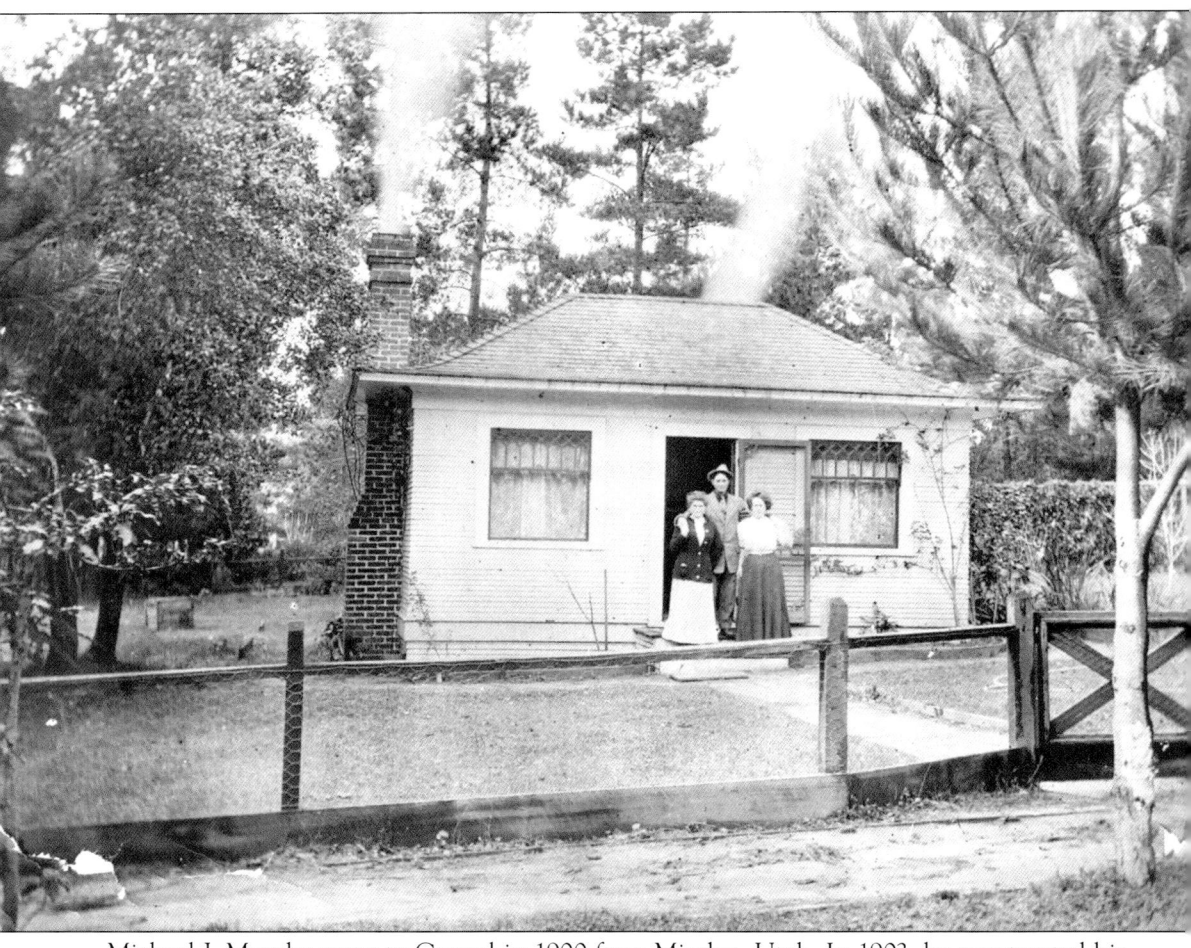

Michael J. Murphy came to Carmel in 1900 from Minden, Utah. In 1902, he constructed his first house, this small hipped-roof cottage, for his mother. Note the early use of narrow clapboard siding and decorative window sash. In 1904, Murphy became the chief builder for the Carmel Development Company. He would erect over 300 buildings in the village during his career. His mother, Emma (left), and wife, Edna, flank the burgeoning contractor in this 1906 image. (Photograph courtesy of the Harrison Memorial Library Collection.)

Four

CARMEL-BY-THE-SEA

The two seminal figures in the successful development of Carmel-by-the-Sea, San Francisco attorney Frank H. Powers and real estate developer James Franklin Devendorf, combined financial resources with managerial skill as well as a shared vision of what Carmel should be. They formed the Carmel Development Company on November 25, 1902. Devendorf's granddaughter, Jane H. Galante, said, "For Frank Powers, Carmel-by-the-Sea was part of the tapestry of his life. For Frank Devendorf, it was his masterpiece." Perry Newberry said of Devendorf, "With a wide benevolence and a deep wisdom, he gave from his experience to make the going easier for us all." By November 1903, there were 30 families living in town; over half were carpenters, plumbers, and so forth who had settled as employees of the company. In November 1904, the total value of lots sold was $60,110. By 1913, promoters noted that over 60 percent of new residents devoted their lives to work connected with the aesthetic arts, broadly defined as college professors, artists, poets, writers, and professional men. Housing was described in Carmel Development Company literature as "artistic in character, reflecting the temperament of the town."

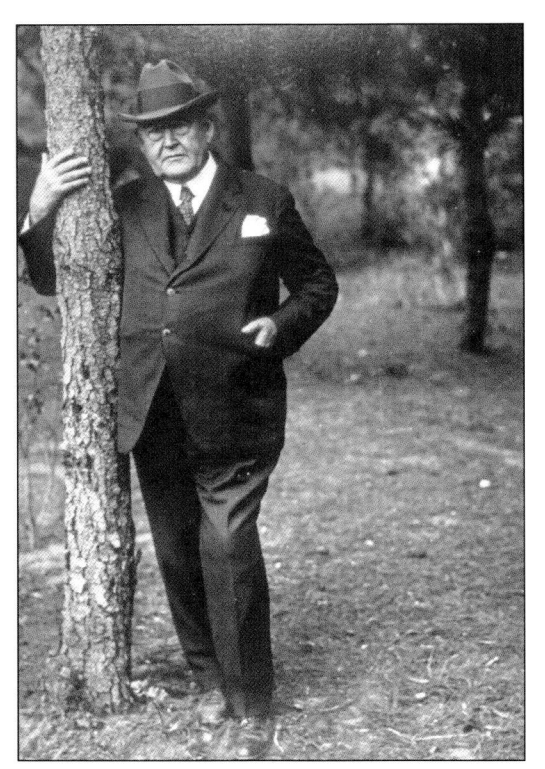

James Franklin Devendorf—"Devy" to his friends and neighbors—was the mainspring that kept things moving in early Carmel. As a seasoned real estate man, he superintended the management of the entire community for the Carmel Development Company. He gave away tree saplings like candy in order to forest the village. (Photograph courtesy of Pat Hathaway, Historic California Views.)

Frank H. Powers, a San Francisco lawyer and club man, was the silent partner and financial genius of the Carmel Development Company. He and his wife, artist Jane Gallatin Powers (right), did much to bring San Francisco's creative bohemian society to Carmel. (Photograph courtesy of the Fassett family archives.)

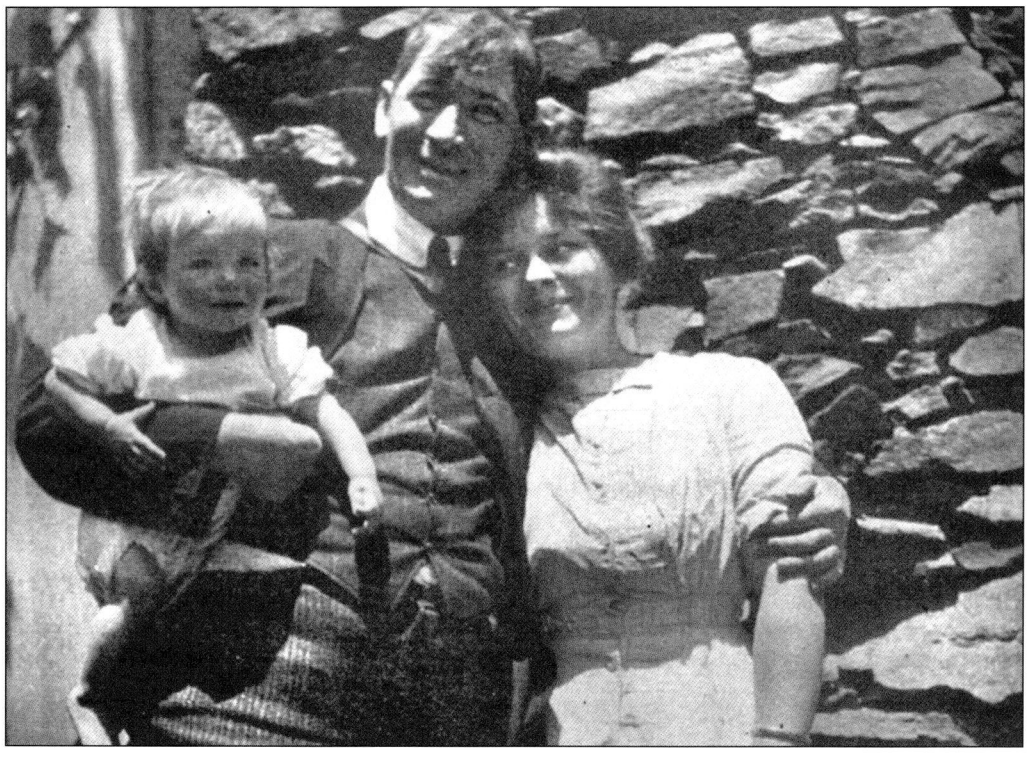

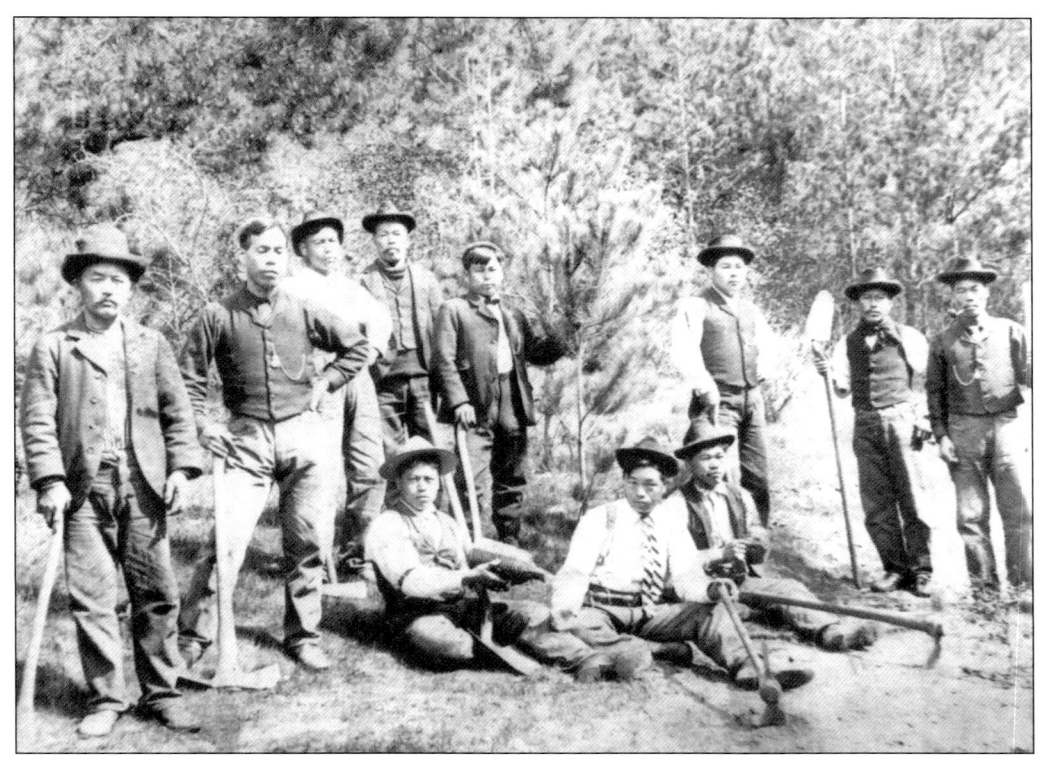

Franklin Devendorf hired Japanese laborers to both clear trees and plant new ones. The gridiron street pattern imposed on the sloping topography of the emerging community invited erosion during the winter rains. Reforestation reduced the problem as well as creating the landscape setting of Carmel as a village in a forest. (Photograph courtesy of the Miyamoto family.)

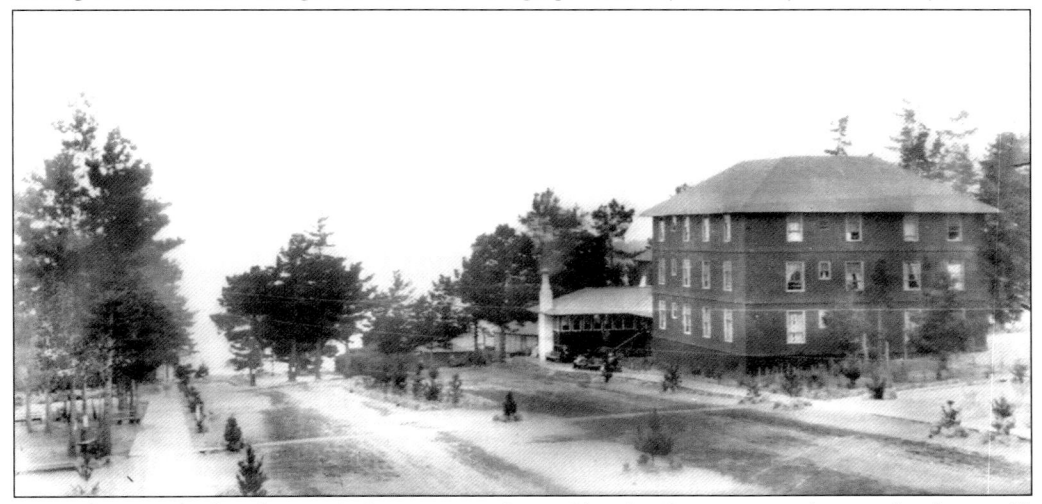

One of Devendorf and Power's first acts in Carmel-by-the-Sea was to relocate the former El Carmelo Hotel. It was rolled on logs by mule power to the northeast corner of Ocean Avenue and Monte Verde Street in 1903, bringing the hostelry much closer to the beach. San Francisco architect Thomas Morgan designed the expanded edifice, renamed the Pine Inn. (Photograph courtesy of the Harrison Memorial Library Collection.)

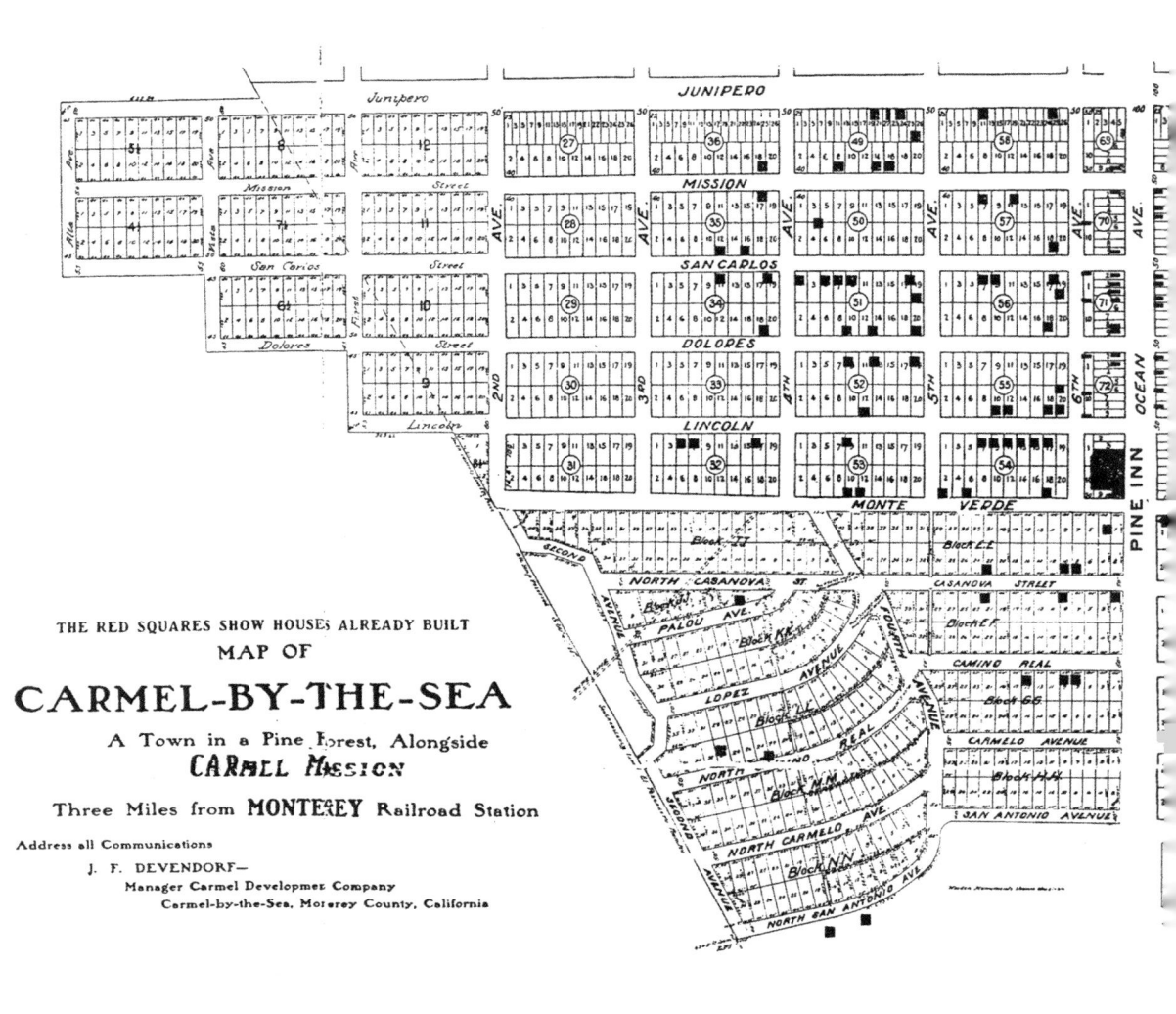

THE RED SQUARES SHOW HOUSES ALREADY BUILT
MAP OF
CARMEL-BY-THE-SEA

A Town in a Pine Forest, Alongside
CARMEL MISSION

Three Miles from MONTEREY Railroad Station

Address all Communications
   J. F. DEVENDORF—
      Manager Carmel Development Company
      Carmel-by-the-Sea, Monterey County, California

The Carmel Realty Company published this map in 1913 as part of an extensive illustrated brochure extolling the virtues of "A town in a Pine Forest." There were over 375 residential dwelling houses. Based on "the milkman's census method," the permanent population was about 400. Promoters boasted of two hotels, several boardinghouses, a general store, butcher shop and greengrocer, a drugstore, candy shop, bakery, and, of course, a barber. There was a post office,

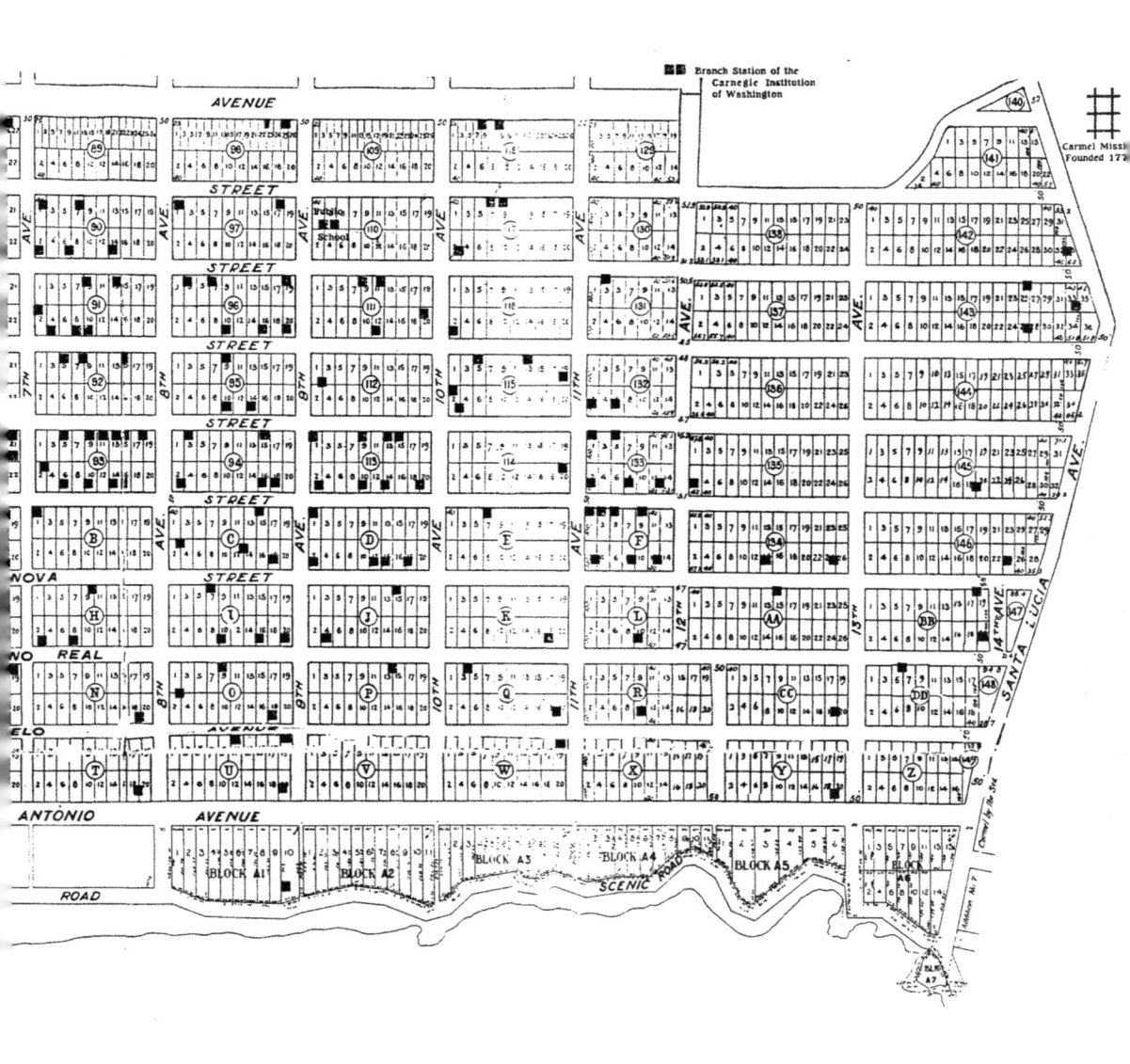

Wells Fargo Express office, public school, and free library. The Carnegie Research Institute of Washington, D.C., even had a branch research laboratory in town. The local civic committee and the Arts and Crafts Club had built a town watering trough for the horses and also worked on creating sidewalks, although the first street paving would not be in place until 1922. (Photograph from the author's collection.)

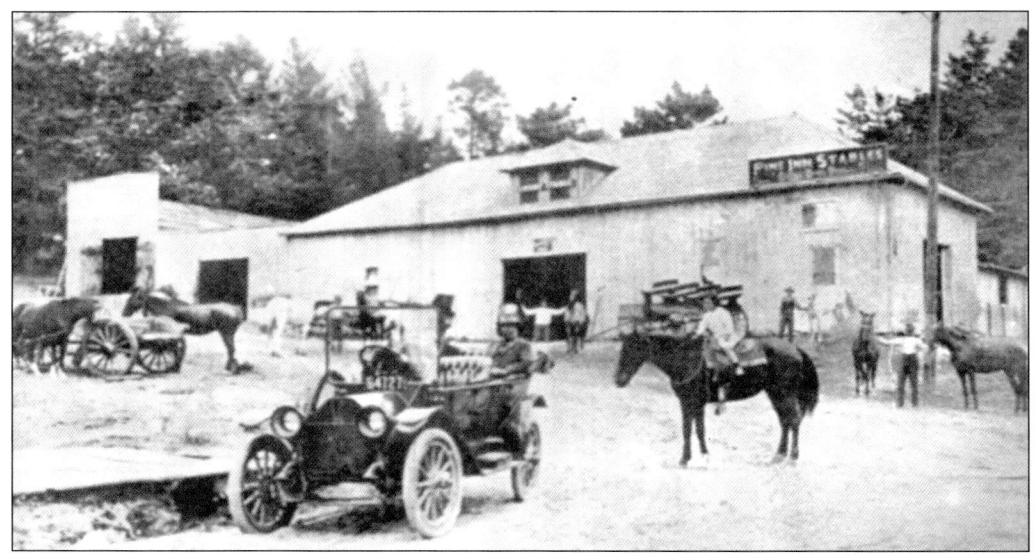

Brothers Oscar and Alfred Coffey built the large livery stable seen here in 1914, on the former site of the El Carmelo, shortly after its move to Monte Verde Street. They ran the Monterey-Carmel stages, a 50¢ round-trip. The Coffeys used the front of the Hotel Carmel as their stage stop and leased saddle horses and buggies for sightseeing trips. (Photograph courtesy of Pat Hathaway, Historic California Views.)

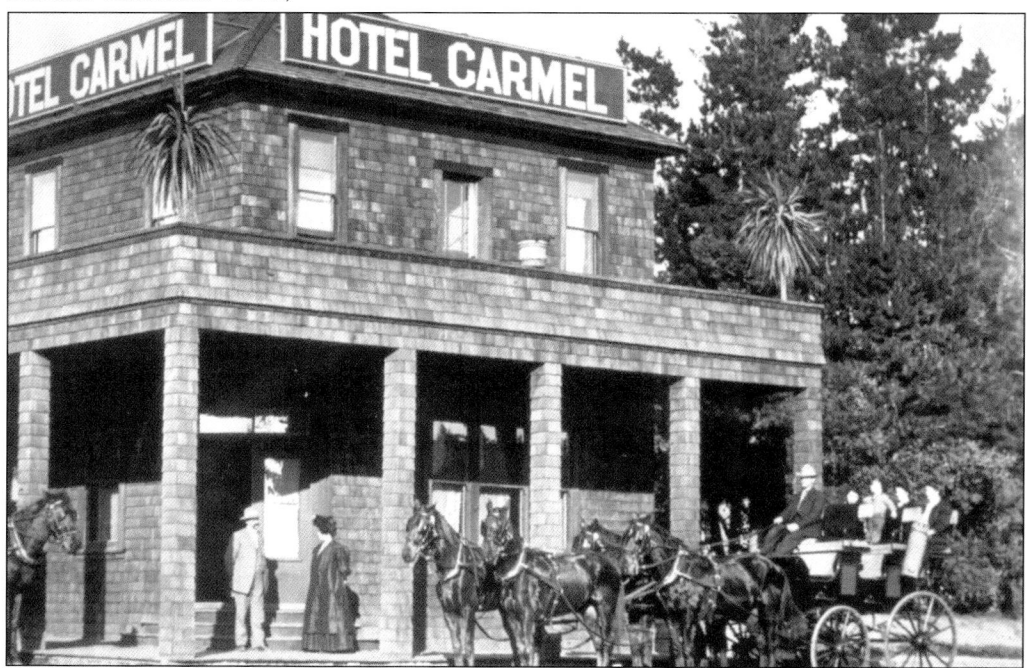

Built in 1898 by D. W. Johnson at the northeast corner of Ocean Avenue and San Carlos Street, the Hotel Carmel was the first known commercial use of wood-shingle siding, associated with the arts and crafts movement, in Carmel. Also referred to as the Bay Area Regionalist style, this use of simple natural materials set the tone for residential design in Carmel into the 1920s. (Photograph courtesy of Pat Hathaway, Historic California Views.)

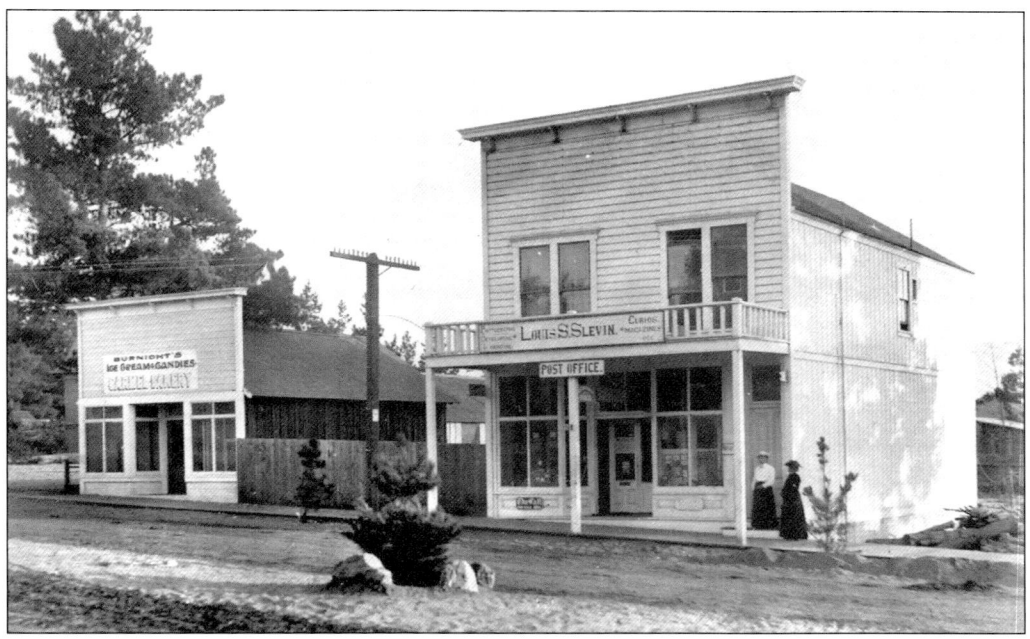

In 1902–1903, L. S. Slevin's was the first general merchandise store in Carmel. It was designed in a wood-framed Western false-front style. These one- and two-story, front-gabled buildings extended their facades vertically to make them look bigger. It was a common building style associated with the settlement of the West. (Photograph courtesy of the Harrison Memorial Library Collection.)

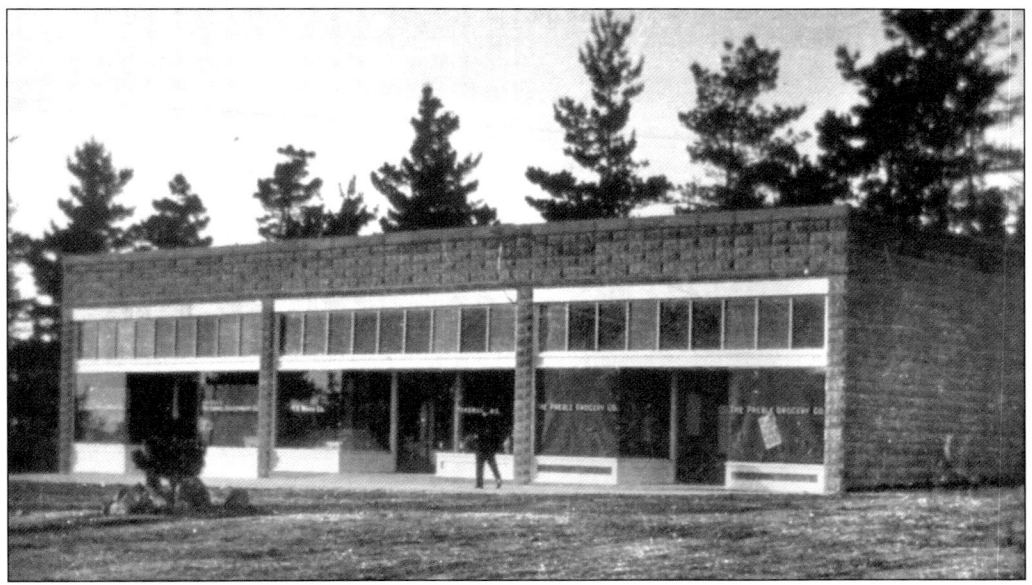

Built in 1903, the Carmel Development Company structure was the first "modern" commercial building block in Carmel. The flat-roofed, stone-faced, concrete-block structure was regarded as fireproof at the time. Pacific Grove real estate investor T. A. Work was responsible for its construction, which was supervised by George Quentel. Carmel carpenter Artie Bowen was part of the building crew. (Photograph courtesy of Pat Hathaway, Historic California Views.)

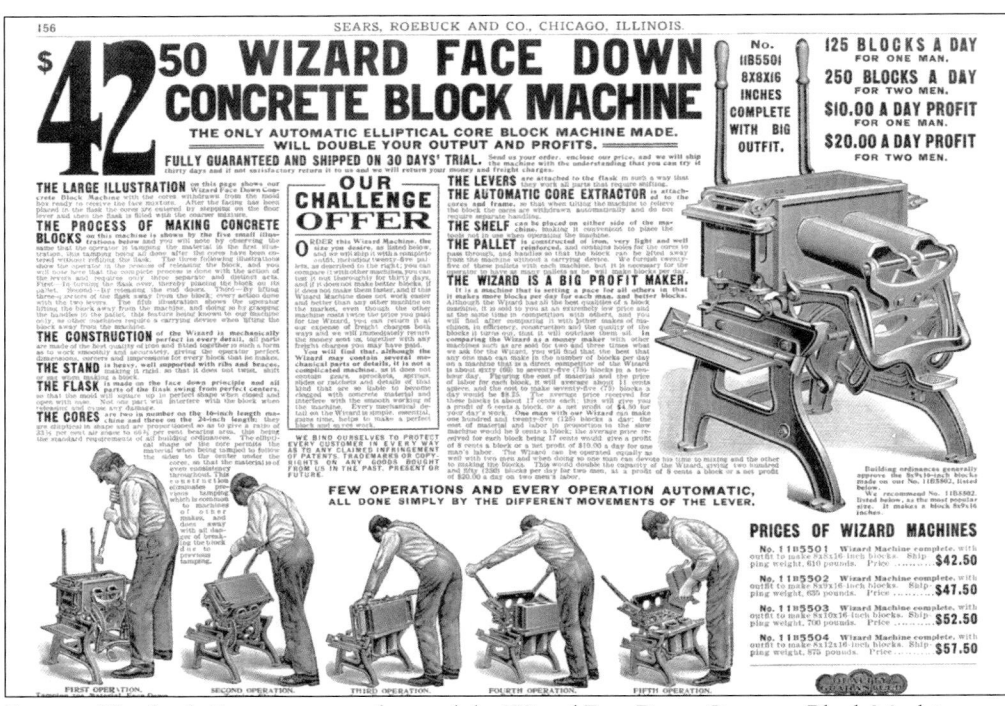

Sears and Roebuck Company manufactured the Wizard Face Down Concrete Block Machine, used in making the concrete wall cladding for the Carmel Development Company building. It was touted as the only automatic elliptical core block machine made and could fabricate 125 blocks a day. This compact modern marvel sold for $42.50 delivered. (Photograph from the author's collection.)

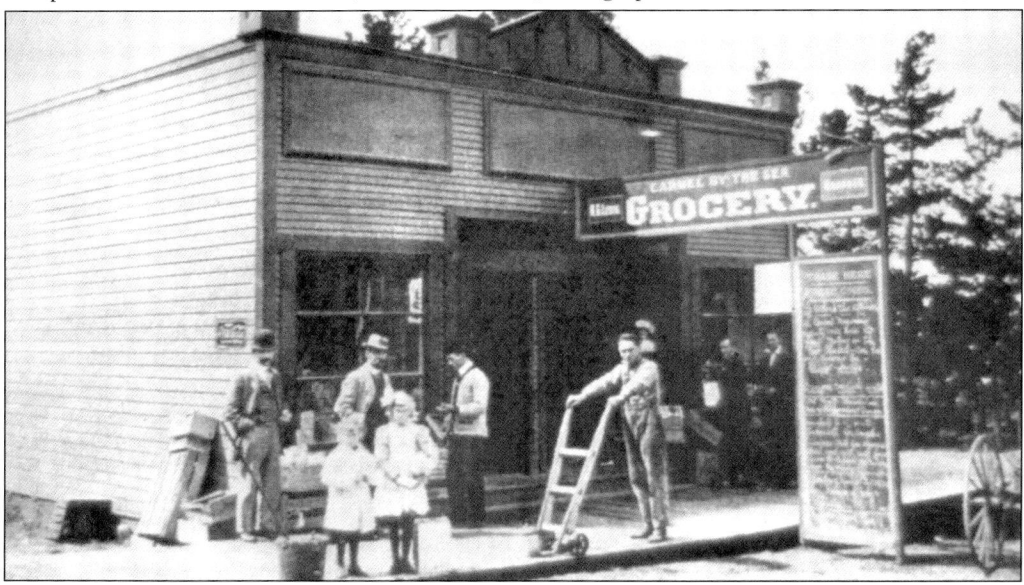

In 1906, two Leidig brothers, Robert and Fred, opened the Carmel-by-the-Sea Grocery Store on the south side of Ocean Avenue just east of Lincoln. The modified false-front building, with its upscale pedimented gable and framed wood panels, provided symbolic evidence of stability in the developing community (Photograph courtesy of Glenn and Marian Leidig.)

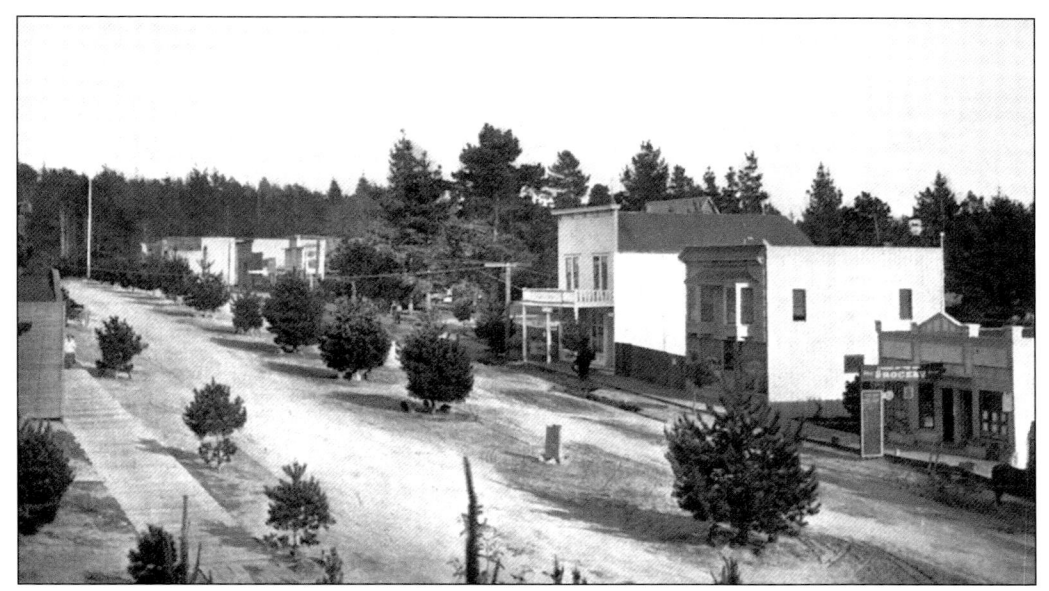

This view looks southeast from the roof of the Pine Inn at Carmel's emerging downtown c. 1910. The building with second-floor bay windows (between the Leidig brothers' market and Slevin's store) is Fritz Schweinger's Bakery. It is one of the few remaining business houses from early Carmel. (Photograph by L. S. Slevin; courtesy of Pat Hathaway, Historic California Views.)

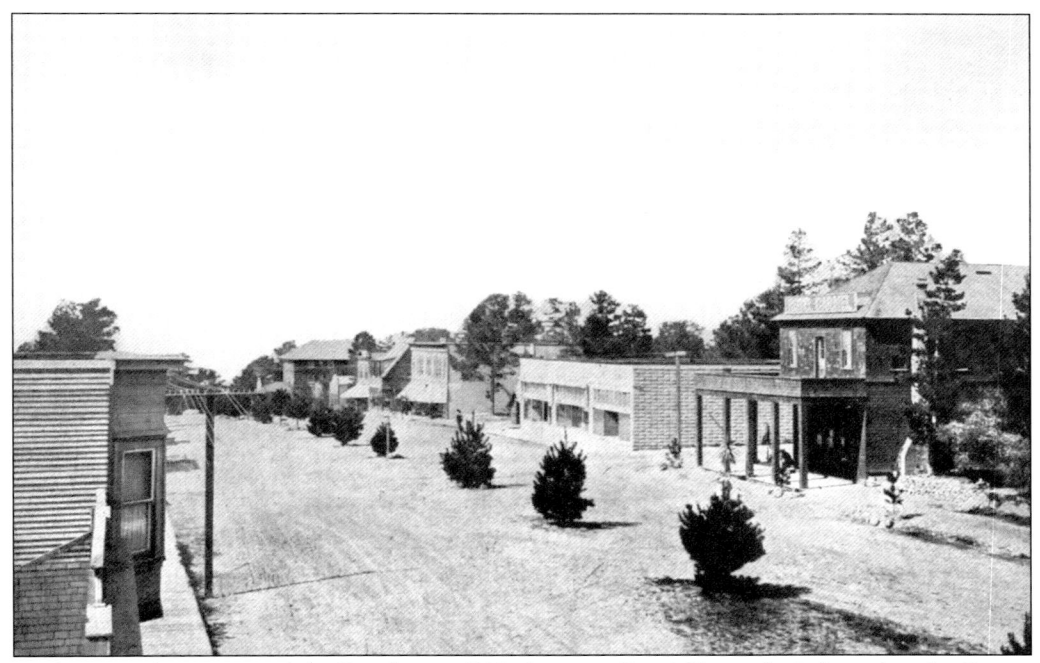

Looking northwest toward the Pine Inn c. 1910, the pines Frank Devendorf planted in the Ocean Avenue median were beginning to take shape, and the forest was growing with the village. Although still raw and not yet quaint, Carmel's commercial frontage was beginning to show some variety. (Photograph by L. S. Slevin; courtesy of the Harrison Memorial Library Collection.)

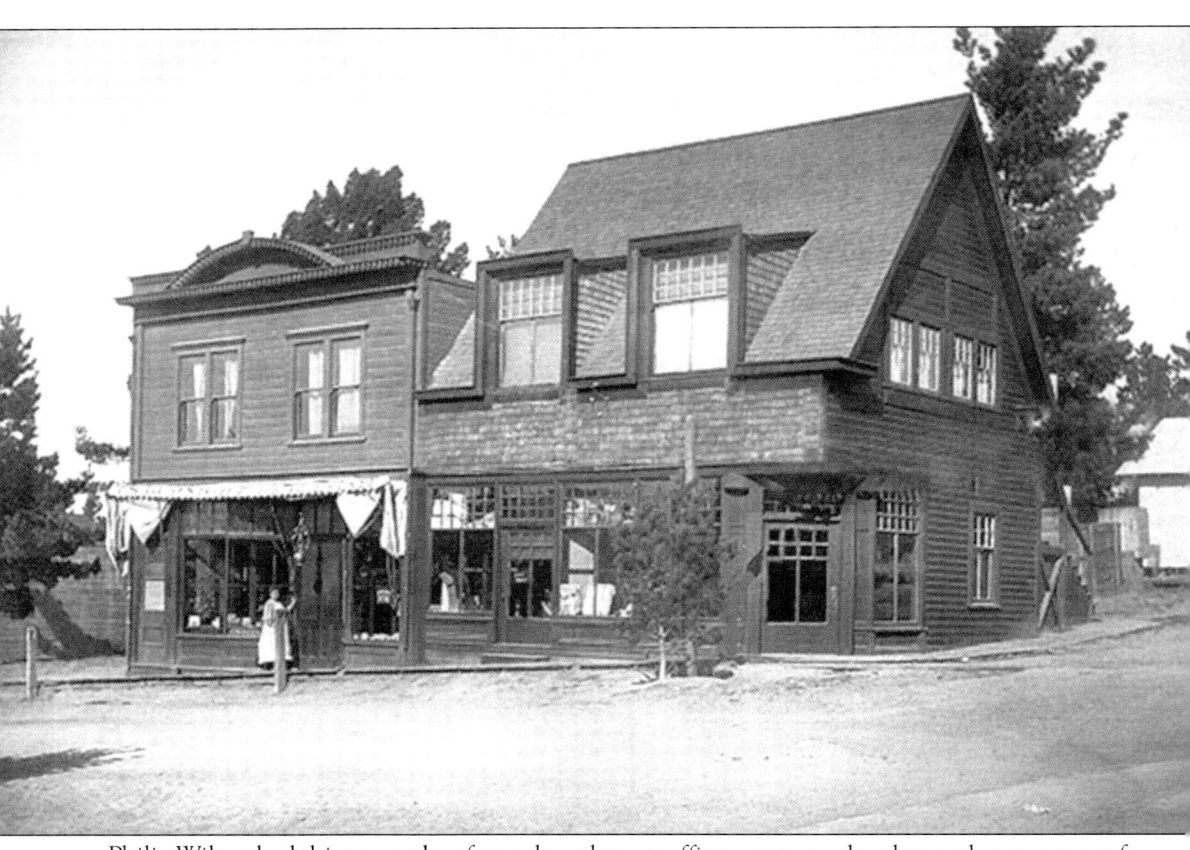

Philip Wilson had this arts and crafts–style real estate office constructed at the northwest corner of Ocean Avenue and Dolores Street in 1905. Although the architect is unknown, its design reflects the emerging Bay Area Regionalist influence. In 1917, the building became Carmel's first city hall. It was also the site of Carmel's first police department. The city's distinctive seal, with its image of Carmel Mission, was adopted here. (Photograph courtesy of the Historic Wilson Building.)

Five

SEACOAST OF BOHEMIA

Rev. Charles Gardner's beautiful board-and-batten vacation home at San Carlos Street and Santa Lucia Avenue is one of the best remaining intact examples of early design reflecting the influence of the arts and crafts movement on Carmel's residential character between about 1905 and the early 1920s. Local housing design came from pattern books, architects, and builders. One of its chief features was simplicity of expression. The use of board-and-batten wall cladding was almost a trademark of the village. Building characteristics of the period included horizontality of proportions; honest reliance on the use of local building materials, clearly expressed in their structural employment; informal building plans with large open porches; and outdoor spaces connected to the interior by horizontal bands of windows to afford a maximum of indoor/outdoor living. Site planning was a key component both in the selection of building orientation and protection of the natural environment. The Carmel Development Company and their chief contractor, Michael J. Murphy, were responsible for much of the residential development for the period but certainly not all. Individual architects, outside contractors, and many owner/builders were equally drawn to Carmel and its unique seaside setting, including women architects like Eugenia Maybury and Julia Morgan, as well as female owner/builders.

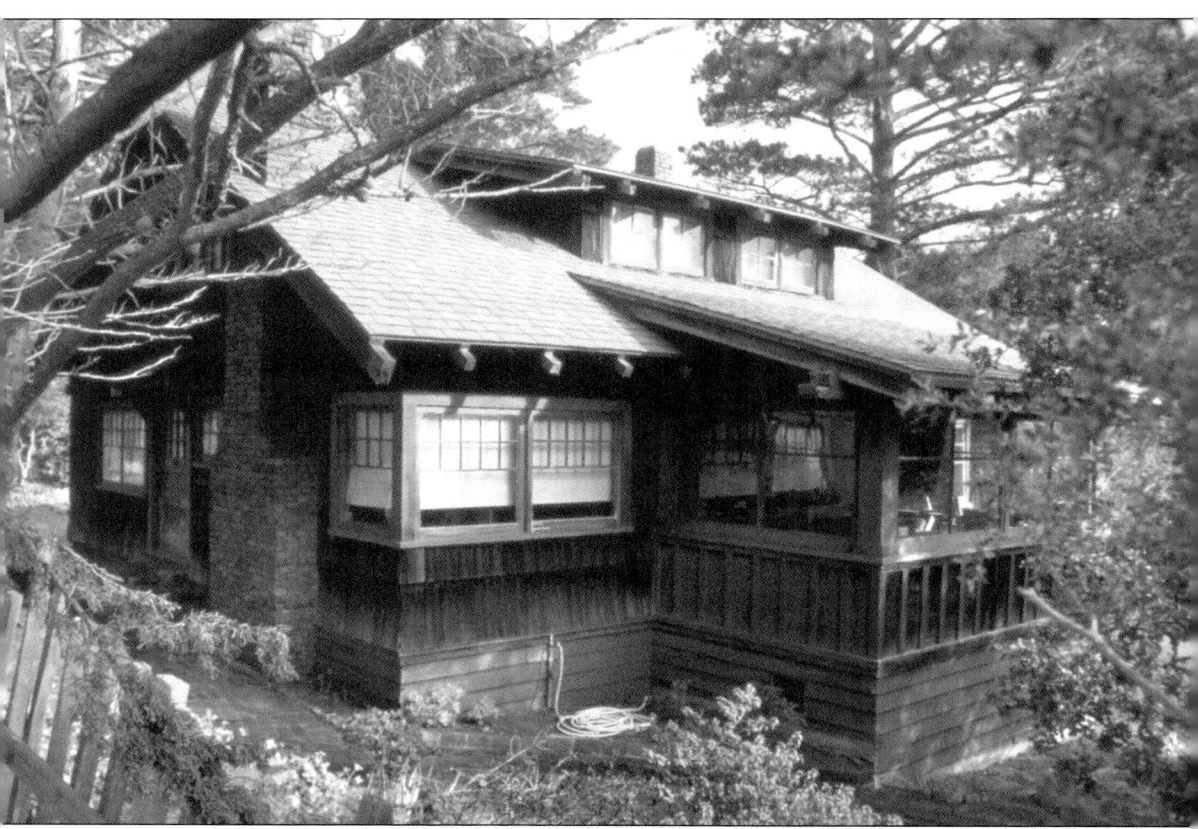

Rev. Charles Gardner was the chaplain at Stanford University in 1905 when he had M. J. Murphy construct this craftsman vacation home on San Carlos Street and Santa Lucia Avenue. Murphy often used horizontal ship-lap siding to visually separate the foundation framing from the main living areas of his houses. The house and its landscape setting may be the least altered of all early Carmel properties. (Photograph by the author.)

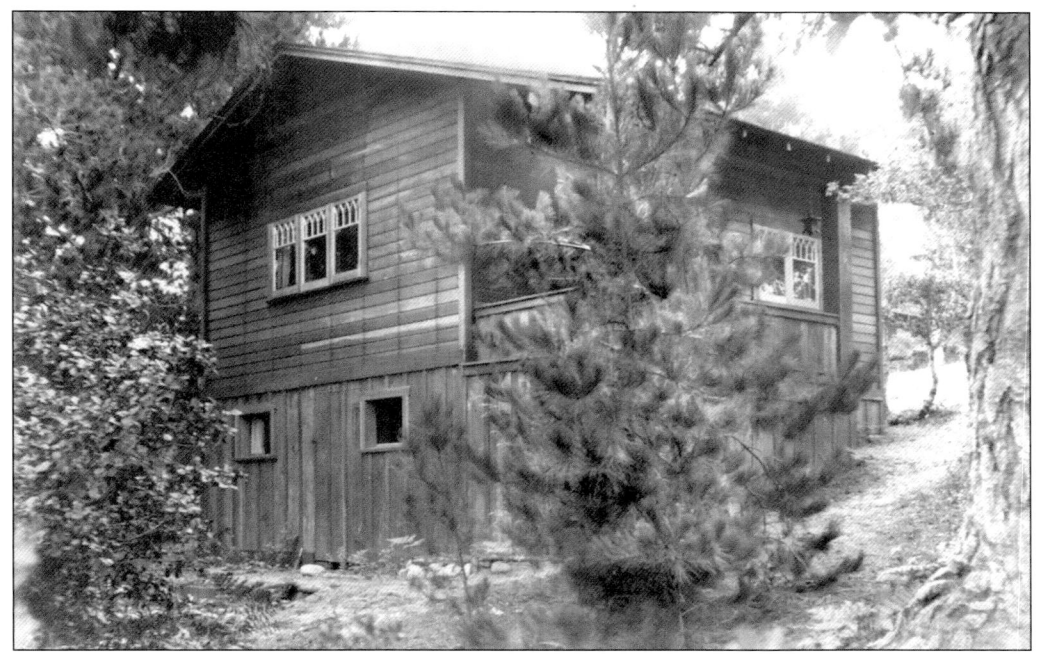

Called by poet George Sterling "Our Lady of Laughter," Mabel Gray Lachmund was Carmel's first music teacher. Trained as a pianist in London, this single mother of two purchased a pair of lots on Lincoln between Fourth and Fifth Avenues in 1902 for $50. In 1905, she hired M. J. Murphy to construct this simple 750-square-foot, wood-framed cottage. (Photograph courtesy of Linda Lachmund Smith Collection.)

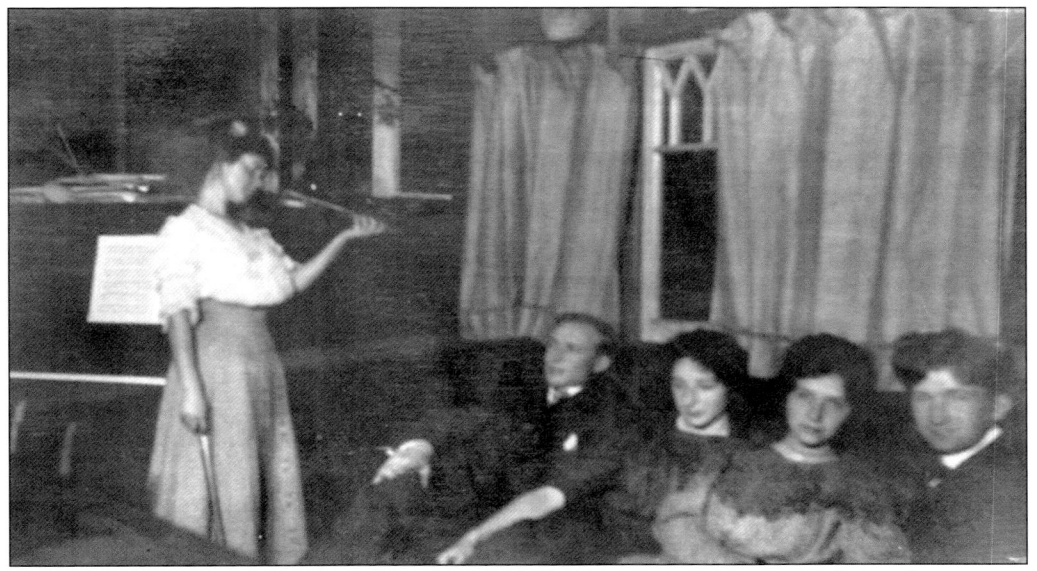

Violinist Adele Hale entertains some of Carmel's bohemian group in the Lachmund cottage c. 1908. Included are her husband, writer Fred Bechdolt, with journalist Jimmy Hopper and his wife to the right. The white-framed Queen Anne–style windows, with their diamond-shaped muntins, tend to be a signature of contractor M. J. Murphy's early work. (Photograph courtesy of Linda Lachmund Smith Collection.)

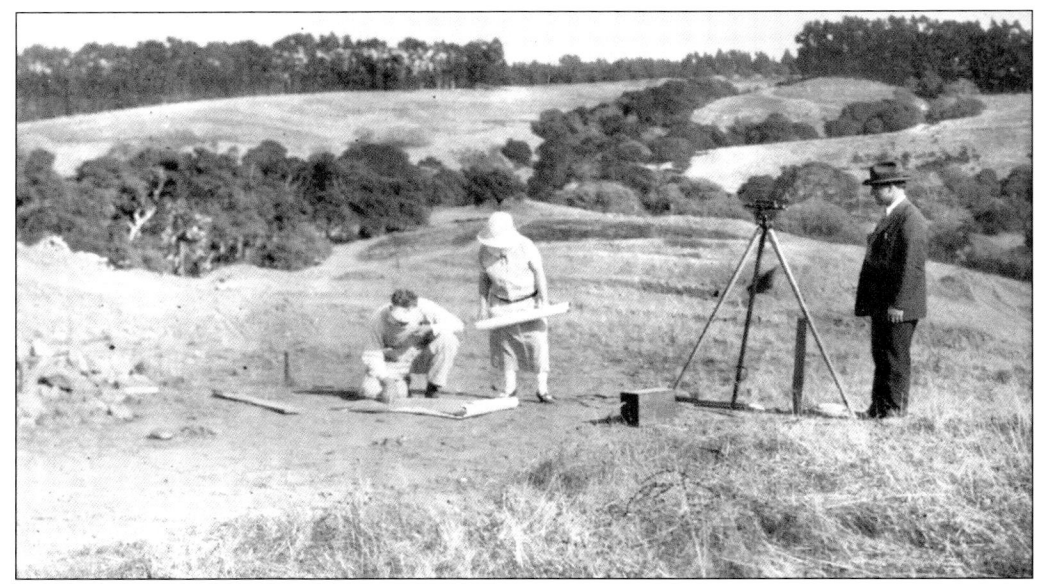

Master builder Michael J. Murphy and his wife, Edna, survey a site in Carmel for a new residence while the draftsman looks on. By 1914, Murphy had established his own contracting firm, and by 1924, he was in the building materials business, with a lumber mill, cabinet shop, and rock crusher. Michael handled the fieldwork, and Edna managed the office. (Photograph courtesy of Thomas Gladney.)

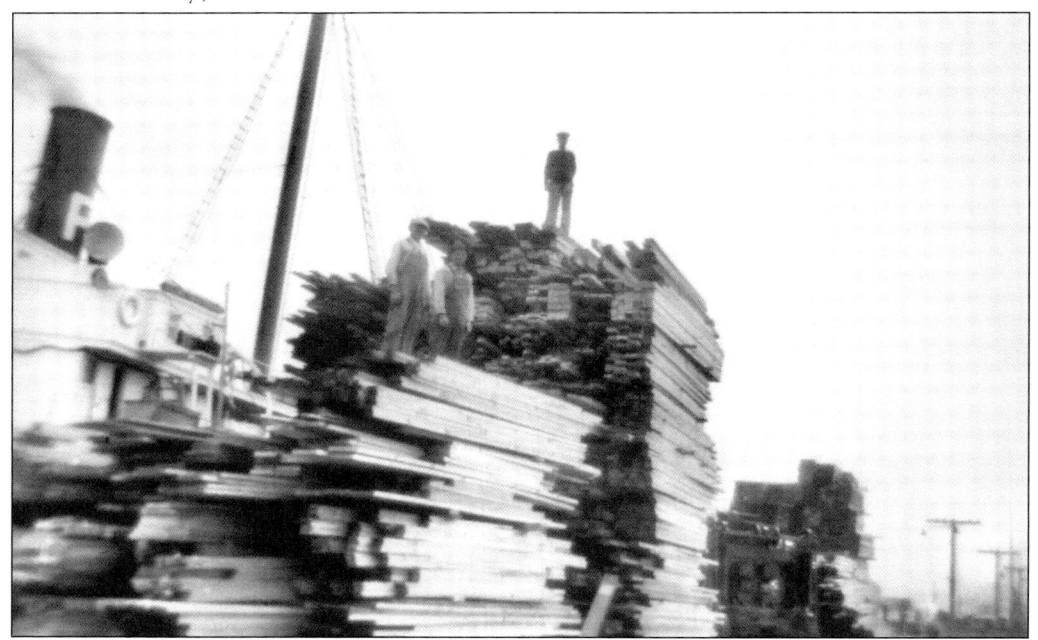

Coastal steamers brought most of the finished lumber from San Francisco to the Monterey Peninsula. Early lumberyards included those owned by Herman Prinz and Thomas Lambert. Albert Hansen's Union Supply Company in New Monterey was established in 1904. The Carmel Development Company bought their material in San Francisco and hauled it direct from the wharf. (Photograph courtesy of Thomas Gladney.)

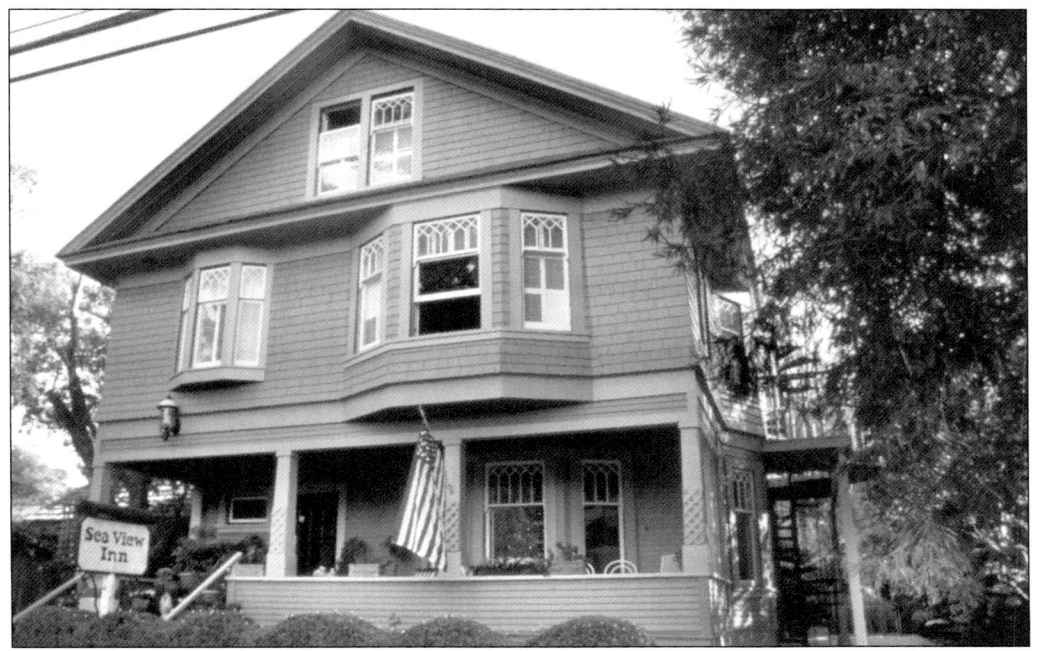

M. J. Murphy built this vernacular suburban cottage for Abbie McDow and Amiee Jones c. 1907. The design was based on the transference of narrow, front-gabled Eastern row houses of the 1880s to wider, stand-alone residences in railroad suburbs in the 1890s. The building reflects vestiges of Queen Anne styling with Colonial Revival details. In 1924, the Stout sisters opened the property as the Sea View Inn. (Photograph by the author.)

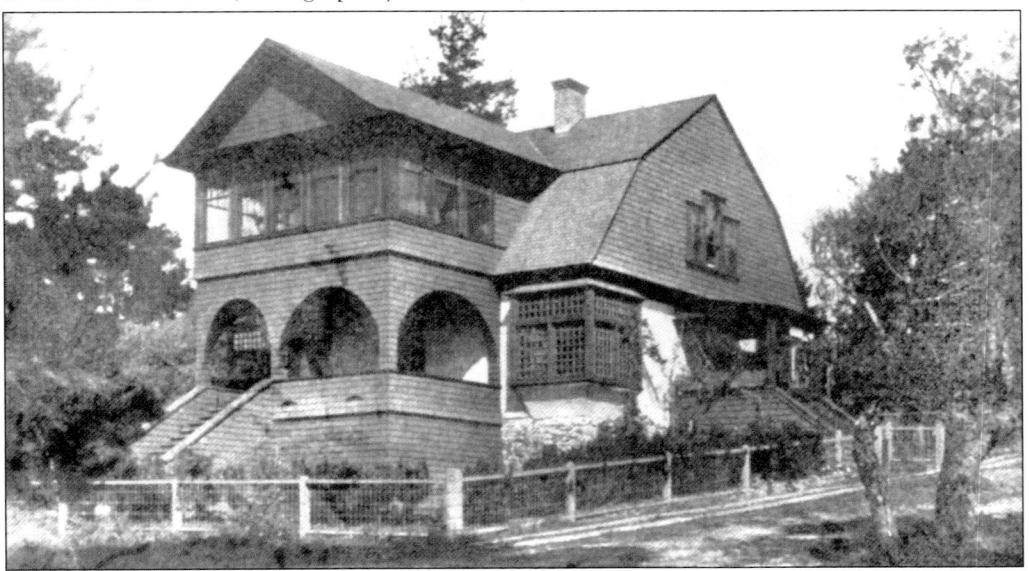

In 1903, M. J. Murphy constructed this example of a pattern-book, gambrel-roofed, Colonial Revival house for Dewitt Johnson, owner of the Hotel Carmel. Johnson became one of the first elected trustees of Carmel in 1916. Located at the northeast corner of Casanova Street and Seventh Avenue, the imposing residence dispels the myth that all of Carmel's early housing was small and quaint. (Photograph courtesy of Pat Hathaway, Historic California Views.)

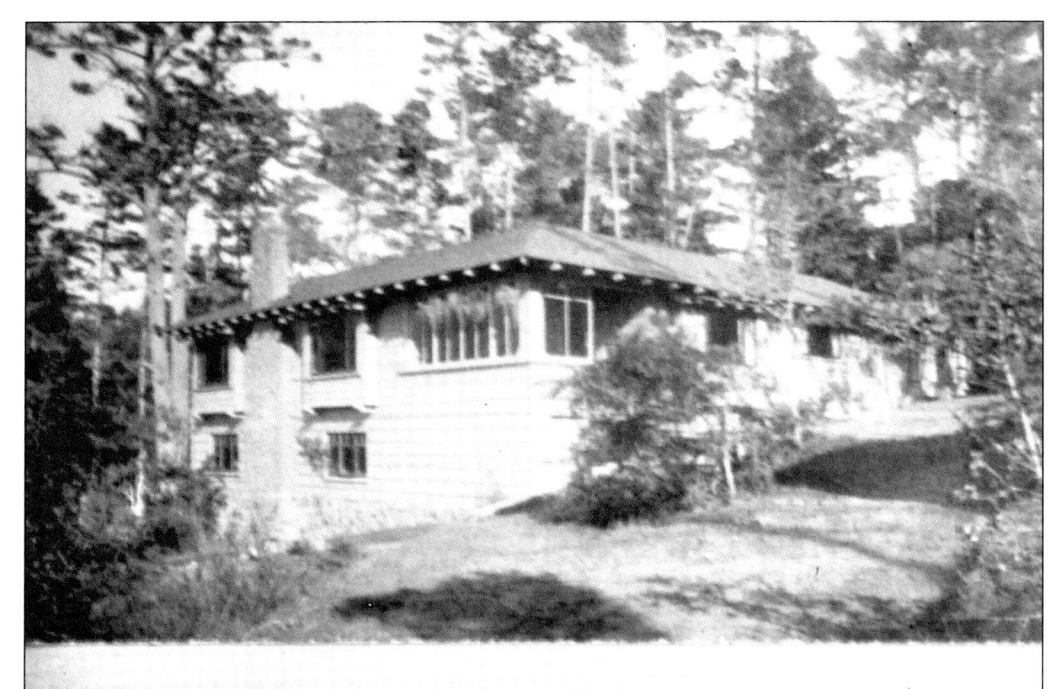

> Mine is a door to which you'll find no key:
> ... The latch-string hangs — come tarry here with me:
> For of my friends, some smile and some are sad,
> Some old tried friends, some new, some poorly clad.
> What matters it — the door swings wide and free.

M. J. Murphy built this hillside cottage called Sleepy Hollow for Peter and Margaret Taylor in 1916. The hipped roof surrounds an open central atrium that provides protection from the elements. Many of the earlier Carmel homes were U-shaped in plan, with the open end of the U facing south. This protected patios from prevailing winds, took advantage of the afternoon sun, and afforded intimate views of the forest and the sea. (Photograph from the author's collection.)

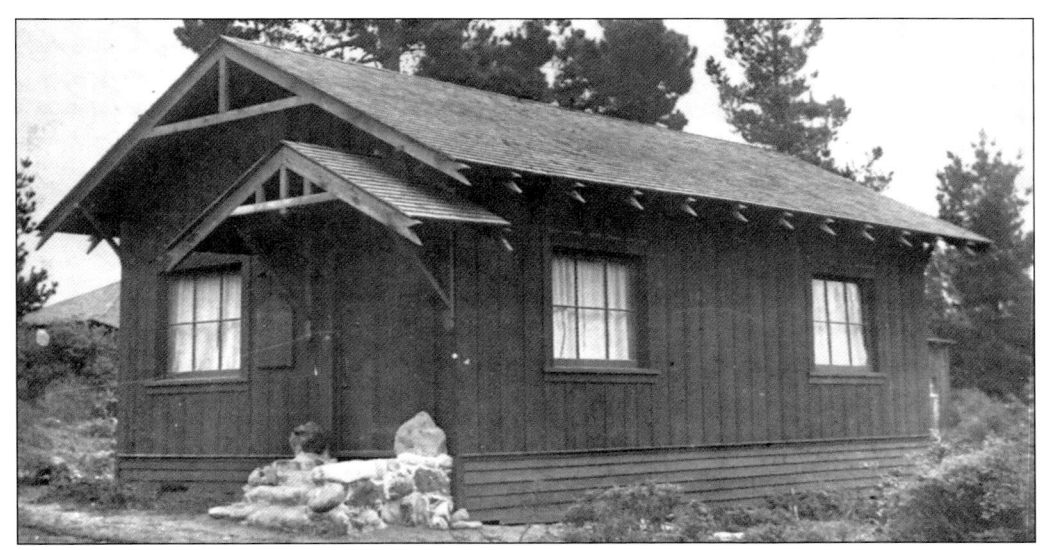

Carmel's early churches were quite informal, as evidenced by this simple craftsman building that housed Carmel Missionary Society's congregation in 1911. M. E. White led the effort to build the church, which met the spiritual needs of about 30 Japanese farmers and fishermen in the Carmel area. (Photograph courtesy of the Harrison Memorial Library Collection.)

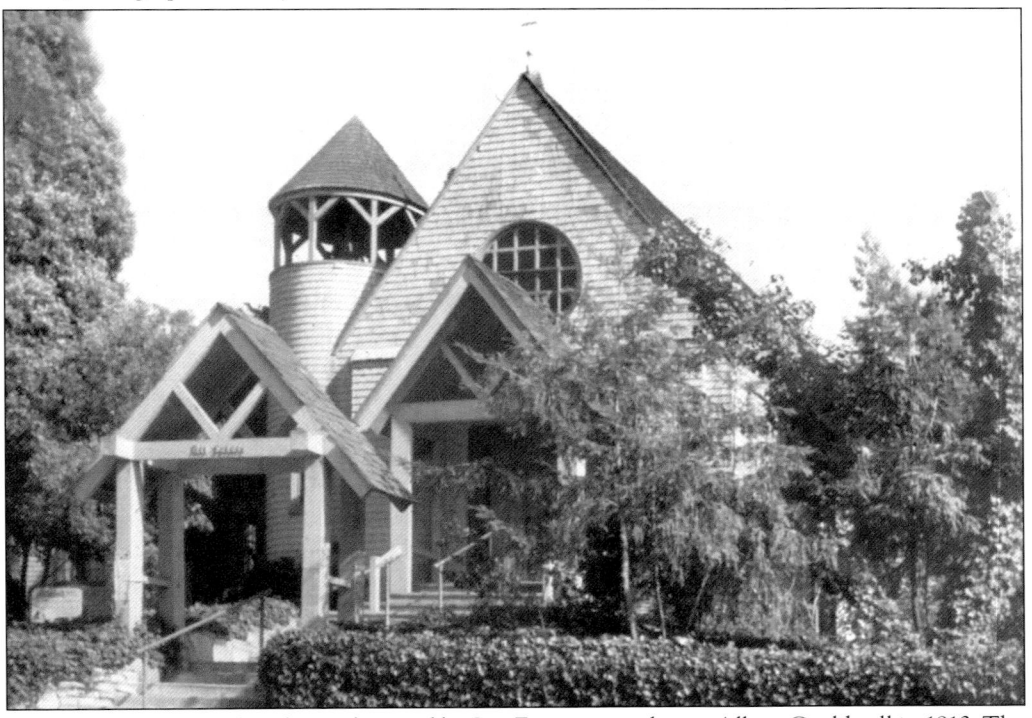

All Saints Episcopal Church was designed by San Francisco architect Albert Cauldwell in 1913. The photograph shows additions made to the shingle-style chapel by M. J. Murphy in 1928. When All Saints built new facilities in 1946, Mayor Fred Godwin and the city council approved the purchase of the church for Carmel's new city hall. The building serves as the seat of local government in Carmel. (Photograph by George Cain; courtesy of the City of Carmel-by-the-Sea.)

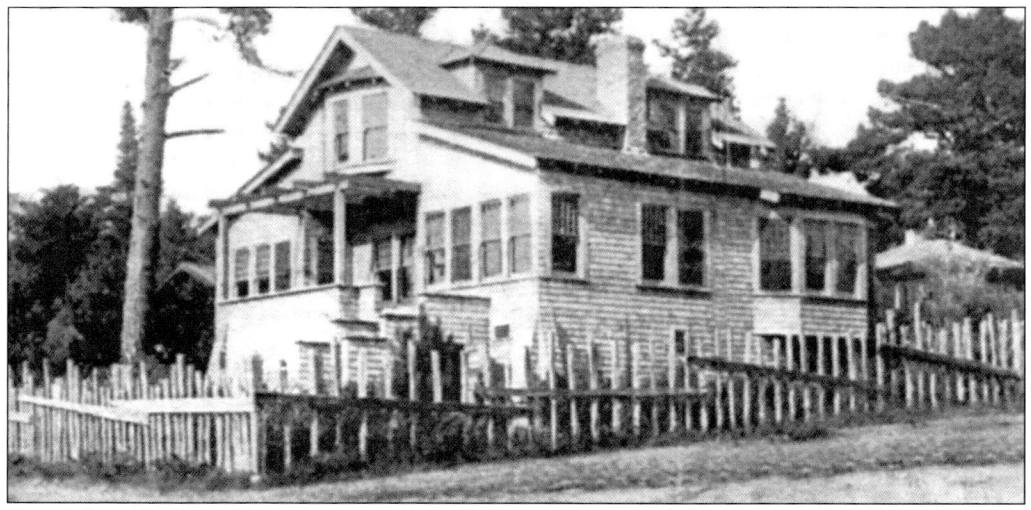

David Starr Jordan, first president of Stanford University, had this shingle-style residence built at the corner of Camino Real and Seventh Avenue in 1905. Gustav Laumeister may have been the designer. Jordan encouraged fellow Stanford instructors to build in Carmel, initiating what came to be called "Professors Row" along the first two blocks of Camino Real off Ocean Avenue. (Photograph courtesy of Pat Hathaway, Historic California Views.)

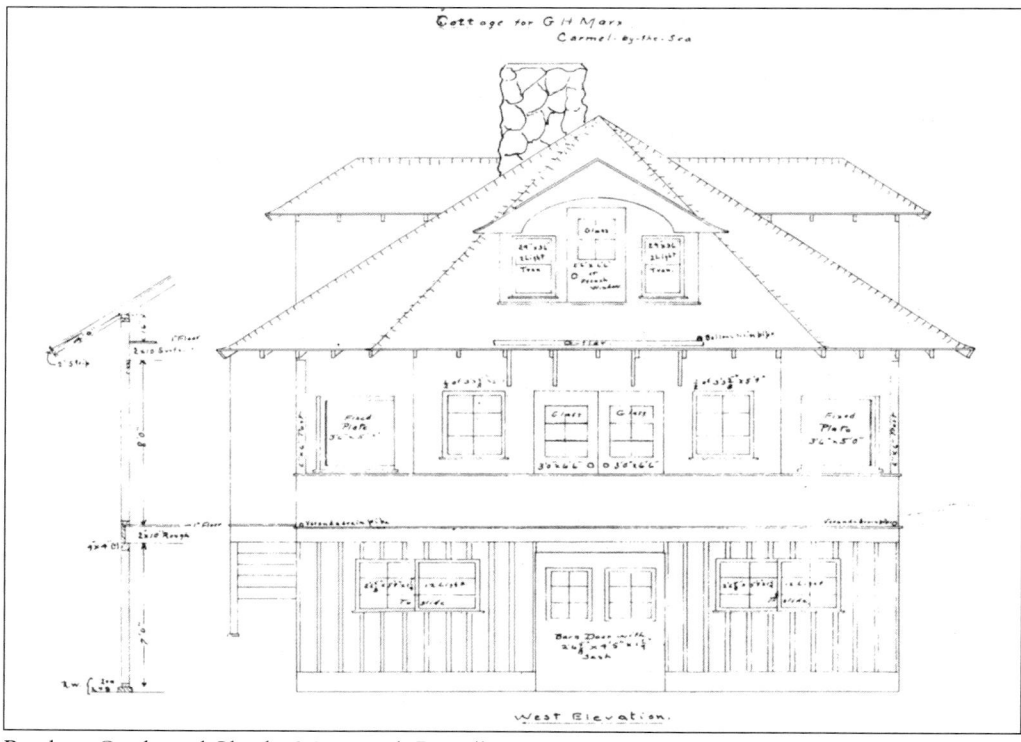

Brothers Guido and Charles Marx, with Dr. Albert W. Smith, established the School of Engineering at Stanford University. In 1905, Dr. Guido Marx purchased two lots along Professor's Row for $100 and constructed a boxy, wood-shingled, American foursquare residence of his own design. Marx may also have been the builder. (Drawing by Dr. Guido Marx; courtesy of Chris Tescher.)

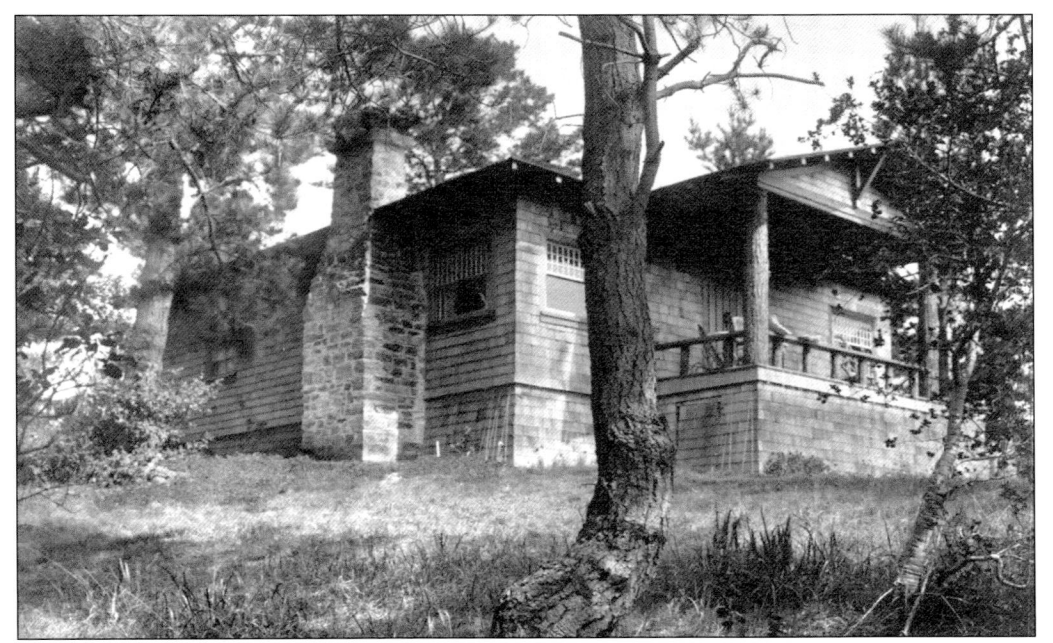

San Francisco poet George Sterling drew the city's bohemian circle to Carmel. In July 1905, Sterling brought his builders, publisher W. W. Woods, the "boss carpenter," and boyhood friend Gene Fenelon to construct a craftsman cottage on the writer's property in the undeveloped Eighty Acres tract southeast of Ocean Avenue and Junipero Street. (Photograph by E. A. Cohen; courtesy of Pat Hathaway, Historic California Views.)

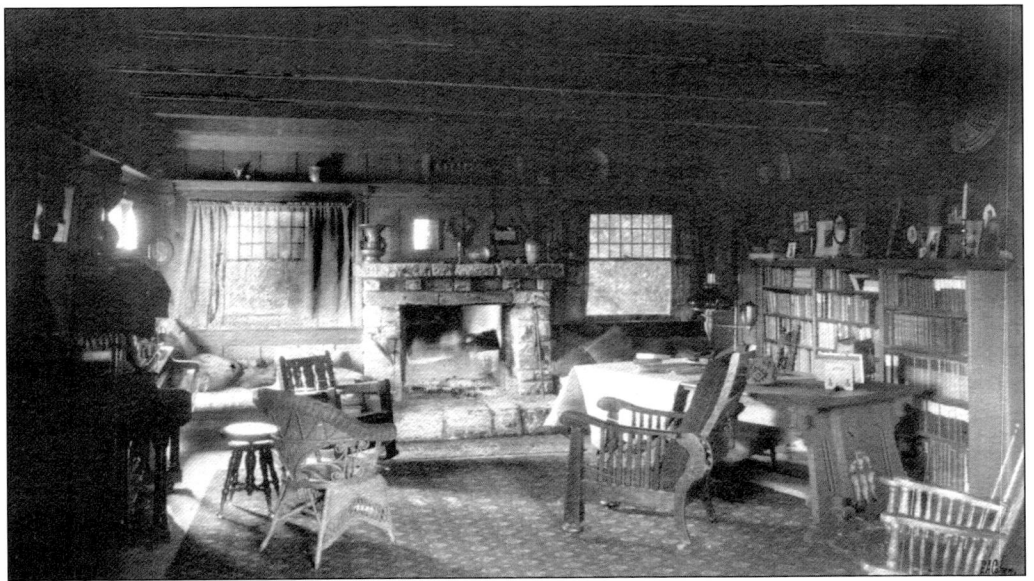

Sterling described the interior of his new house, completed in October 1905: "My 'living room' is 30 by 18 ft., 'finished' oiled redwood, and with a huge fireplace and chimney. The chalk-rock for which I obtained by making several trips to a ranch a few miles up the Carmel Valley. The first fire was lit in late September." (Photograph by E. A. Cohen; courtesy of Pat Hathaway, Historic California Views.)

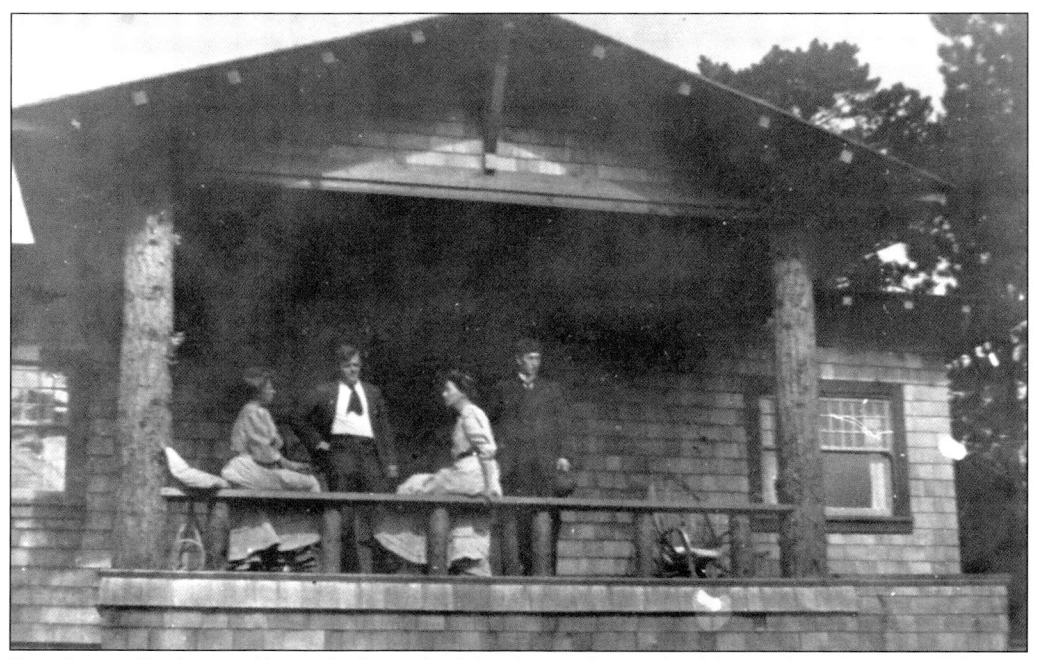

Poet George Sterling and his wife, Carrie (right), relax on the porch of the Sterling cottage with friends Charmian and Jack London. Carmel Bay, which Sterling described as "blue as sapphire," was just half a mile away. In 1913, Jimmy Hopper and his wife purchased the Sterling cottage when the poet returned to San Francisco. (Photograph courtesy of the Harrison Memorial Library Collection.)

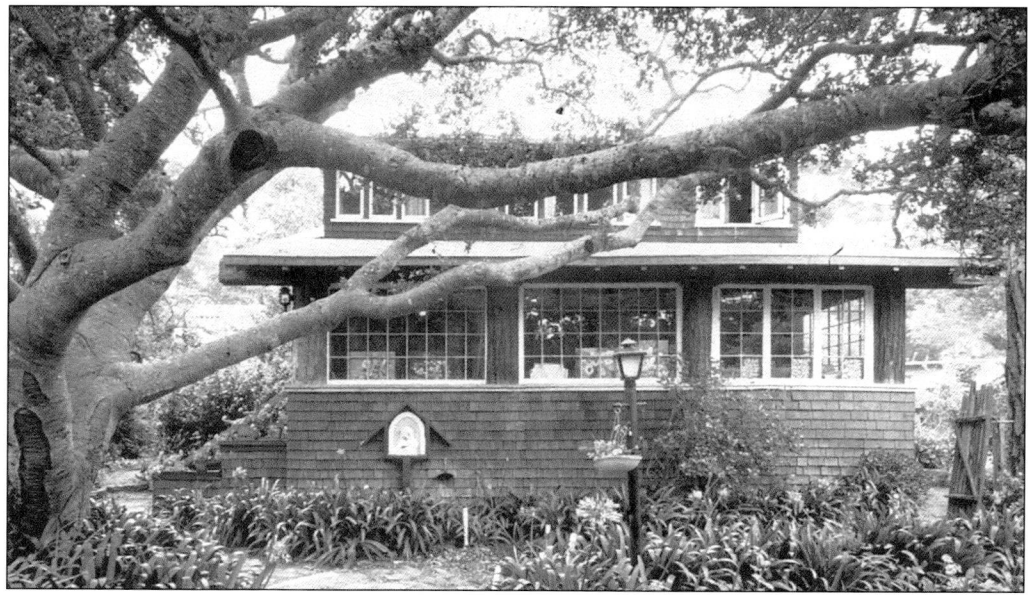

Renowned photographer Arnold Genthe was a Bohemian Club friend of both Frank Powers and George Sterling. Genthe designed and built the wood-shingled bungalow he had always wanted at Carmel in 1906. His full-width open porch was supported by four large redwood tree trunks, facing Carmel Bay from Camino Real. (Photograph by Morley Baer; courtesy of Monterey Peninsula College.)

Natural light from the skylights in the redwood ceiling of Arnold Genthe's studio/living room highlight its craftsman furniture. The photographer had the first cement basement in Carmel. He used it to develop his photographs of the 1906 earthquake and fire, having lost his San Francisco home to the conflagration. (Photograph courtesy of Pat Hathaway, Historic California Views.)

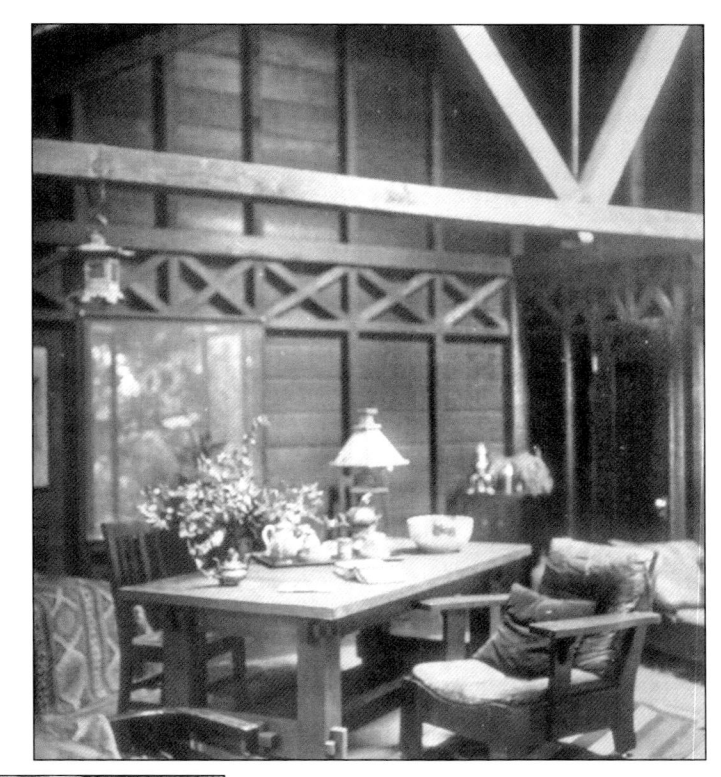

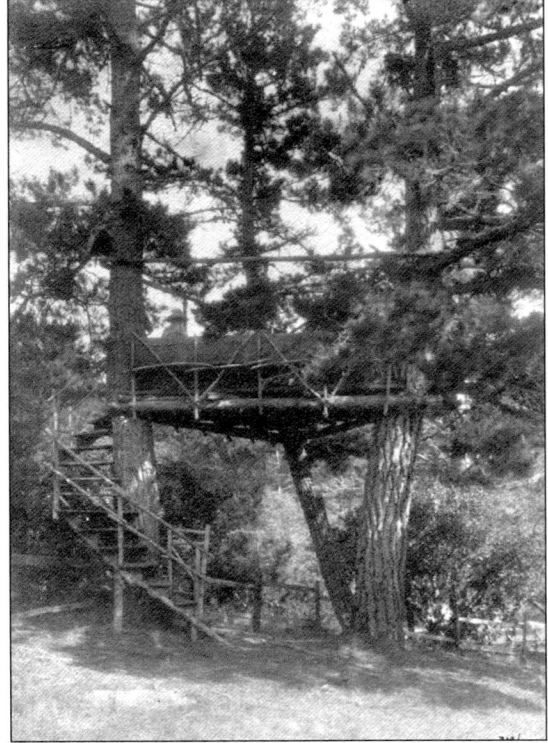

Carmel was an early haven for creative and independent women. One of the founders of its bohemian art colony was novelist Mary Austin. When the author settled in the village in 1906, she rented a log cabin and did much of her writing in a tree house, possibly designed by Louis C. Mullgardt, that she called her "Wick-i-up." (Photograph by E. A. Cohen; courtesy of Pat Hathaway, Historic California Views.)

57

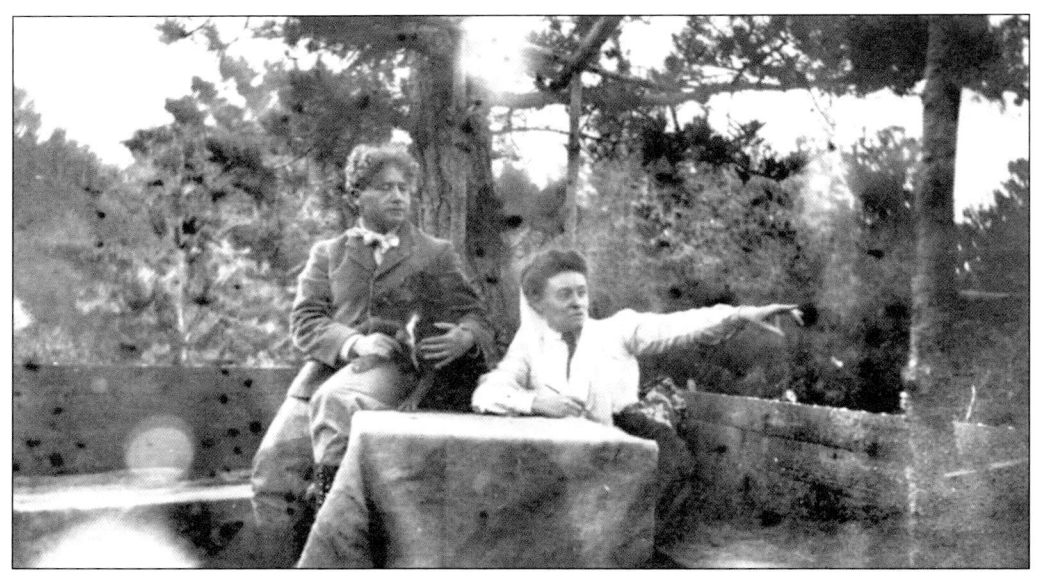

Mary Austin visited Carmel in 1902 while researching her novel *Isidro*, partially set at the Carmel Mission. She was prone to wearing Grecian robes or the beaded leather costume and long braids of a Native American princess. Austin is seen here in more conventional dress at her writing desk with fellow author Jimmy Hopper. (Photograph courtesy of the Harrison Memorial Library Collection.)

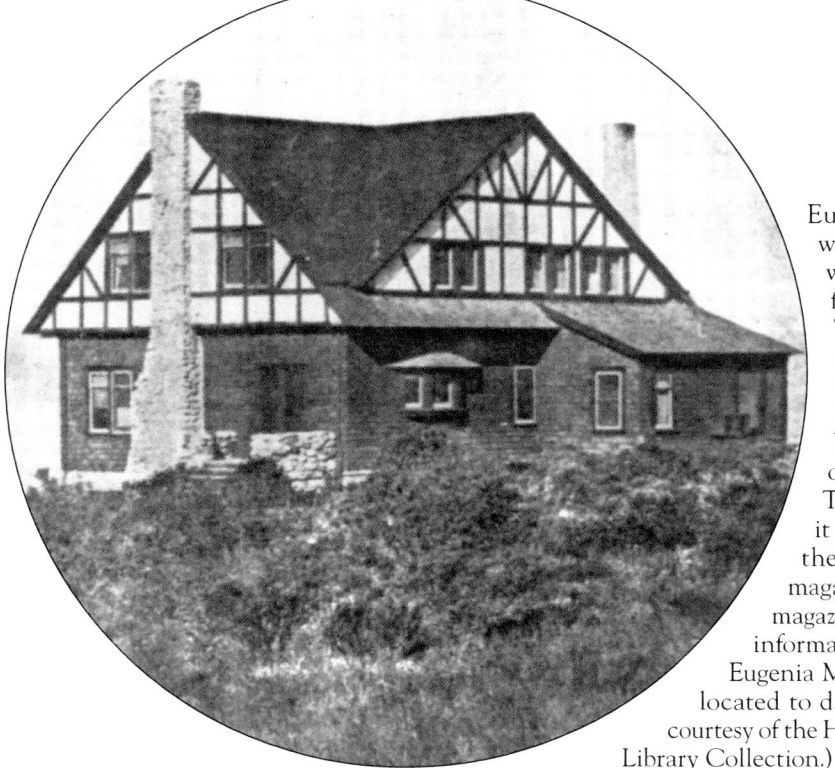

Eugenia Maybury was the architect who designed the first half-timbered Tudor Revival residence in Carmel in 1905. Ben Turner was its builder. Located on the north side of Thirteenth Avenue, it was published in the *House Beautiful* magazine. Neither the magazine article nor any information on architect Eugenia Maybury has been located to date. (Photograph courtesy of the Harrison Memorial Library Collection.)

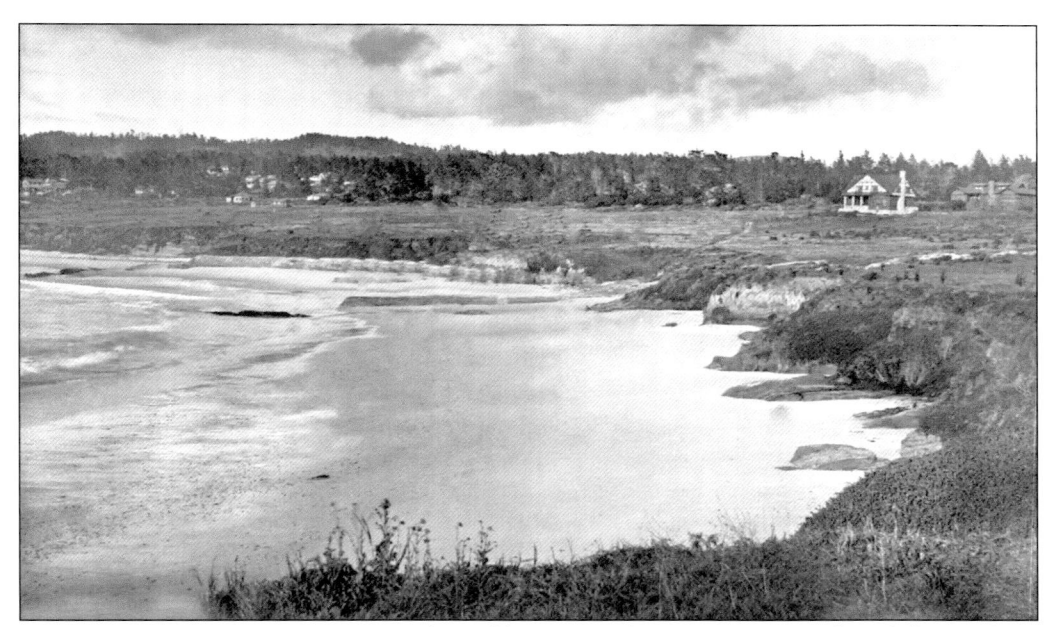

In 1908, writers Grace McGowan Cooke and her sister Alice McGowan purchased the Maybury house. They called the place Locksley Hall, as there were no street numbers in Carmel. The house became a rallying point for the creative artists from the village on their way to Cooke's Cove for a beach supper of mussels, abalone, Spanish beans, red wine, and coffee. (Photograph courtesy of Pat Hathaway, Historic California Views.)

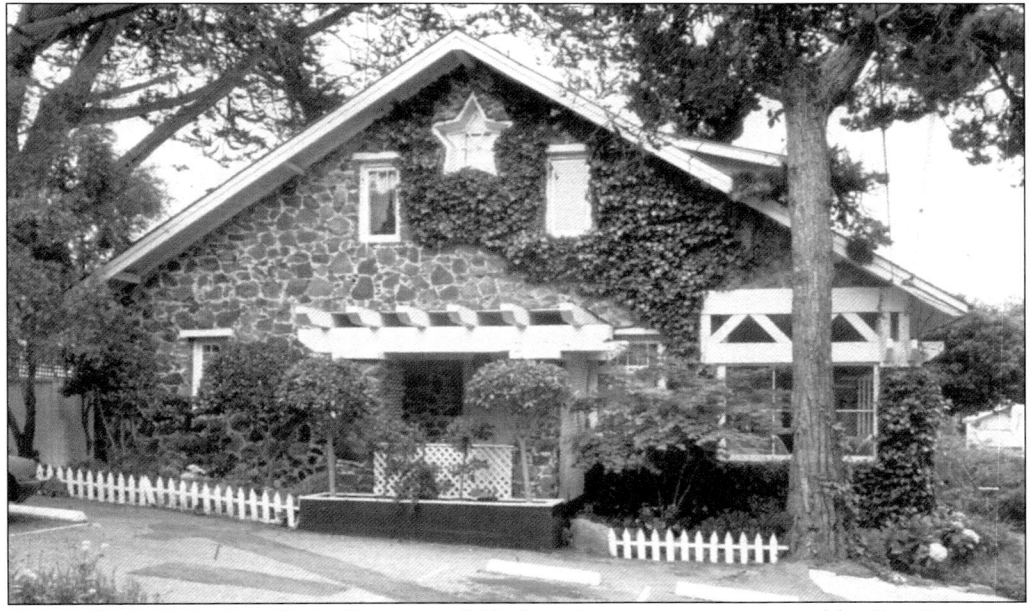

Originally built for Josephine Foster in 1906, Stonehouse was constructed by San Francisco contractor W. W. Wood. The stonemasonry appears to be the work of Ben Turner. Note the star window in the gable apex. Foster, a writer, was a patron of the arts in Carmel, often entertaining the village literati in her handsome craftsman residence. (Photograph by Morley Baer; courtesy of Monterey Peninsula College.)

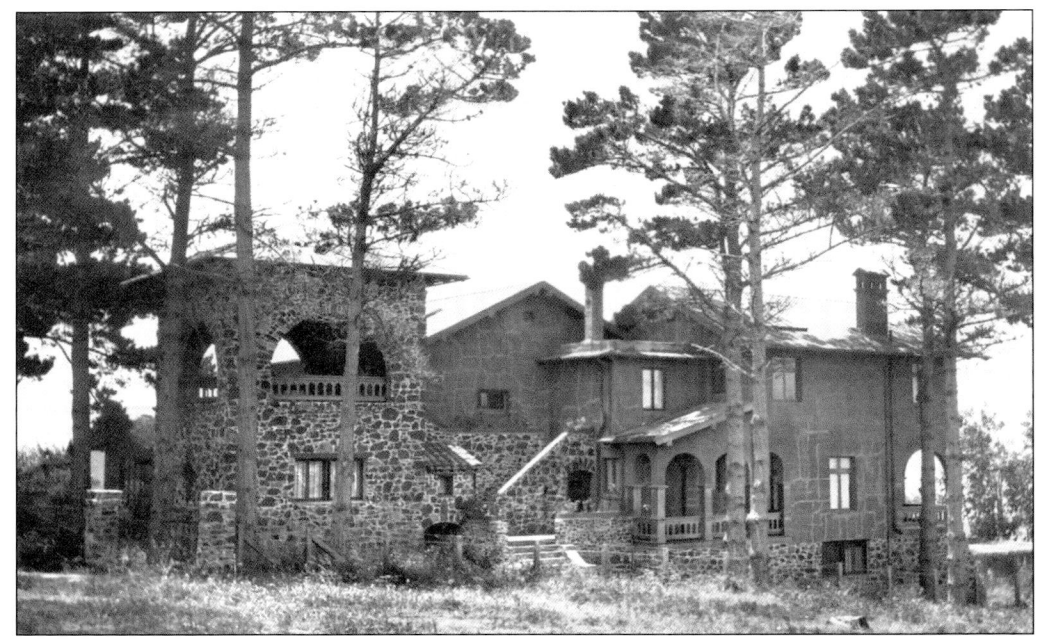

Artist Christian Jorgensen and his wife, Angela Ghirardelli, constructed La Playa in Carmel in 1906. Jorgensen provided the design, and Ben Turner built the distinctive stone tower with its quatrefoil window, paying homage to the Carmel Mission. Seaweed was employed to insulate the walls, and the place had one of the first swimming pools in Carmel. (Photograph courtesy of the Harrison Memorial Library Collection.)

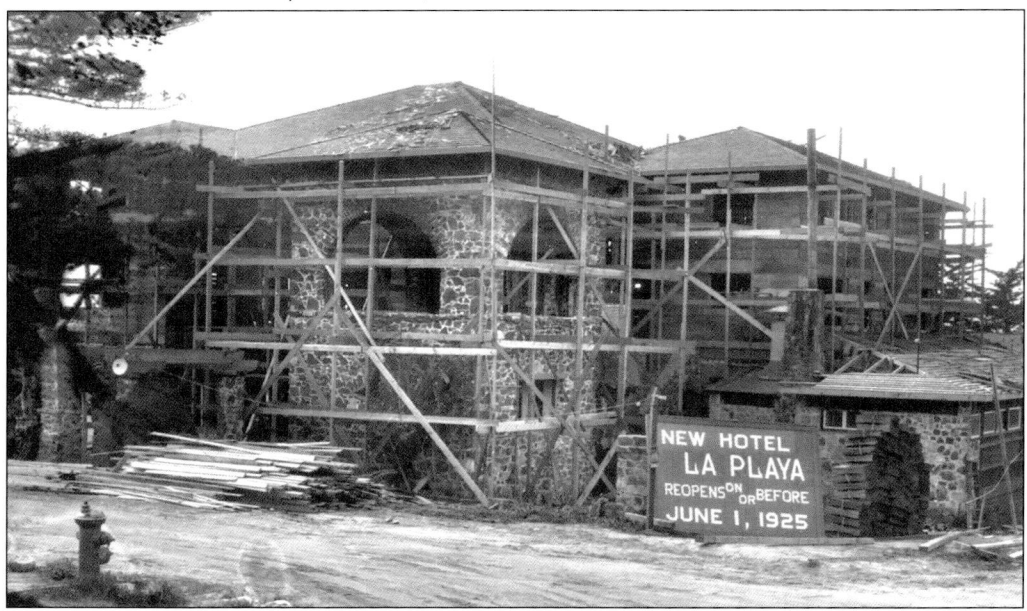

In 1909, Angela Ghirardelli's niece drowned in Carmel Bay. The loss precipitated the couple's departure from Carmel. La Playa was leased to Agnes Signor, who added rooms and operated it as a hotel. Signor bought the property in 1916. A fire in the mid-1920s required rebuilding. M. J. Murphy was the contractor. (Photograph courtesy of Pat Hathaway, Historic California Views.)

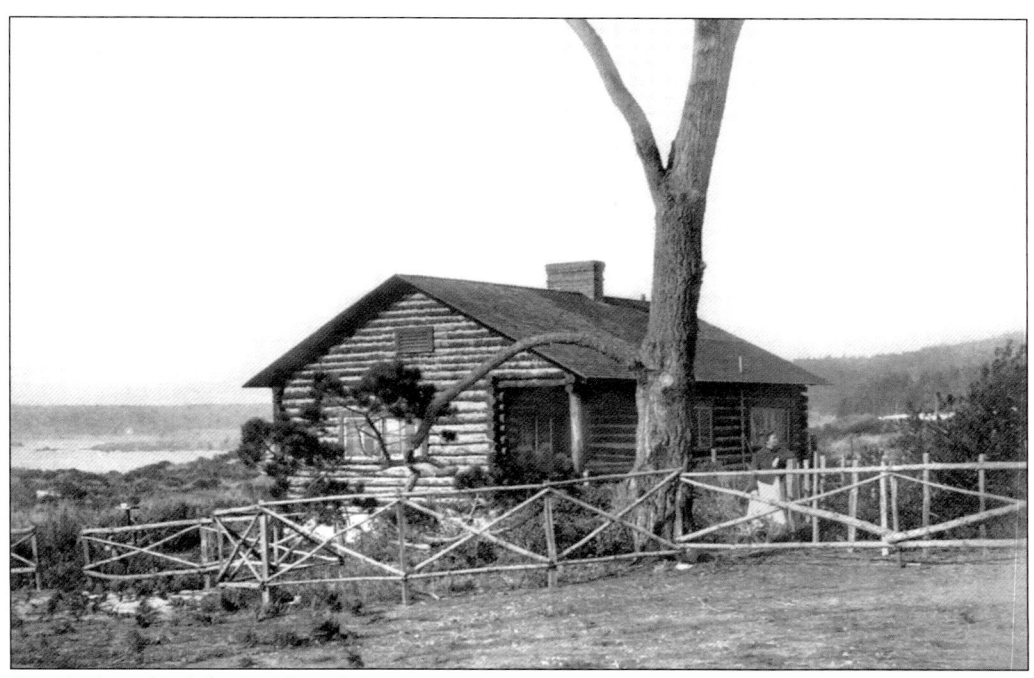

Stanford medical doctors Levi Lane and Virginia Smiley had Log Haven constructed about 1907 on the north side of Eighth Avenue near Carmelo Avenue. Note the open space beyond the rustic cabin. The property was incorporated into a commercial development called Cottages by the Sea in 1941 by Adolph LaFrenz, with contractor Ernest Bixler as builder. (Photograph courtesy of Pat Hathaway, Historic California Views.)

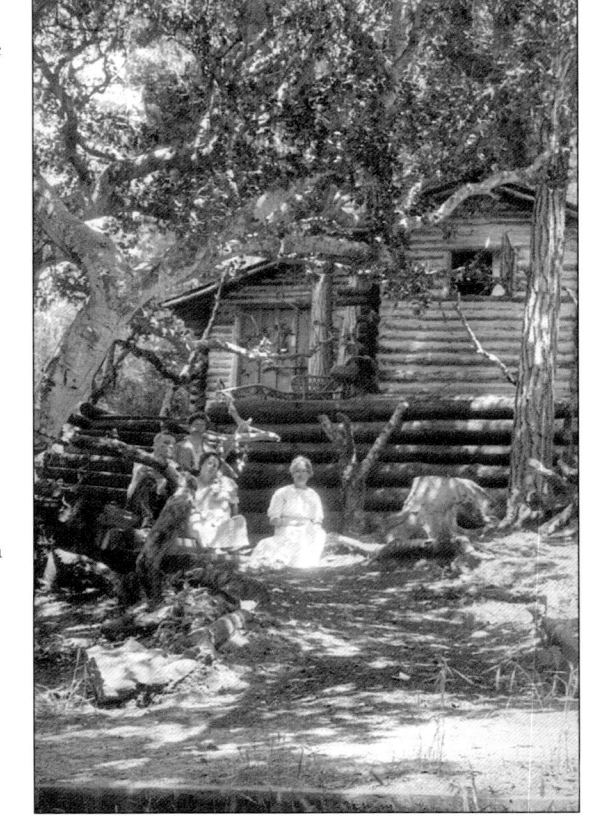

Alameda attorney George H. Richardson built this log cabin on Monte Verde Street about 1903. It was one of four or five log houses in early Carmel. In 1914, newly married Robinson Jeffers and his wife, Una, rented it as their first Carmel home. Jeffers and family members are seen on the porch. (Photograph courtesy of the Tor House Foundation Archival Collection.)

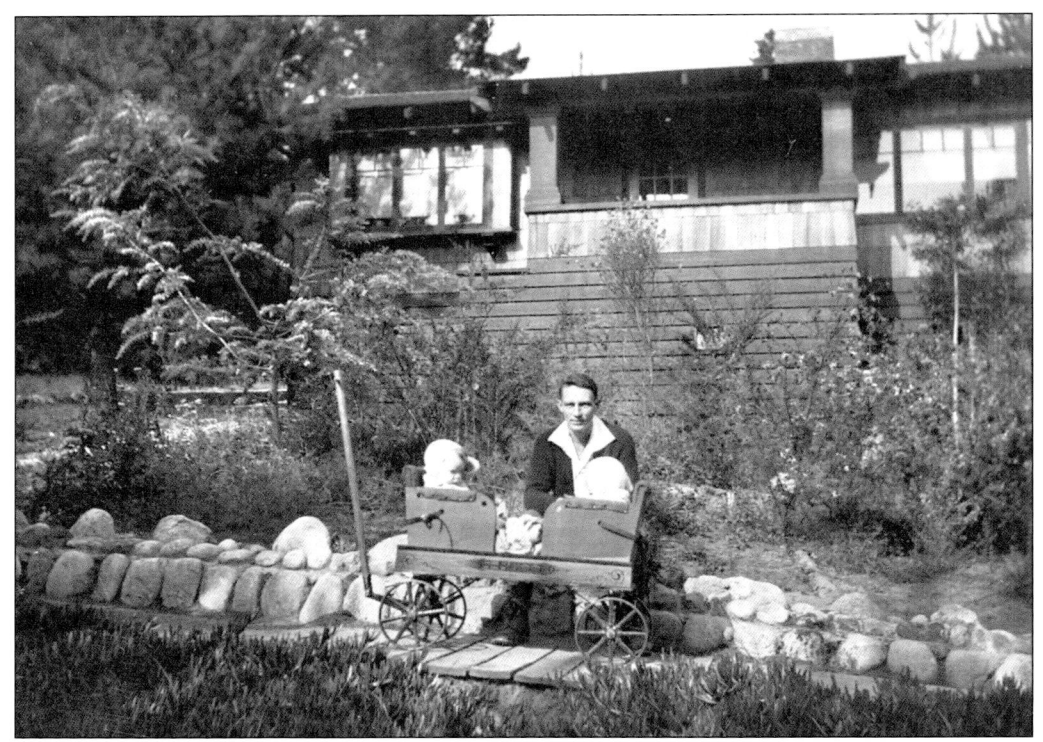

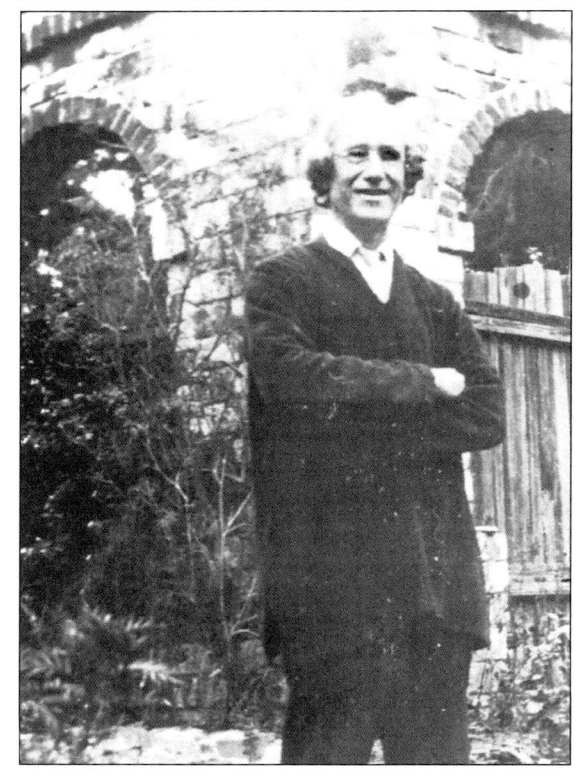

Constructed in 1914 for Adelaide J. Trethaway, this craftsman cottage became the second Carmel home of the Robinson Jeffers family in 1917, after the birth of their twins Donnan and Garth, seen here with their father. Sited on Lopez Avenue, the cottage afforded excellent views of Carmel Point, where Jeffers was building Tor House. (Photograph courtesy of Tor House Foundation Archival Collection.)

Architect Charles Sumner Greene, who had precipitated California's bungalow movement with his brother Henry in Pasadena at the beginning of the 20th century, moved to Carmel in 1916. Like Robinson Jeffers, the architect's family lived in rented quarters for a considerable period before Greene designed a permanent home in the village. (Photograph courtesy of Pat Hathaway, Historic California Views.)

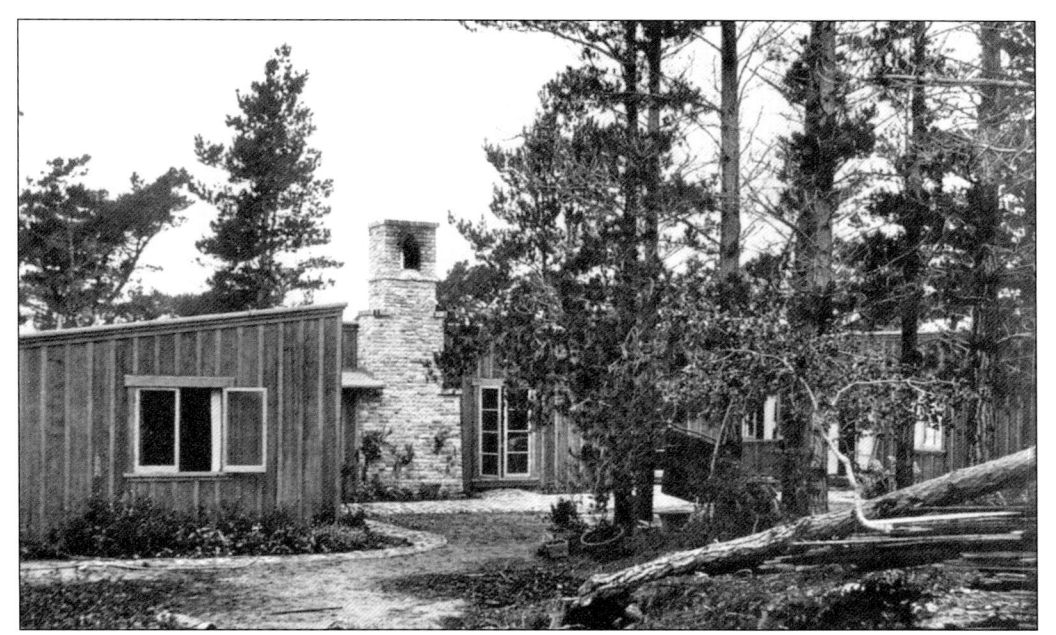

In 1919, Greene purchased seven lots along Lincoln Street south of Thirteenth Avenue. In 1921, he designed and built this small, shed-roofed, U-shaped, board-and-batten cottage based loosely on his 1903 Arturo Bandini House in Pasadena. The walls were fabricated on the ground and lifted into place, and the concrete foundation was one of the first in Carmel. (Photograph courtesy of the Gamble House Foundation.)

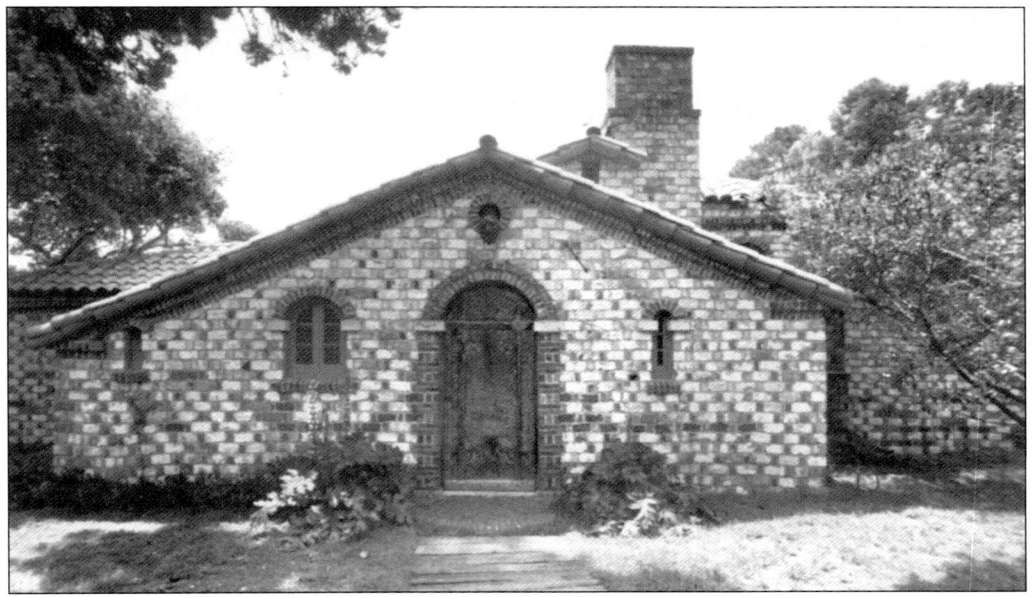

Greene and his son, Nathanial, did much of the work building a studio in 1924. The used-brick wall cladding came from the old El Carmelo Hotel in Pacific Grove, and the oak and teakwood for flooring and doors were a gift from the White Lumber Company of San Francisco. The roof tiles were left over from the James house job. Charles Greene did all the woodcarving. (Photograph by Morley Baer; courtesy of Monterey Peninsula College.)

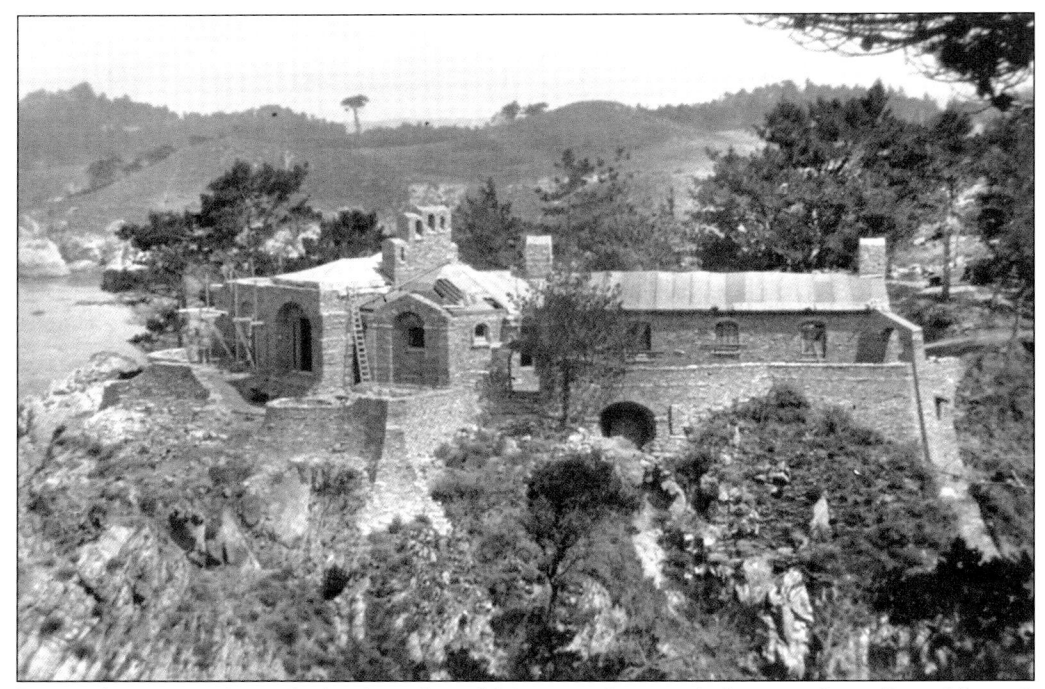

Battered stones tied into bedrock anchored Missouri china and glass merchant Daniel James's Carmel Highlands residence into a cliff face as if it had grown there. Built between 1917 and 1922, C. S. Greene personally supervised every aspect of its construction. It was his only building done entirely in stone. (Photograph courtesy of Pat Hathaway, Historic California Views.)

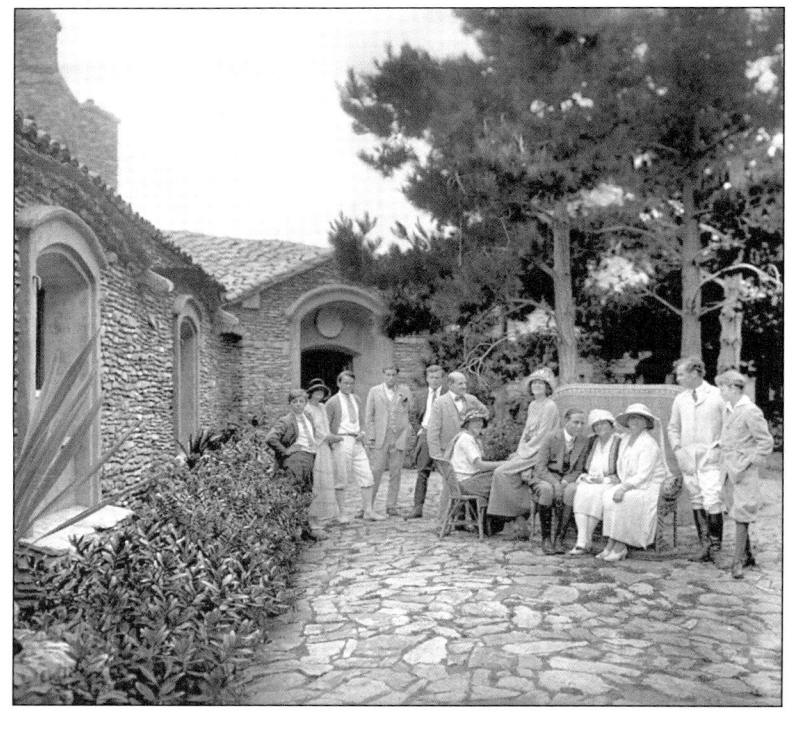

Daniel James and his wife, Lillie, (seated at the left end of the wicker bench) entertain friends in 1925 in the courtyard of Tintagel, their newly completed summer home near Carmel. James came to the Carmel area to be a writer. His son Dan (standing, far right) also took up the pen, winning high praise for his novels under the nom de plume Danny Santiago. (Photograph courtesy of Pat Hathaway, Historic California Views.)

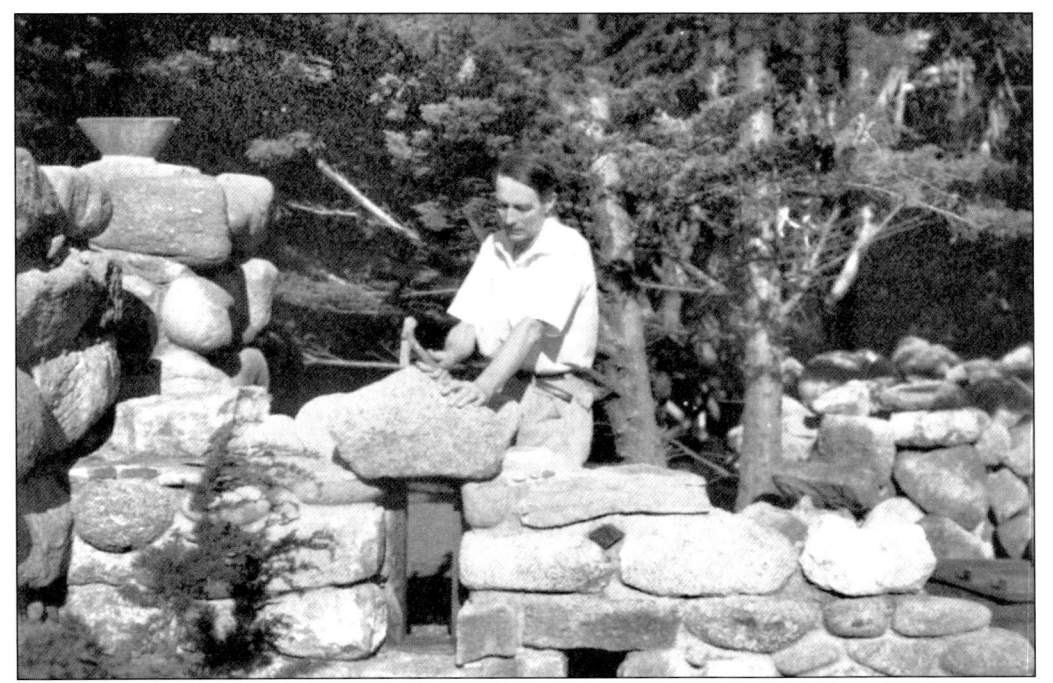

Robinson Jeffers built his Carmel home on five acres of windswept land at Carmel Point that he purchased in 1914 for $500. Called Tor House, construction began in 1919 from local granite rock. Jeffers apprenticed as a laborer with the project stonemason, a man named Pierson, in order to learn the masons' craft. (Photograph courtesy of the Tor House Foundation Archival Collection.)

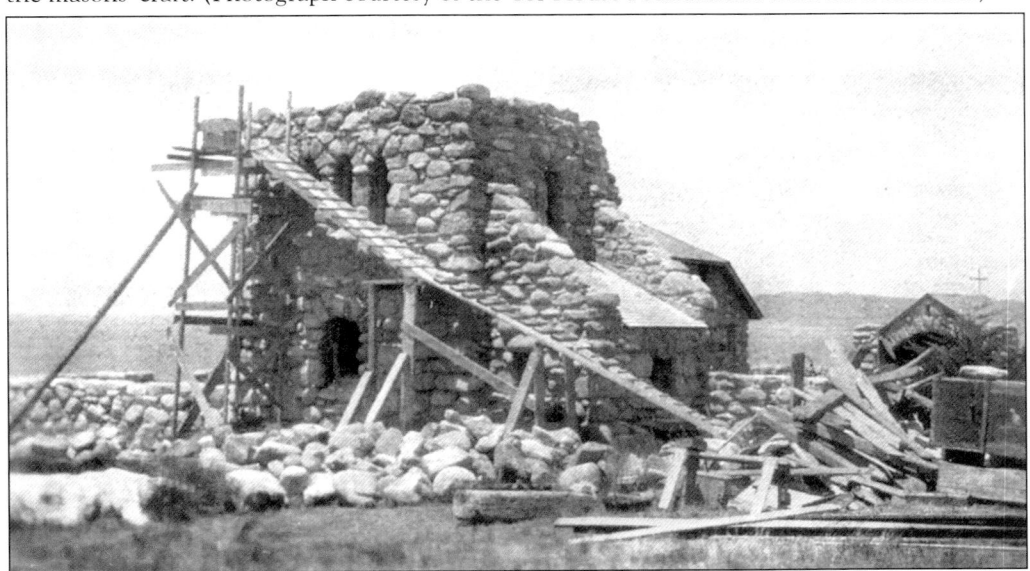

Robinson Jeffers developed his stone-setting skills on a detached garage, then on a low stone wall enclosing the courtyard at Tor House before he undertook the daunting task of building Hawk Tower. The poet worked alone on his stone aerie between 1920 and 1924. At first he rolled its granite building stones up the inclined ramp seen here. (Photograph courtesy of the Tor House Foundation Archival Collection.)

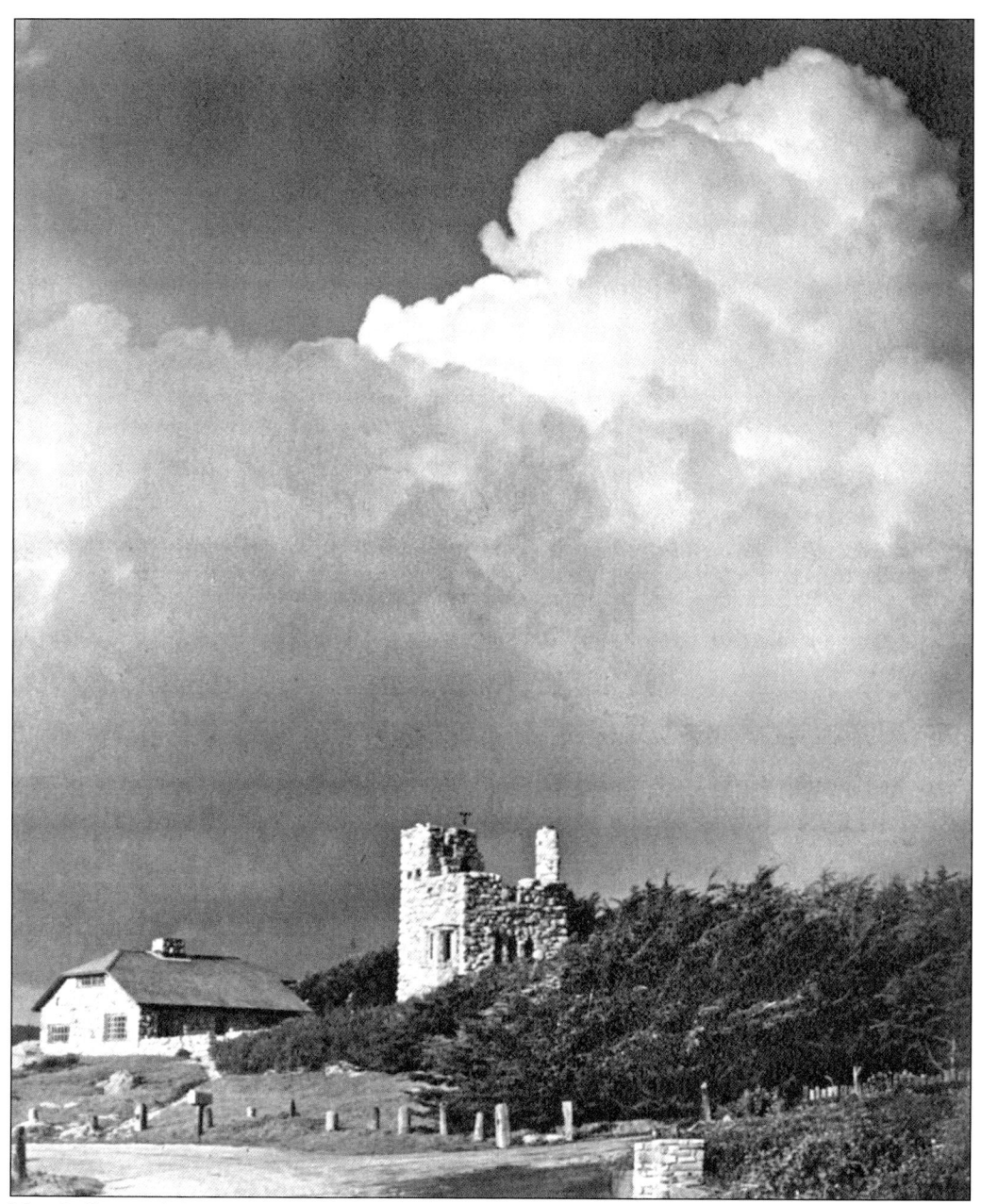

Una Jeffers said that Hawk Tower "rose out of our dreams of old Irish towers." Cemented into its granite fabric were numerous cultural artifacts, steeped with personal meaning, collected from around the world. Framing the base of Tor House are some of the 2,000 trees planted by the poet and his family over time. (Photograph by Horace B. Lyon; courtesy of the Tor House Foundation Archival Collection.)

The Jefferses' teenage son, Donnan, was as much an Anglophile as his famous parents. He is seen here in the 1940s trimming the formal cypress maze he created near Tor House as a young man. Unfortunately little remains of the large grove of trees Robinson Jeffers planted on his five-acre parcel at Carmel Point. (Photograph by Raymond Bates, courtesy of Jeffers Literary Properties.)

The inspirational source for Donnan Jeffers's cypress maze may have been England's Hampton Court or the popular topiary maze in the south garden of Monterey's Hotel Del Monte, designed by landscape architect Rudolph Ulrich. Seen here from above, its geometric composition is a strong counterpoint to the informal character of the Jeffers grove. (Photograph courtesy of Pat Hathaway, Historic California Views.)

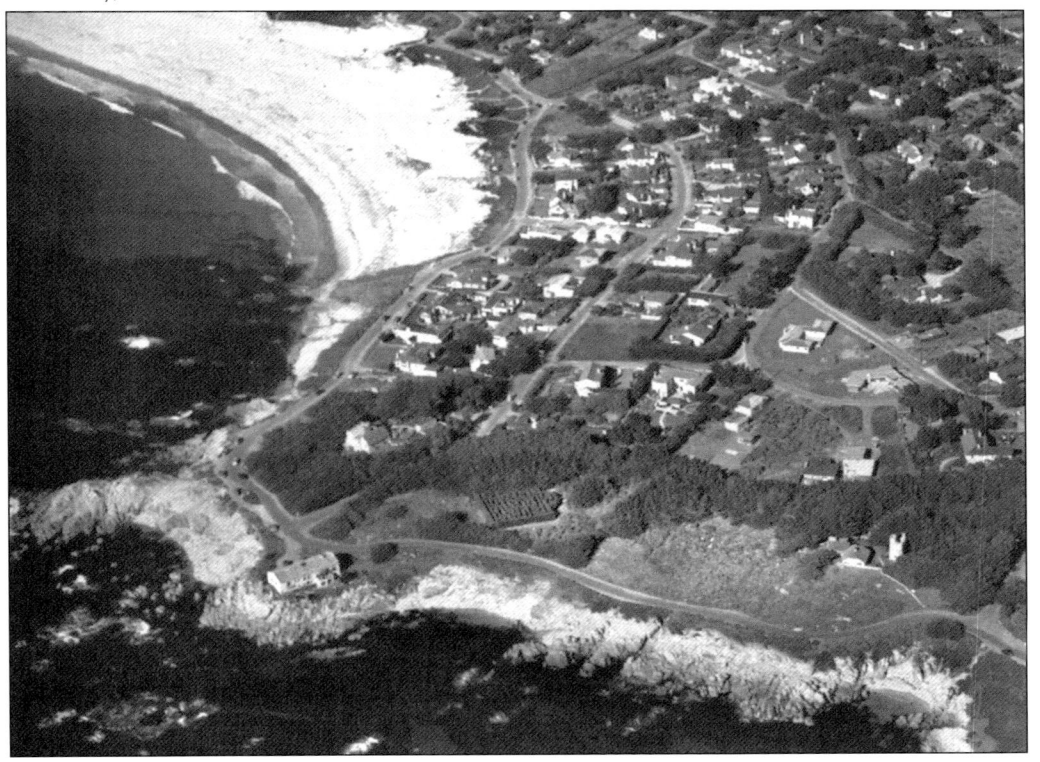

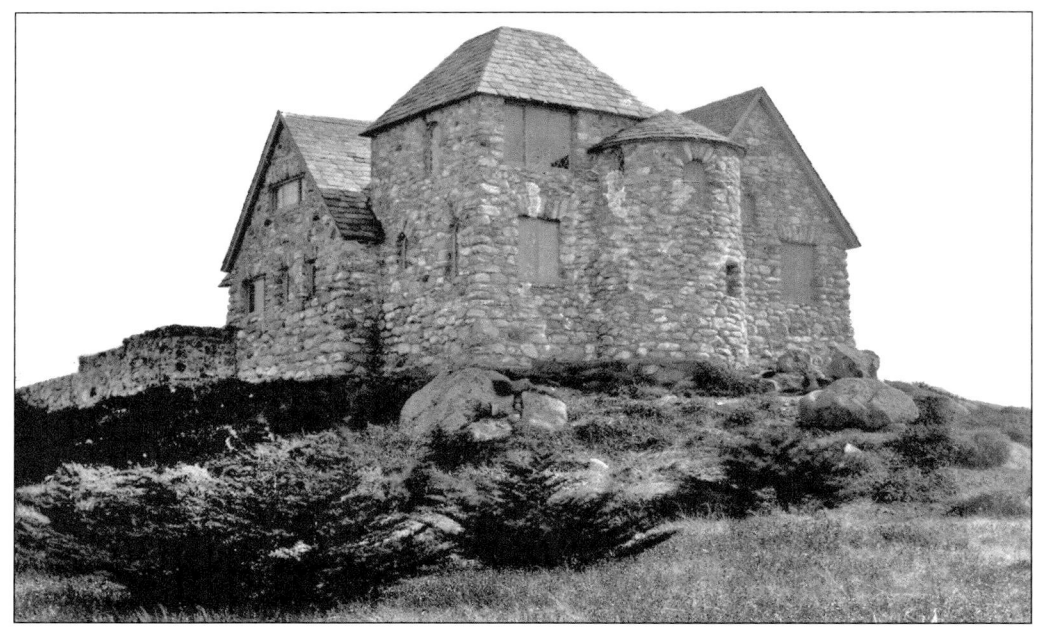

One of Lee Gottfried's early commissions was the construction of Edward Kuster's stone house on Carmel Point in 1920. Both Kuster and Gottfried were very familiar with medieval European architecture, and the Norman-style keep Kuster designed was in perfect harmony with next-door neighbor Robinson Jeffers's Tor House. Kuster had been Una Jeffers's first husband. (Photograph courtesy of Pat Hathaway, Historic California Views.)

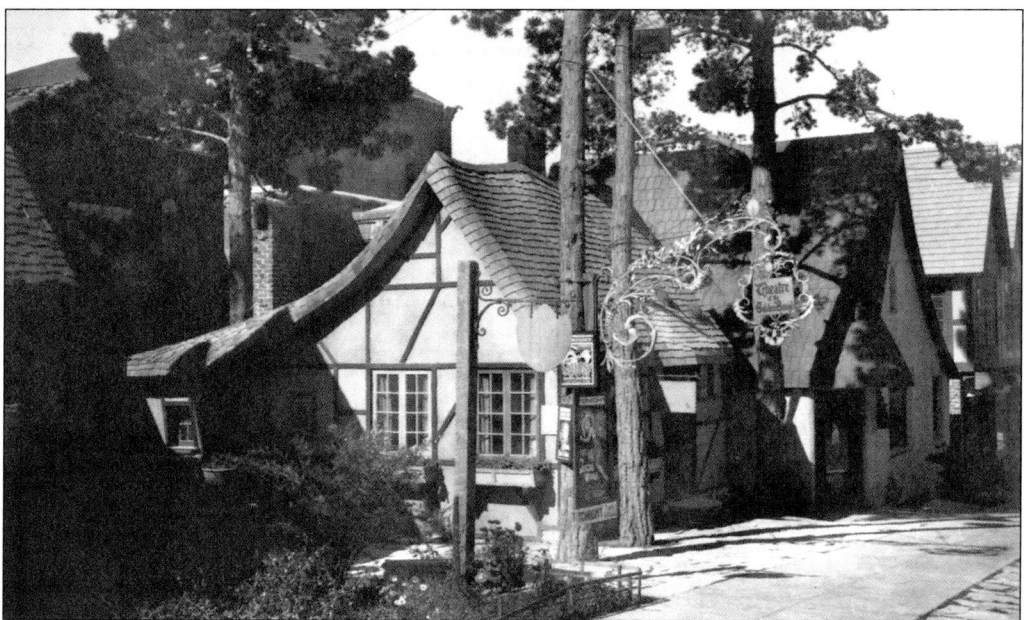

Between 1922 and 1925 Carmel's business district, and subsequently its residential neighborhoods, saw a sea change in the architectural expression of the village. It began with Edward Kuster's Theatre of the Golden Bough and its surrounding courtyard of small commercial shops. (Photograph by Lewis Josslyn; courtesy of Pat Hathaway, Historic California Views.)

Six

THE COURT OF THE GOLDEN BOUGH AND BEYOND

Writing for the *San Francisco Bulletin* in April 1924, Daisy Bostick noted, "there is a group of little shops that might well be transferred to an artist's canvas and labeled 'A bit of old Europe.' They have curving graceful roofs, some with mottled colors. Some are thatched, some reflecting copper tints when the sun filters through the pine trees." Carmel's vocal civic leader and journalist, Perry Newberry, nominated Edward Kuster to Carmel's Hall of Fame as the individual responsible for transforming the main street from a typical small western town "into an Ocean Avenue of beauty and artistry." Both the art interests who sought to preserve Carmel as a community devoted to the art of living and the business interests who saw the potential for profit in the well-healed tourists who liked their holidays rustic recognized the value of architectural excellence. The *Carmel Pine Cone* put it simply in a 1926 editorial: "Line, color and appropriateness in business sections are active salesmen, inviting trade and enlarging trading areas. Architecture is the most important window dressing of a community." By 1924, M. J. Murphy had established a building supply business in the village to meet the demands of the rapid growth.

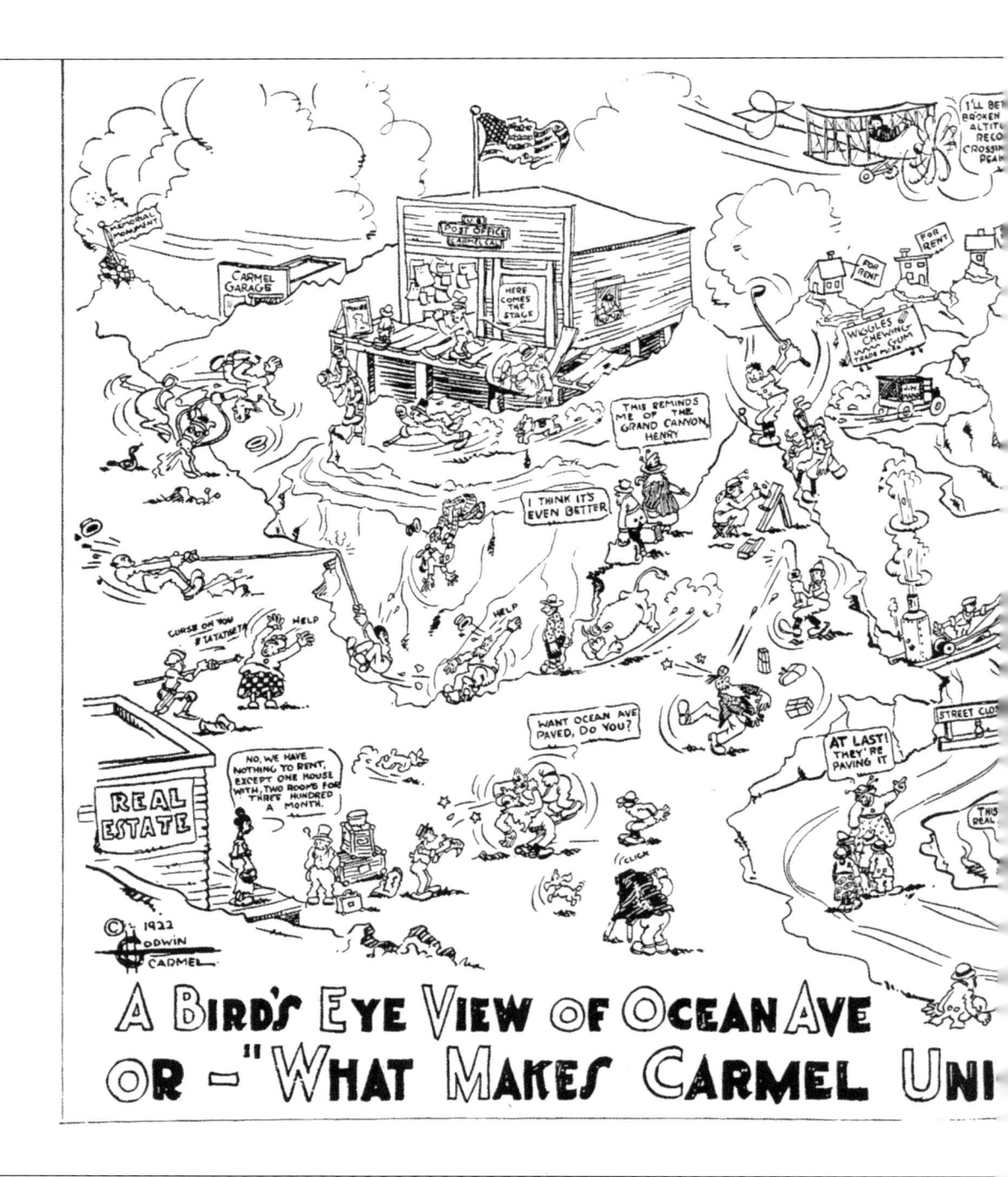

La Playa Hotel manager Harrison Godwin, an excellent cartoonist, took a satirical look at the paving of Carmel's main street in 1922. Sydney Ruthven of Monterey was the contractor. A dust bowl in summer and quagmire in winter, the unpaved roadway had individual names for its numerous travel hazards, including the "Devil's Staircase." Response to its paving through the efforts of the business interests saw the art interests placed in public office with Perry Newberry as mayor. The first city planning commission was established in 1922 to control commercial growth. In 1928, a traffic pattern was proposed that would route cars around the residential area and out to Highway 1. Outraged, the business interests regained control of city government. In 1929, a zoning law was passed stating that business development should forever be subordinate to the residential character of the community. (Drawing courtesy of the Harrison Memorial Library Collection.)

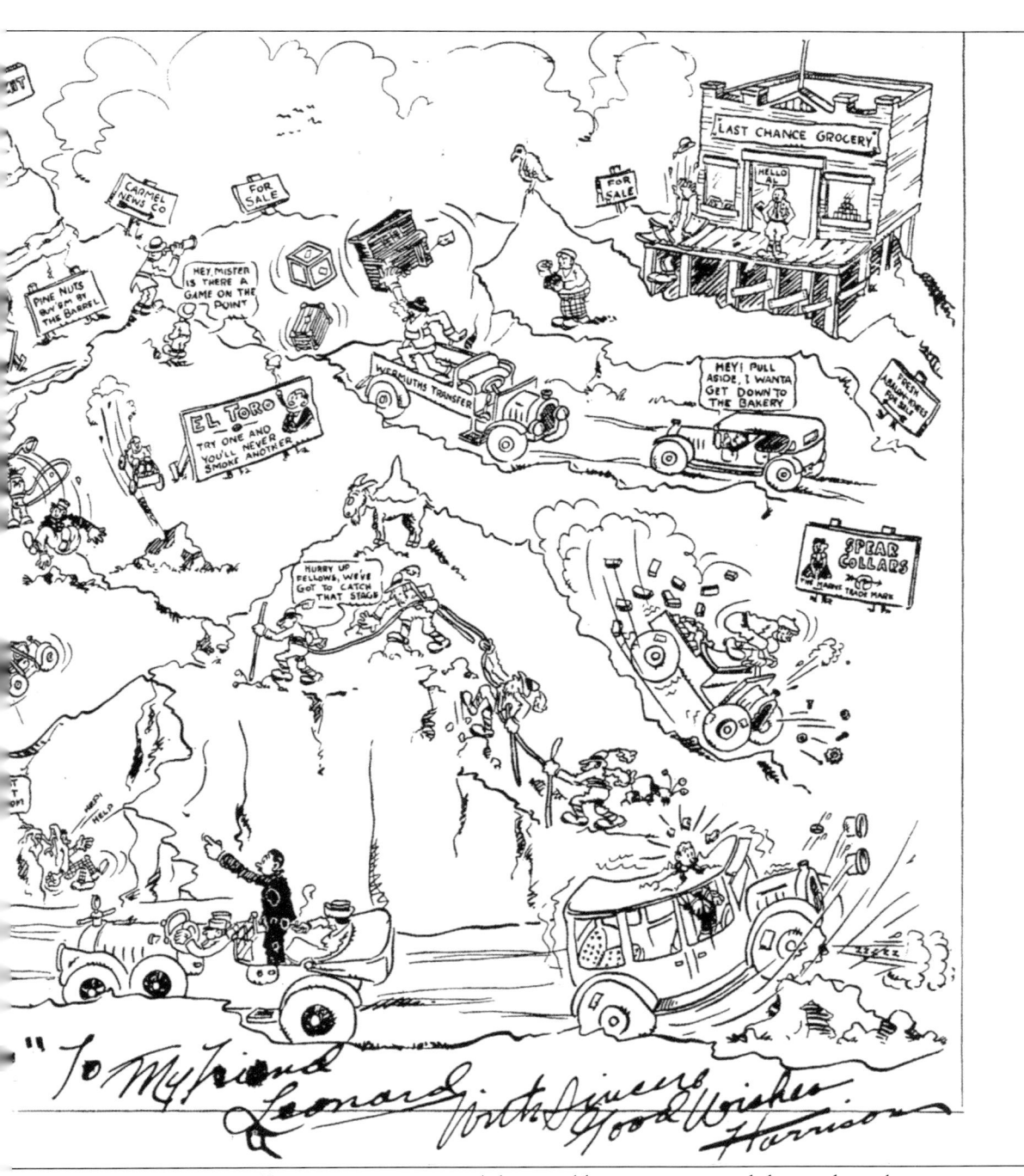

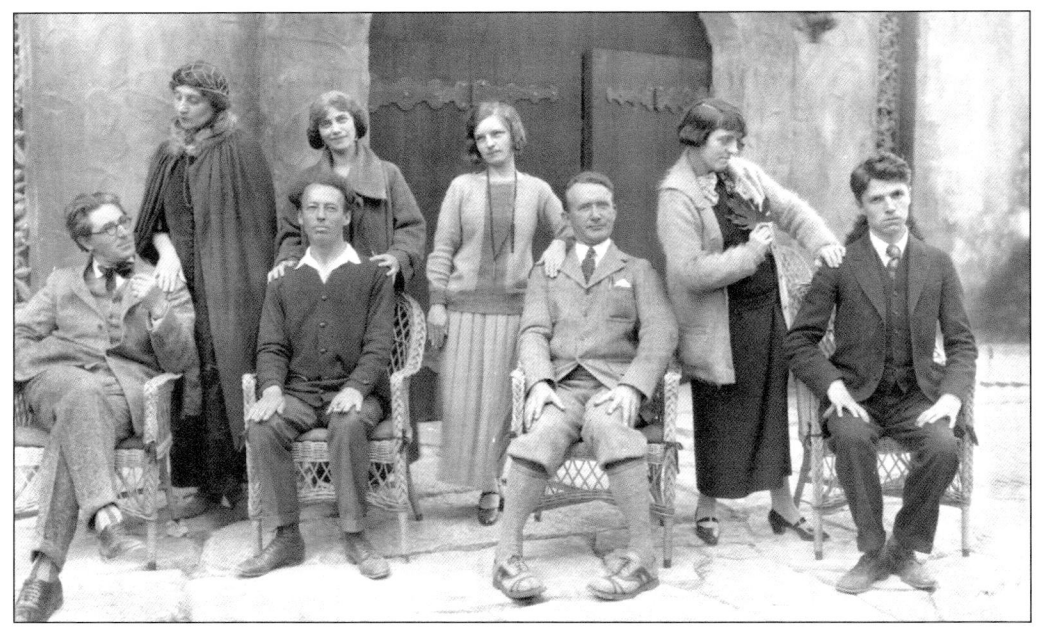

Edward Kuster (third from right) left a successful law practice in Los Angeles to come to Carmel because of the community's overwhelming commitment to local theater. He determined to provide the village with an experimental theater and professional drama school. Kuster's Theatre of the Golden Bough was named after a classical symbol for the imagination. (Photograph courtesy of Pat Hathaway, Historic California Views.)

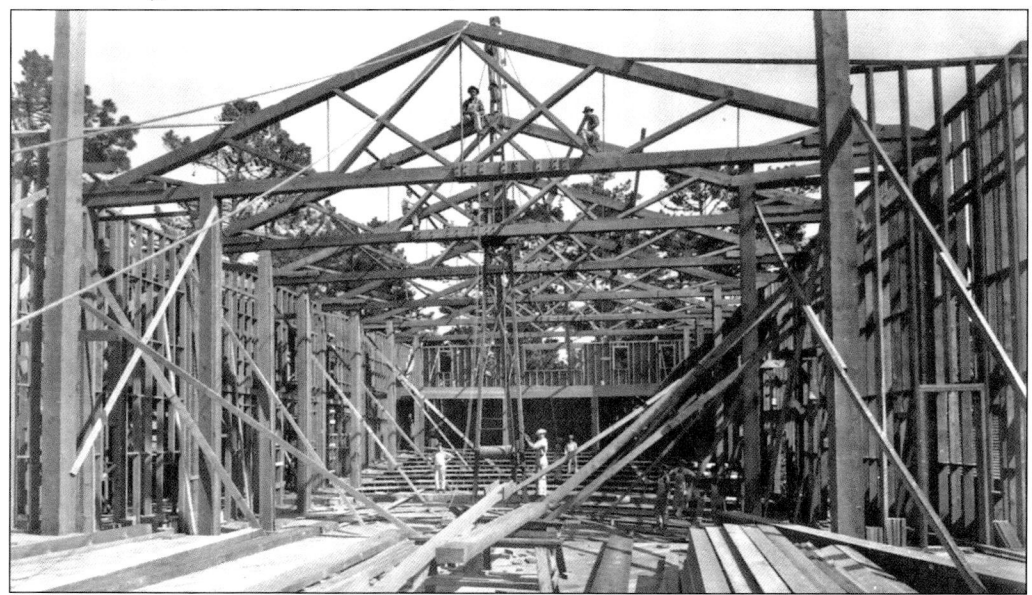

Edward Kuster designed the 1923 Golden Bough. It included a projecting semicircular platform connected to the main stage by wide shallow steps, indirect lighting, and small balconies. Lee Gottfried was his contractor. Theater expert Maurice Browne described the theater as the "most beautiful and perfectly equipped intimate playhouse in America." (Photograph courtesy of the Harrison Memorial Library Collection.)

The boxy mass of "Ted" Kuster's experimental theater was set at the rear of the commercial courtyard, allowing small "old world" shops and mature pine trees to screen its size from Ocean View Avenue. It was said to resemble early ecclesiastical buildings of Lombardy. Its rough textured exterior, simple lines, and arched doorways fit seamlessly into the fabric of the village. (Photograph courtesy of Pat Hathaway, Historic California Views.)

The Carmel Weavers Studio was constructed in the fall of 1922 at the southeast corner of Ocean Avenue and Dolores Street by Lee Gottfried to house a group of local weavers. The following July, the English cottage with its faux half-timbering and steamed wood-shingle roof, suggesting thatch, was moved to the Court of the Golden Bough, one of the first Tudor-style shops in the complex. (Photograph courtesy of Pat Hathaway, Historic California Views.)

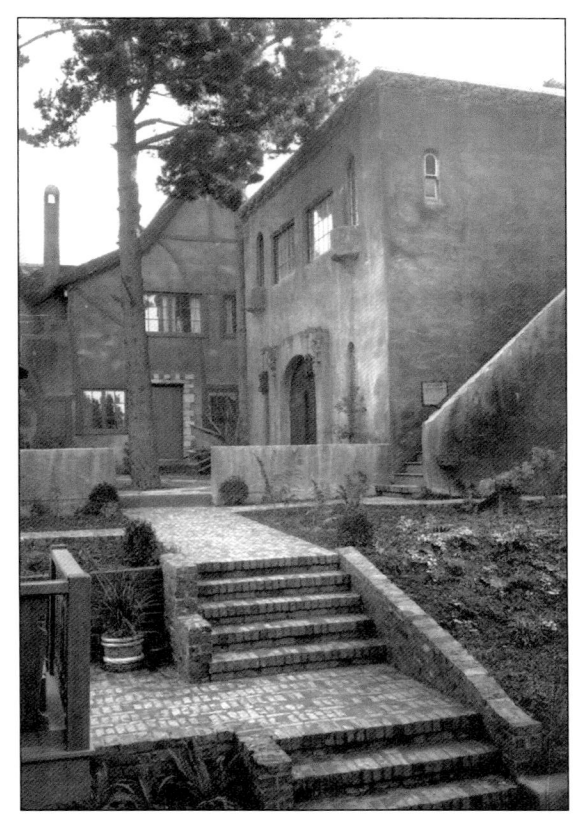

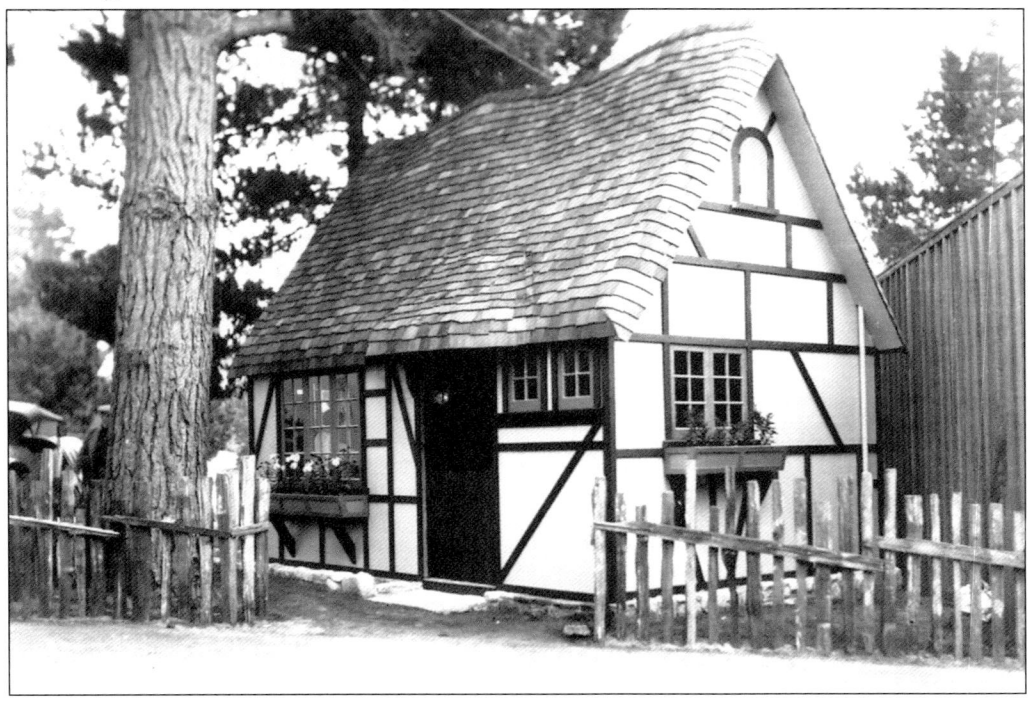

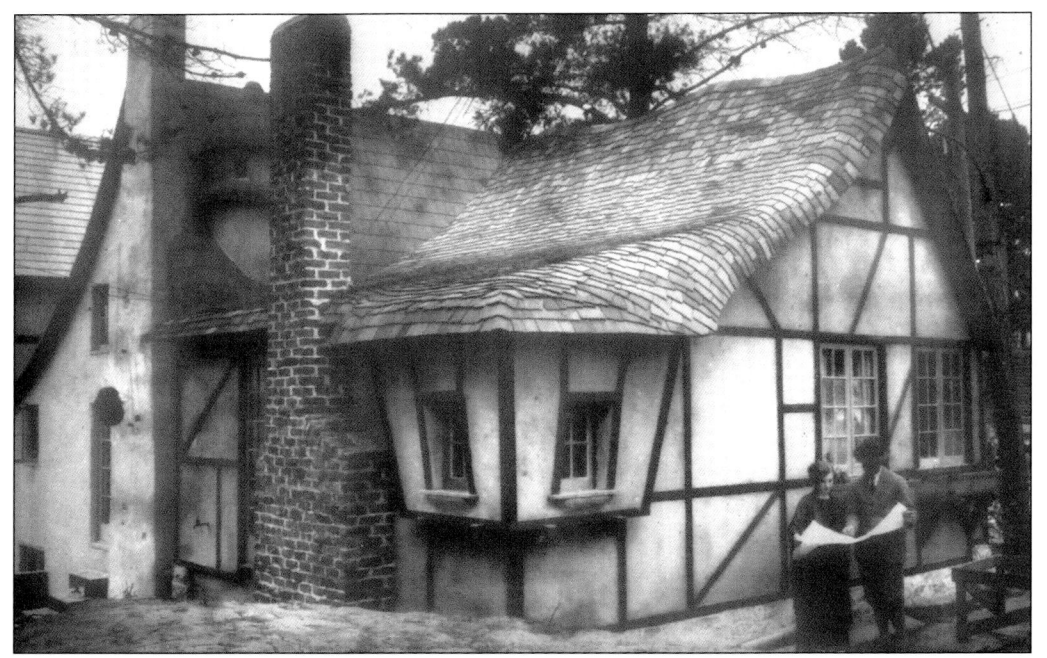

In 1923, the tiny Carmel Weavers Studio was moved to center stage, fronting the Theatre of the Golden Bough. It was enlarged by contractor Lee Gottfried to accommodate a brick fireplace and a fanciful ticket booth for the playhouse. Master builder M. J. Murphy and Emma Otey are seen reviewing plans for another shop in the courtyard. (Photograph courtesy of Pat Hathaway, Historic California Views.)

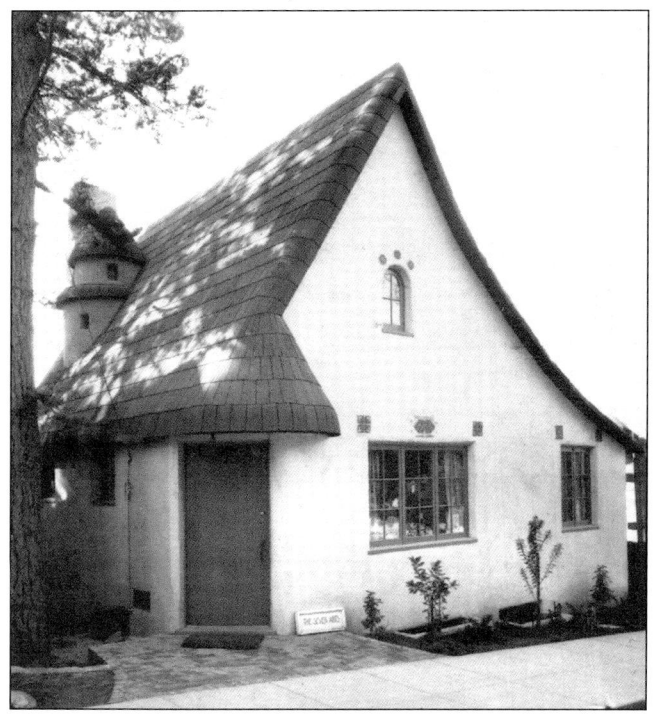

Edward Kuster looked to the illustrations of Edmond Dulac in a book of Swedish folk tales for the design of the Seven Arts Shop in the Court of the Golden Bough. Built by Michael J. Murphy, the tiny building included miniature turrets and colorful tiles placed in the stucco above the windows. It later became a Christian Science reading room. (Photograph courtesy of Pat Hathaway, Historic California Views.)

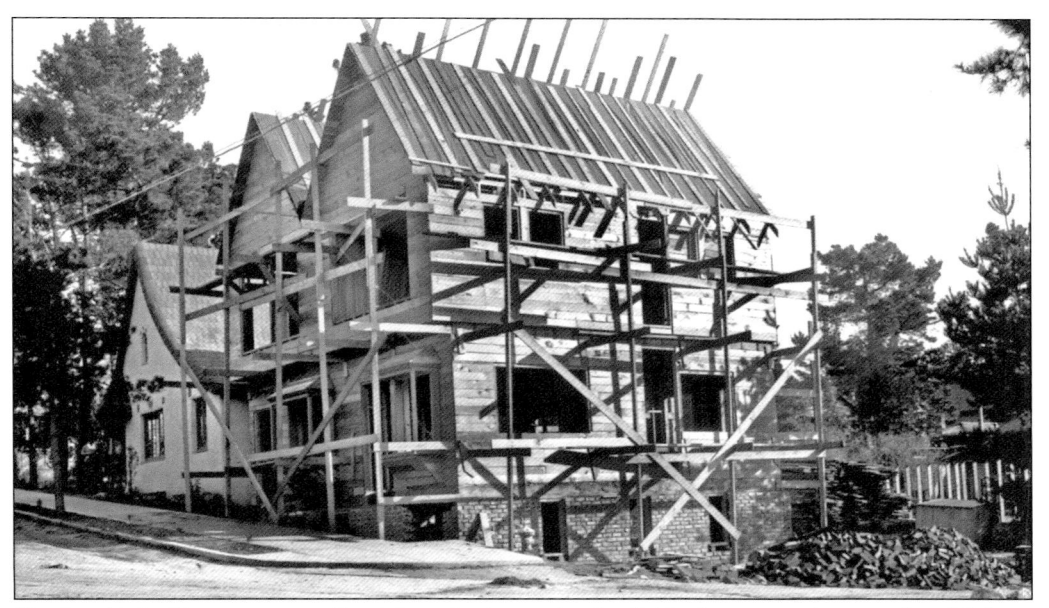

Dr. Amelia L. Gates was a pediatrician. A pioneer in the field of preventative care for children, she retired to Carmel in 1922, and in 1924, Dr. Gates designed and supervised construction of the commercial building anchoring the west end of the Court of the Golden Bough. Its design was based on prototypes she had seen in Austria. Fred McCrary was the builder. (Photograph courtesy of Pat Hathaway, Historic California Views.)

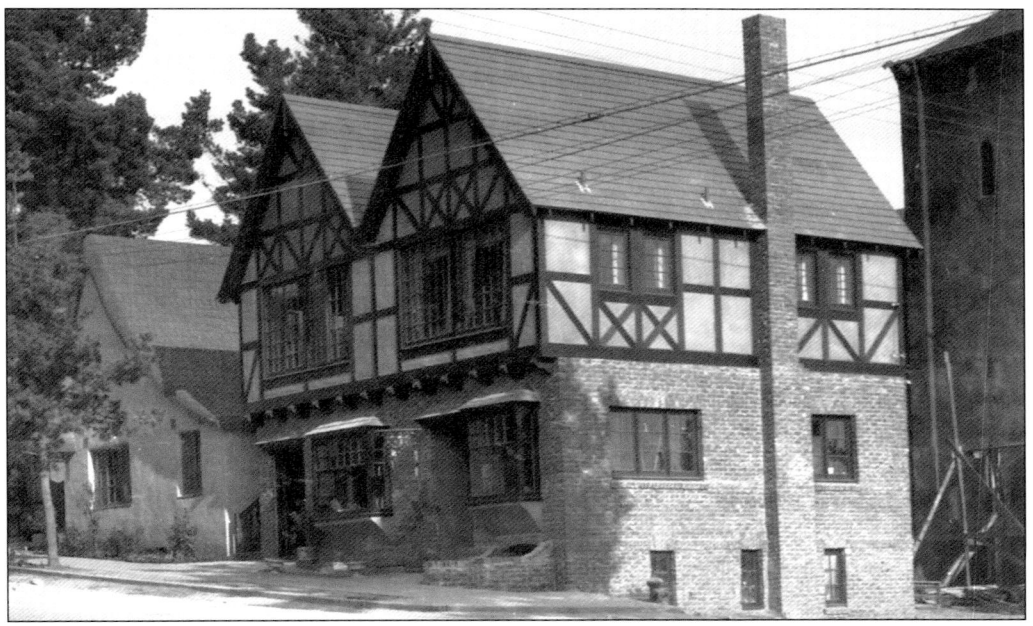

Dr. Gates and her husband had come to Carmel in 1910 and built a cottage on Camino Real. Her commercial building was a retirement investment property. It had retail shops on the ground floor and a studio apartment above. The clinker brick veneer, faux half-timbering, and paired gable roofs create a strong presence on the street. (Photograph by Lewis Josslyn; courtesy of Pat Hathaway, Historic California Views.)

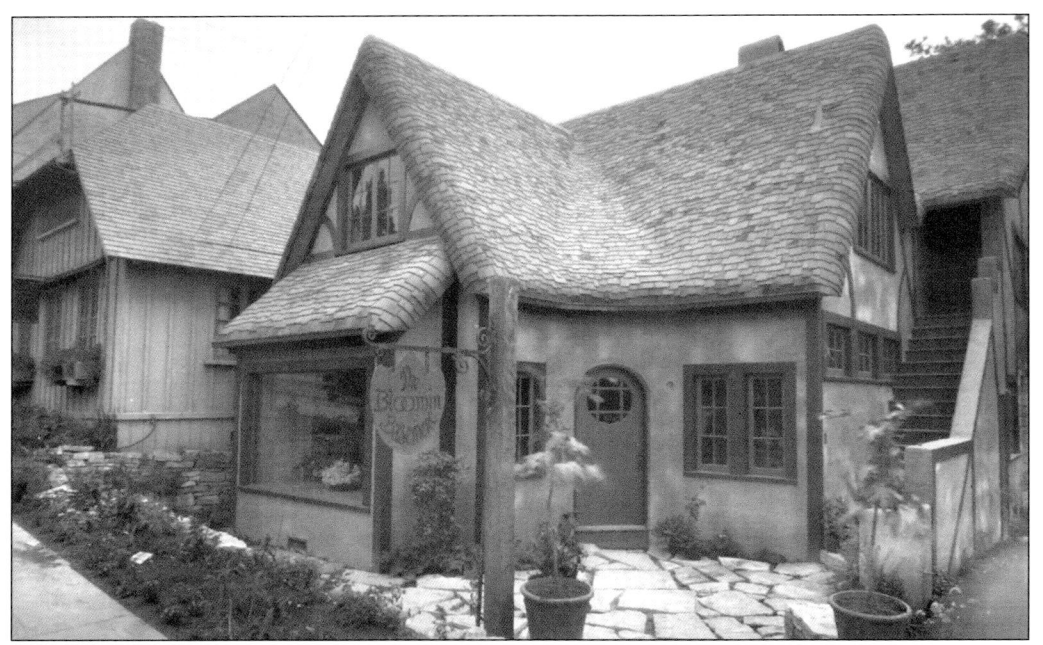

Novelist Harry Leon Wilson had Lee Gottfried design this Tudor-style building in 1925 for his wife Helen's flower shop, The Bloomin' Basement. Gottfried noted that "the roof swings steeply to three ridges. . . . The ridges and eaves are undulated giving the place the appearance of being thatched." The first floor bar, called Sade's, was a social center for actors and musicians. (Photograph courtesy of Pat Hathaway, Historic California Views.)

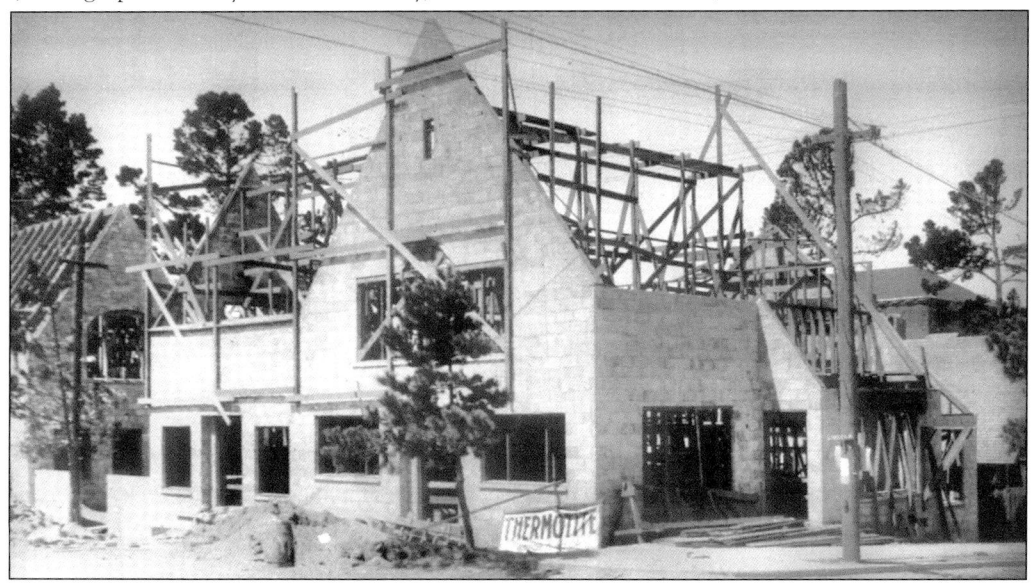

Theatrical entrepreneur and publisher Herbert Heron had architect Albert B. Coats design his new Seven Arts Building at the southwest corner of Ocean Avenue and Lincoln Street in 1926. Earl Percy Parkes was the contractor. It was one of the first buildings in Carmel to employ Thermotite, a locally produced cement block said to be fireproof, waterproof, and practically everlasting. (Photograph courtesy of Pat Hathaway, Historic California Views.)

As noted in the advertisement, there was little one could not construct with Thermotite. The parent company for the building material, the Thermotite Construction Company of San Jose, franchised their product in Monterey County to Albert Otey and his wife, Emma, as Carmel Thermotite, Inc., for $25,000 in 1925. (Photograph from the author's collection.)

THERMOTITE

The Very Best of Construction At No Greater Cost.

A Few of the Things Built With Thermotite:

Theaters	Laundries	Swimming Pools
Homes	Service Stations	Veneer Walls
Garages	Stores	Retaining Walls
Churches	Refrigerators	Garden Walls
Club Houses	Stairways	Hydrating Plants
Factories	Septic Tanks	Columns
Floors	Curbs	Etc., Etc.

The SUCCESS of Thermotite is based on superior merit. It has met with opposition from critics who do not know what it is. We have yet to meet the man, who, when he honestly looks into the matter, will go away anything but a booster.

We welcome anyone to the Carmel plant to make any kind of a test he desires. Bring along any other building material supposed to be superior to Thermotite and test them together.

We Can Meet Any First-Class Construction Figure Get Our Prices Before You Build

FRANK T. CARTER

Designer — Sales and Construction Mgr. Caramel Thermotite Inc. Carmel. — Builder

The Polk directory for Carmel in 1926 noted that "The Seven Arts Building was . . . the first devoted to beauty and utility instead of utility alone." Local artists George and Catherine Seideneck did the initial decoration. It housed the Carmel Institute of Art, the Carmel Press, and the *Carmel Cymbal* newspaper. Photographer Edward Weston had his studio in the building. (Photograph courtesy of Pat Hathaway, Historic California Views.)

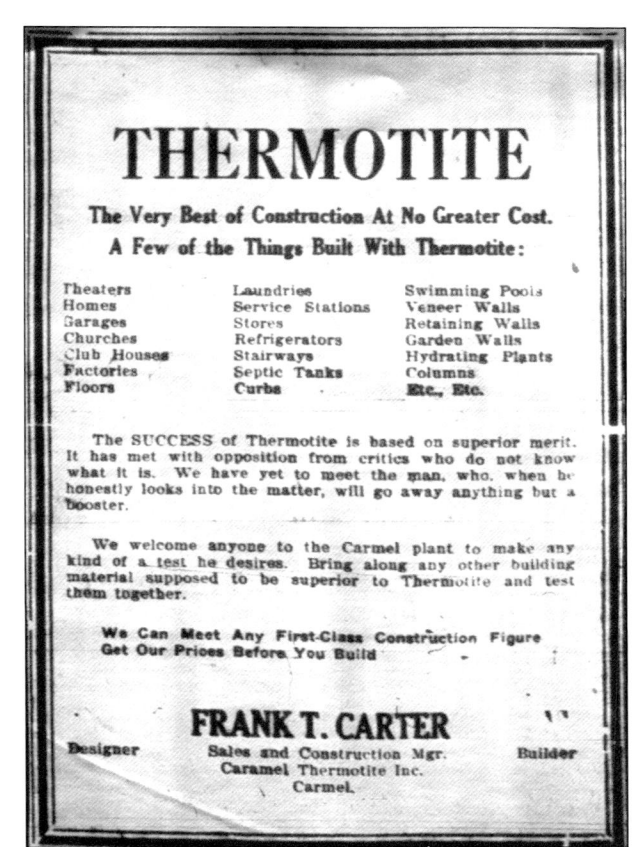

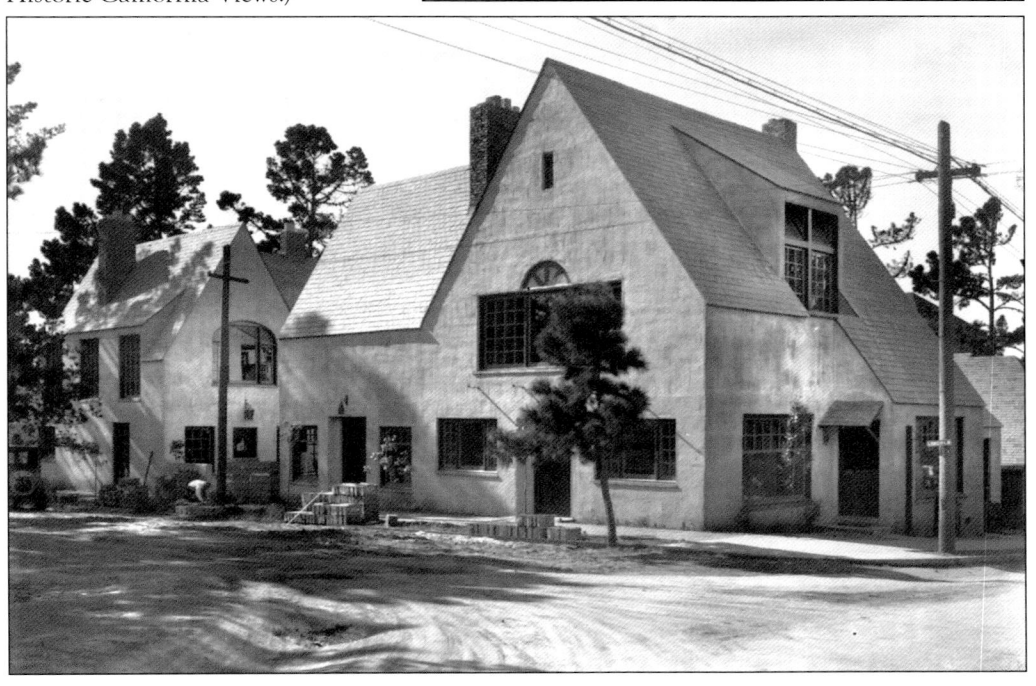

77

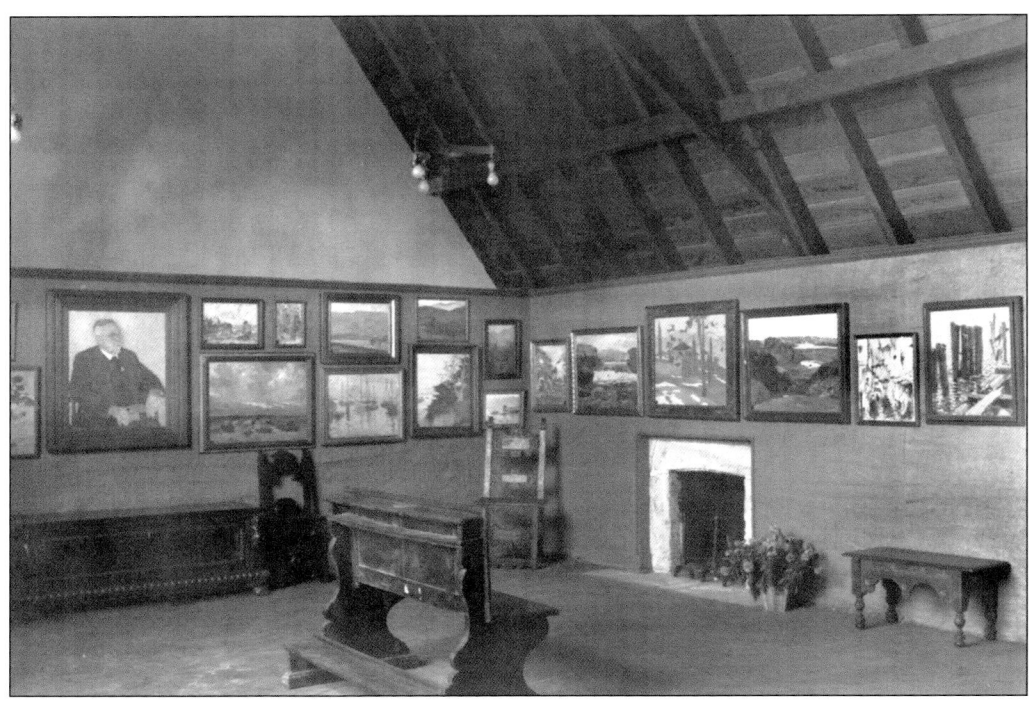

Modeled on the Laguna Beach Art Association, a group of Carmel artists formed the Carmel Art Association in August 1927. The organization's purpose was "for the advancement of art and for cooperation among artists." Their first formal gallery was on the second floor of the Fine Arts Building. The association is still going strong as the oldest artists' cooperative in the West. (Photograph courtesy of Pat Hathaway, Historic California Views.)

The contractor for Paul Flanders's Outlands was Fred Ruhl of the San Francisco firm of Dowsett and Ruhl. The builder had come to the Monterey Peninsula in 1916 and became the principal contractor for the Pebble Beach Villa Estates. He was responsible for the construction of the Pebble Beach Lodge and a number of well-known residences in the resort community. (Photograph from the author's collection.)

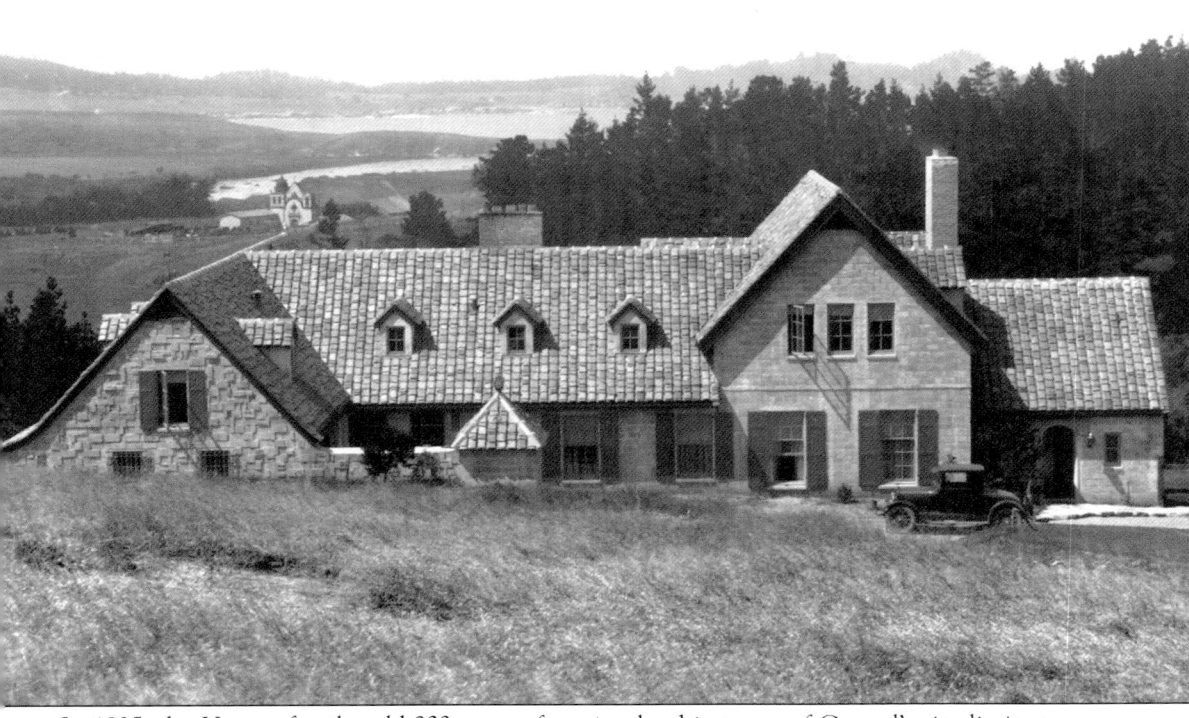

In 1925, the Hatton family sold 233 acres of grazing land just east of Carmel's city limits to a group of investors for residential development. Local capitalists Paul Flanders and Charles Van Riper and writer Harry Leon Wilson were the principals. Flanders set the architectural tone for the project by bringing well-known San Francisco architect Henry Higby Gutterson in to design his own home, Outlands, a Tudor Revival manor house. (Photograph by Lewis Josslyn; courtesy of Pat Hathaway, Historic California Views.)

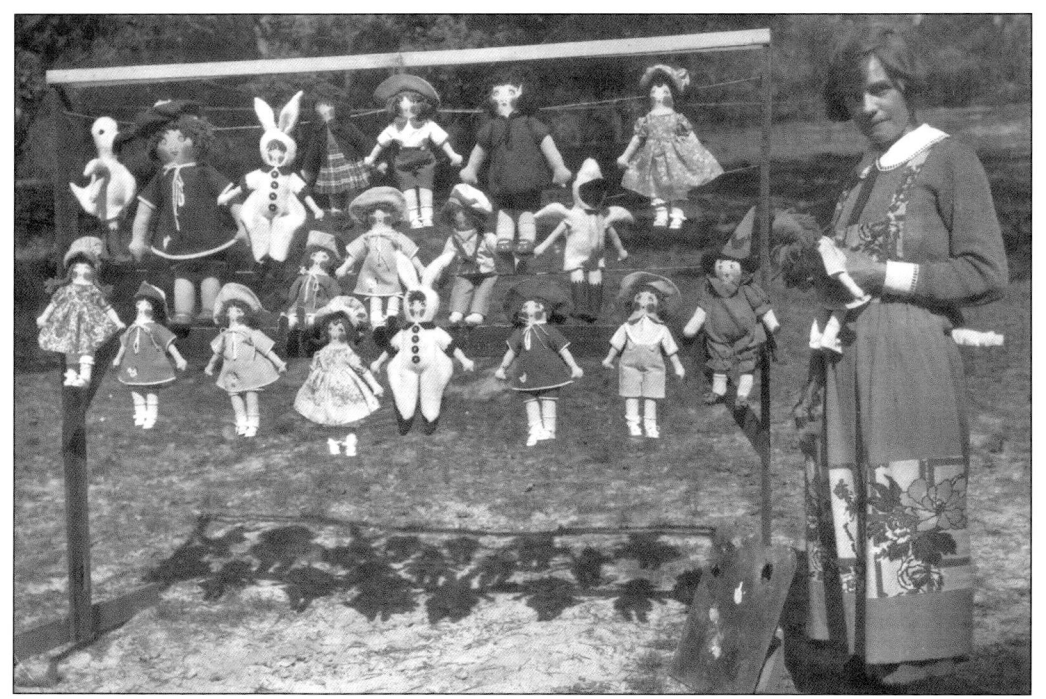

Rancher Hugh Comstock had no architectural training and only basic carpentry skills when he came to Carmel in 1924 to visit his sister. She introduced him to Mayotta Brown, a local doll maker, whose popular "Otsy-Totsy" felt dolls would initiate a sea change in the residential design of the village and make Comstock Carmel's "builder of dreams." (Photograph courtesy of Pat Hathaway, Historic California Views.)

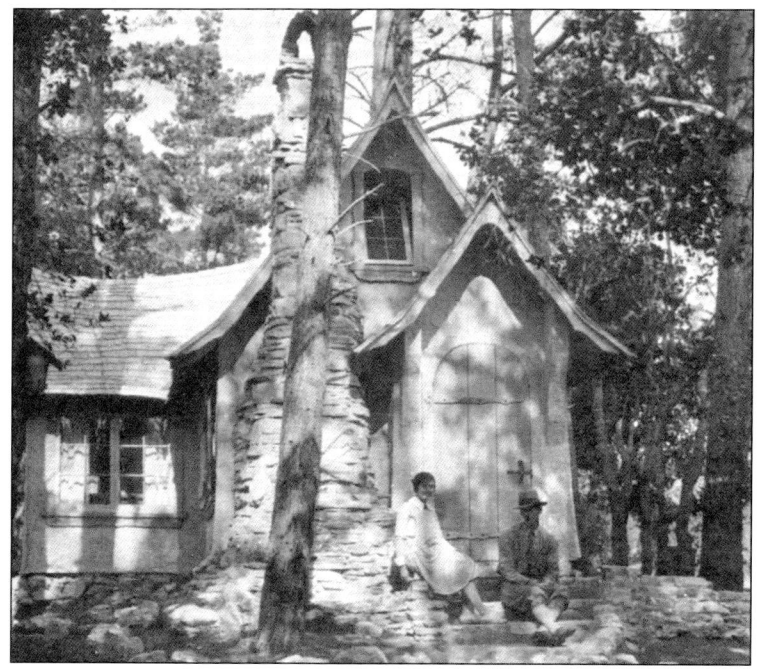

Comstock soon married Mayotta. Drawing inspiration from children's book illustrations, the couple handcrafted a whimsical cottage to showcase Mayotta's dolls. It had a sagging roof, hand-carved window and door casings, and rustic Carmel stone chimney. Plaster mixed with pine needles was toweled over burlap on the walls to create a rough exterior surface. (Photograph courtesy of the Monterey Public Library, California History Room Archives.)

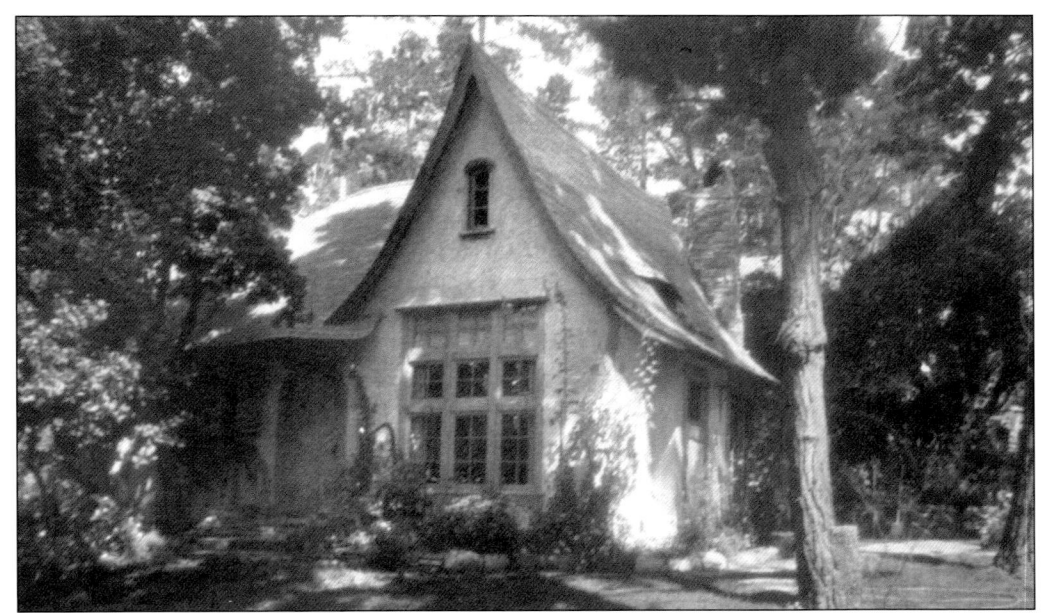

Comstock's Doll House, later renamed Hansel, struck a chord within Carmel's artistic community. Everyone wanted his own fairy-tale cottage. Soon Comstock found himself in the construction business. His early works, like his own home Obers of 1925, were highly imaginative and individual. Comstock was quite sensitive to protecting the natural landscape setting. (Photograph courtesy of Pat Hathaway, Historic California Views.)

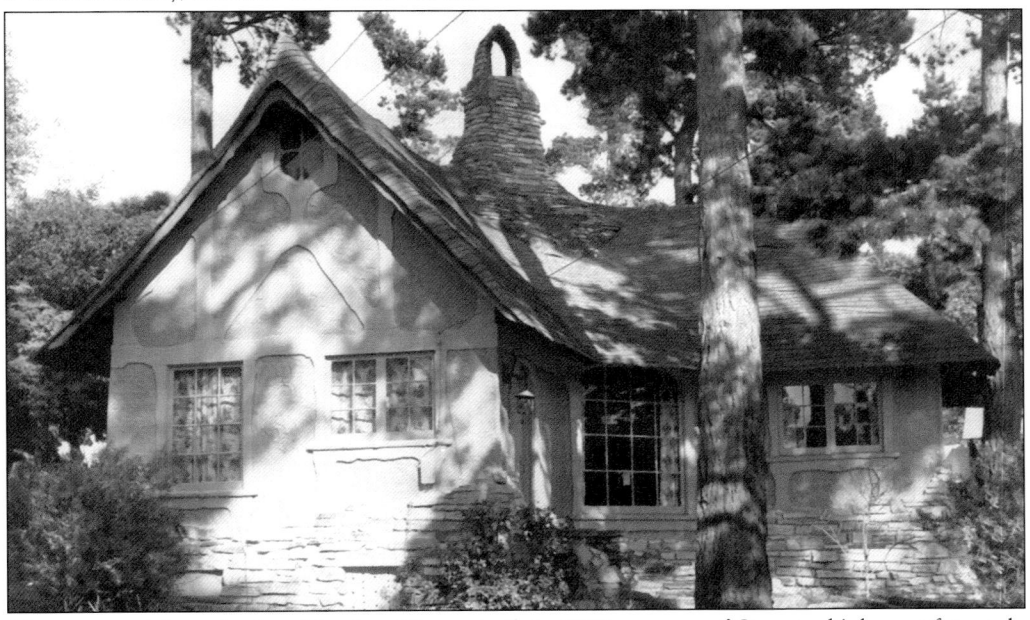

This cross-axial confection, Marchen House, built in 1928, was one of Comstock's largest fairy-tale cottages. Fred Coleman, the mason on the D. L. James house, built the Carmel stone fireplace. A local critic noted, "The chimney is neither round, square or rectangular. It is fantastic in its grotesque mis-shapen form." (Photograph courtesy of the Monterey Public Library, California History Room Archives.)

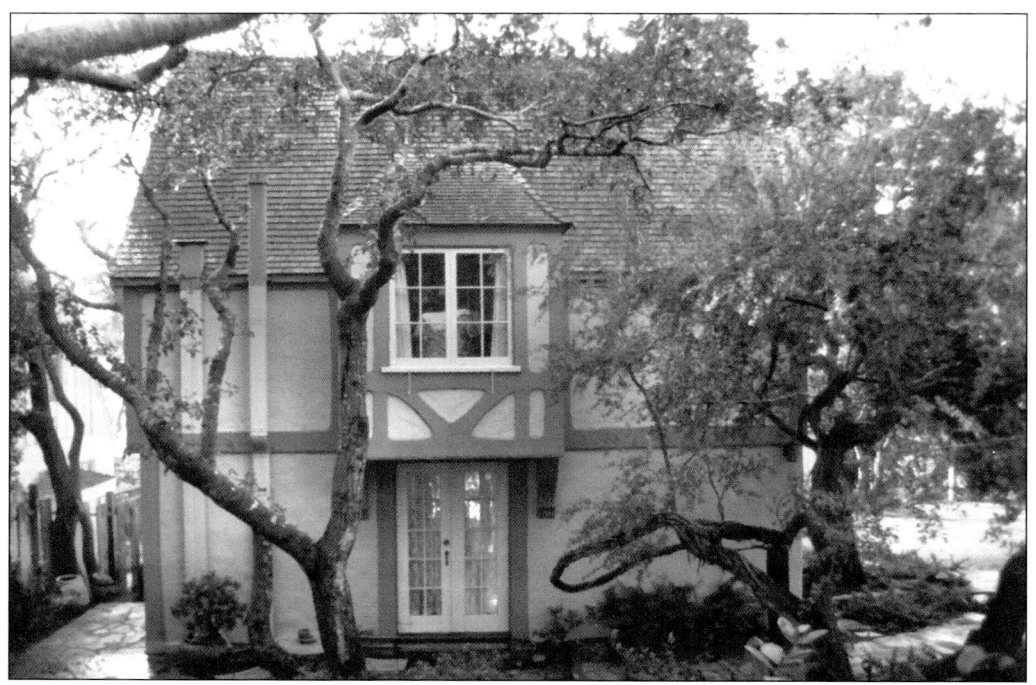

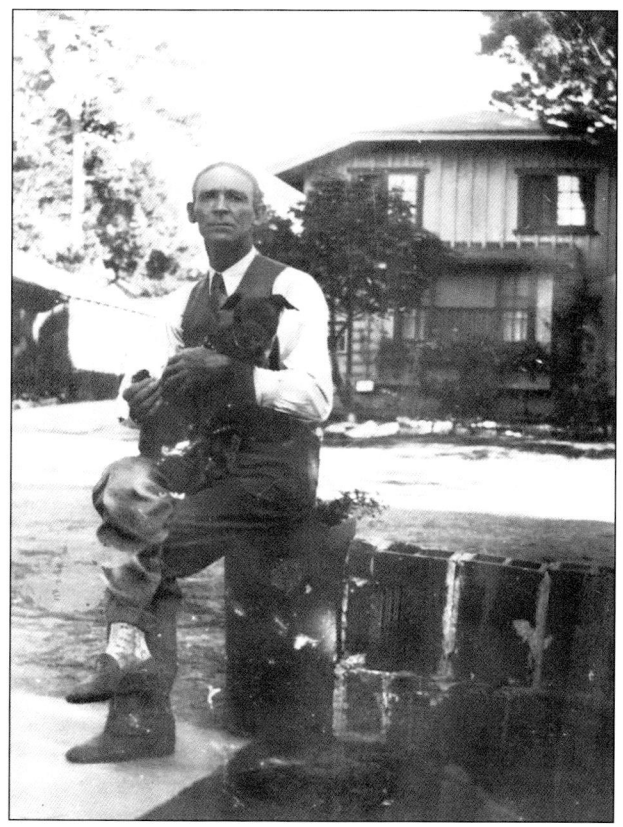

In 1928, Eastern investor W. O. Swain convinced the Carmel City Council to allow him to develop a small, five-unit subdivision based on the English garden city plan, as Swain noted, "with a feeling of spaciousness about them, as in a park." The five houses form the largest single concentration of Comstock fairy-tale cottages left in Carmel. The Birthday House anchors the corner of Santa Fe Street and Sixth Avenue. (Photograph by the author.)

Contractor Jess Nichols was a charter member of Carmel's first board of trustees in 1916 and Carmel's first elected city clerk. Author Grant Wallace had Nichols build a fairy-tale cottage on Sixth Avenue near Torres Street in 1927 that was, according to Wallace, "so arranged that every small detail in regard to practicality and artistry had been taken care of." (Photograph courtesy of the Harrison Memorial Library Collection.)

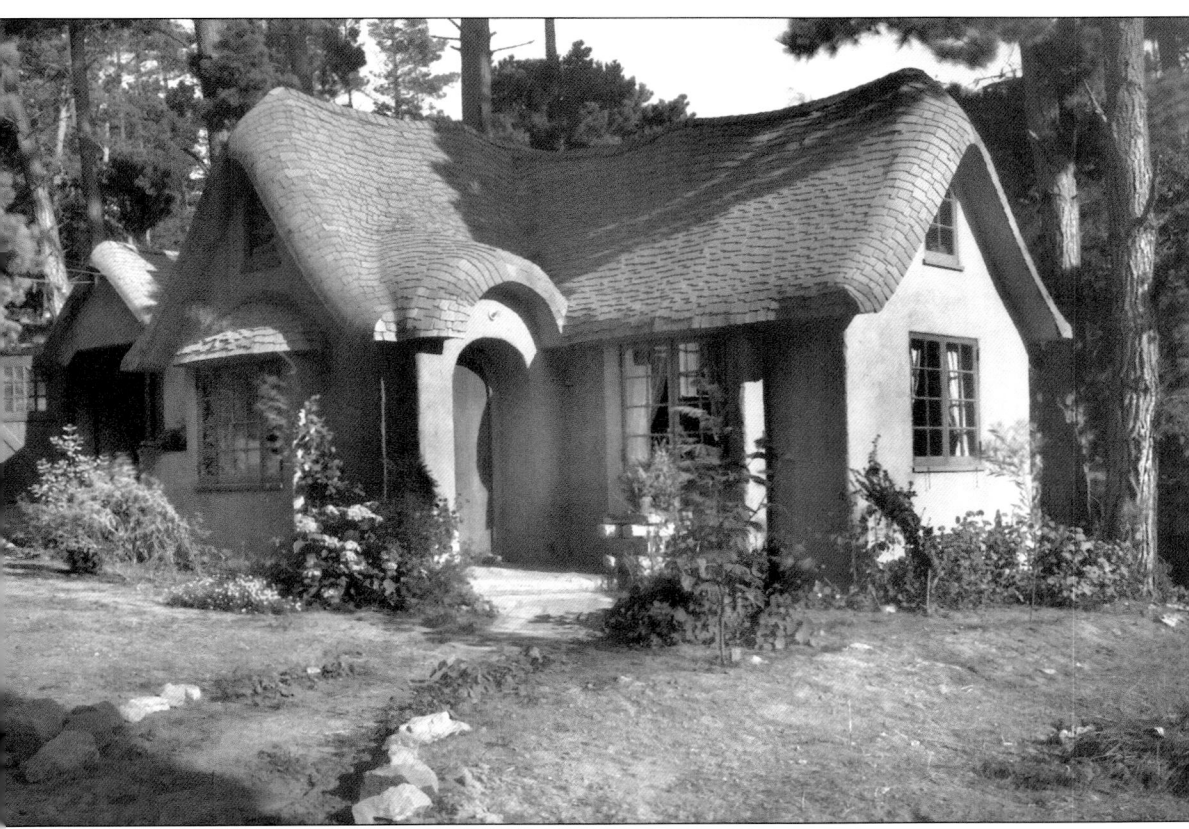

The success of Comstock's fairy-tale cottages created a growth industry in Carmel. Local contractors began building them, including Jess Nichols. Noted writer and naturalist Grant Wallace, who designed his own cottage, had Nichols build directly across Sixth Avenue from Comstock's own home. (Photograph courtesy of Pat Hathaway, Historic California Views.)

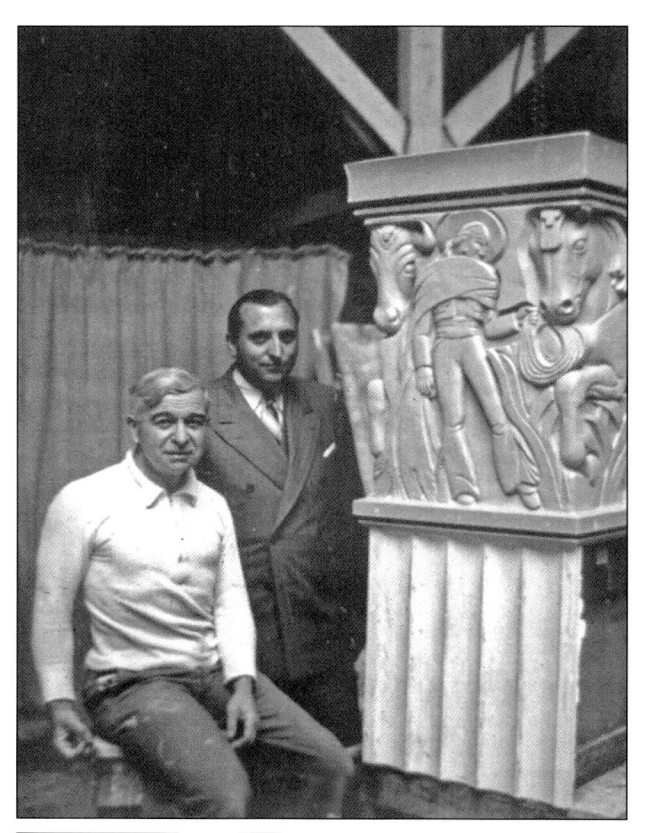

Robert Stanton (right), with artist Jo Mora, left Carmel in 1927 to work for Southern California architect Wallace Neff. He returned in 1936, becoming a leading architect in the area. He trained a generation of local architects in his Carmel office. Stanton helped found the Monterey Bay Chapter of the American Institute of Architects in the early 1950s and was its first fellow. (Photograph from author's collection.)

Robert Stanton first came to Carmel in 1925 as a contractor. His office building on Monte Verde Street was constructed by Fred Ruhl. The miniature French Norman chalet, with its half-timbering, turrets, and conical roof caps, was in keeping with the romantic Tudor Revival direction in which Carmel's commercial core was heading in the 1920s. (Photograph from author's collection.)

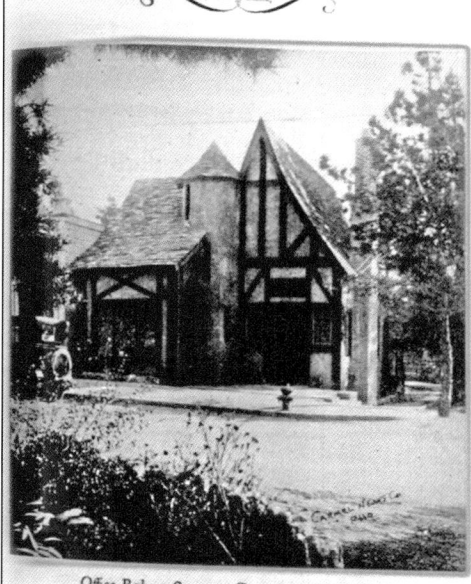

Office Robert Stanton Company, Carmel.

The Robert Stanton Company

CARMEL, CALIFORNIA

SPECIALIZING in the designing and construction of Pebble Beach and Monterey Peninsula Country Club homes.

The work of this firm is characterized by artistry of design and quality of construction.

We would be pleased to consult with anyone contemplating the building of a home on the Monterey Peninsula.

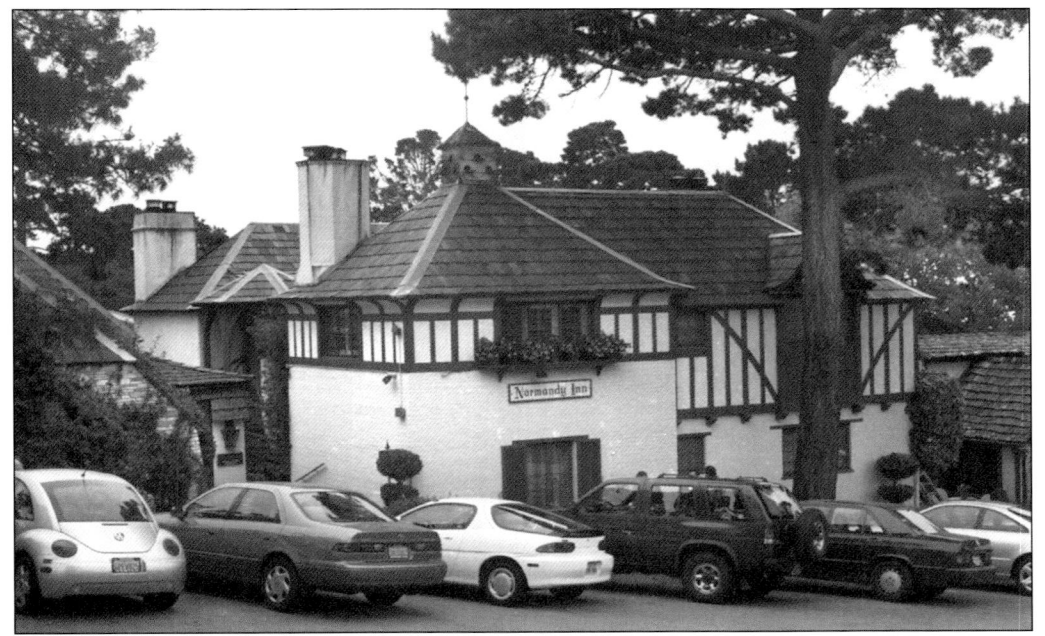

Robert and Virginia Stanton, a noted interior designer, spent a lifetime developing the Normandy Inn at the southwest corner of Ocean Avenue and Monte Verde Street into one of Carmel's most attractive and popular hotels. It was an ongoing expansion of Robert's original Carmel office that continued the Tudor Revival theme. (Photograph by the author.)

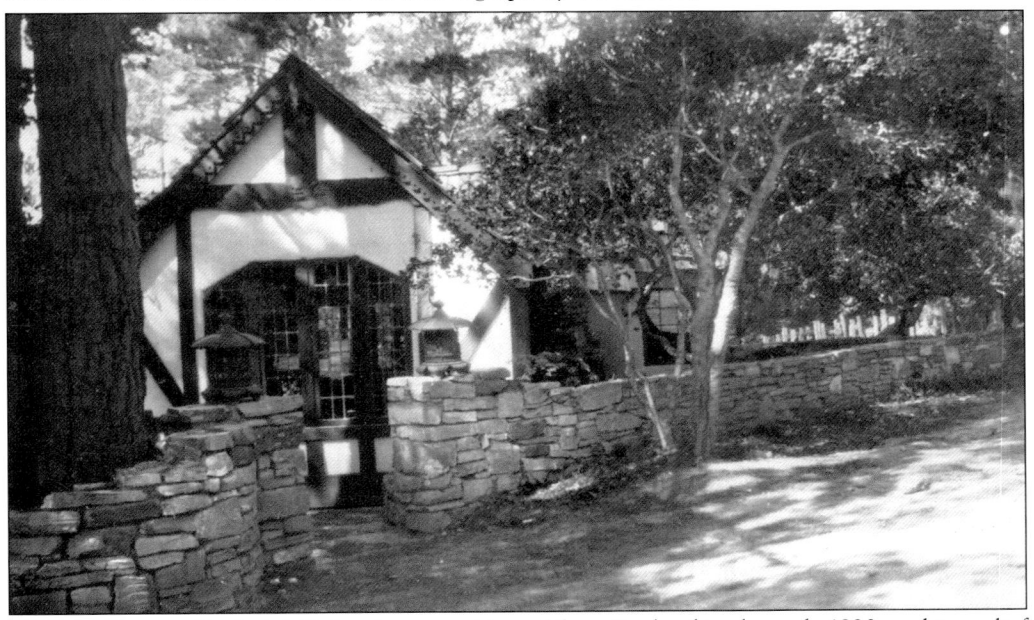

Building designer Frederick Bigland came to Carmel from England in the early 1920s seeking relief from asthma. He established himself as a prominent builder for the quality of his craftsmanship and familiarity with the English arts and crafts tradition. Hermes House, his own half-timbered cottage on Mountain View Avenue, was an excellent advertisement for his building skills. (Photograph courtesy of Debbie Sharpe.)

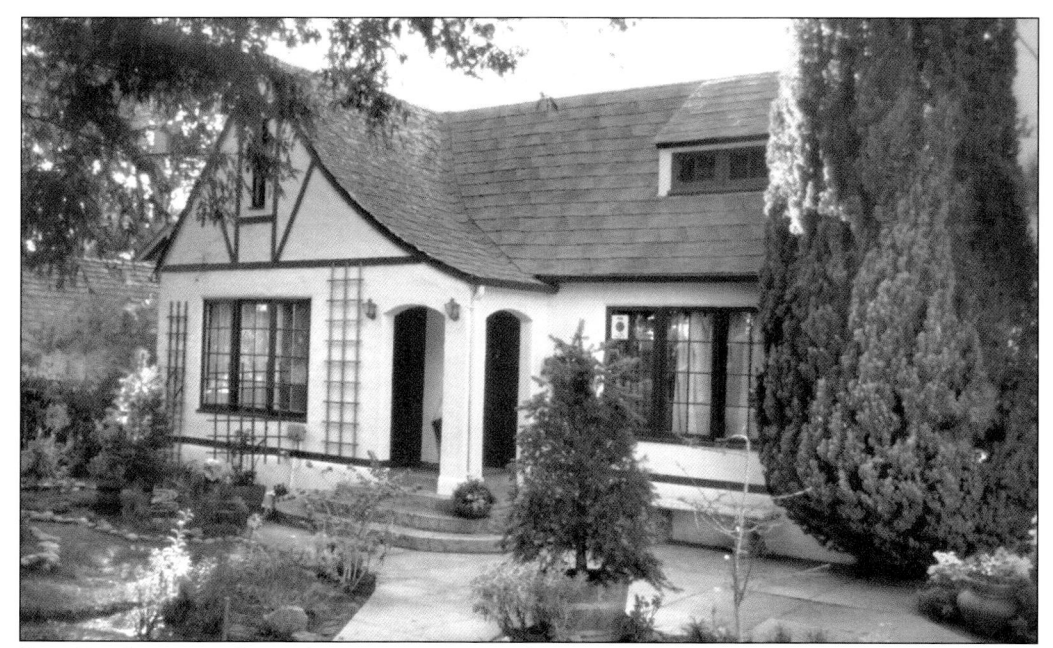

Ross Bonham was Carmel's mayor in 1929, when Ordinance 96 established just two zoning districts, one residential and the other commercial. Designer-builder George Mark Whitcomb, who designed and built Bonham's house in 1926, came to Carmel in 1919 after service in World War I. He was a popular builder because of his interest in meeting the needs of his clients. (Photograph by the author.)

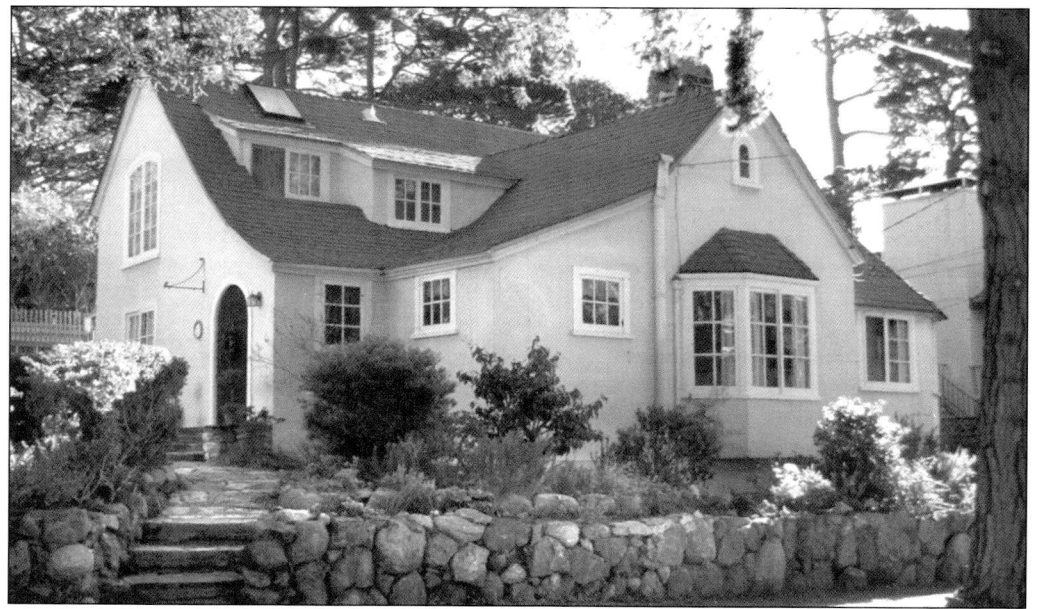

M. J. Murphy's 1922 Tudor Revival office was also a model home, capitalizing on the wave of interest in romantic and pictorial residential design sweeping the country in the early 1920s. Murphy employed most of the basic design elements of the style, employing stucco, a newer fire-resistant material for the exterior wall cladding. (Photograph by the author.)

M. J. Murphy was a prodigious worker. He was the most active designer-builder in Carmel between 1902 and 1940, erecting as many as 350 buildings of all types. Murphy did more to give the village its basic architectural character than any other single person. Quality of materials and workmanship were his watchwords, as was preservation of the natural environment. (Photograph courtesy of Thomas Gladney.)

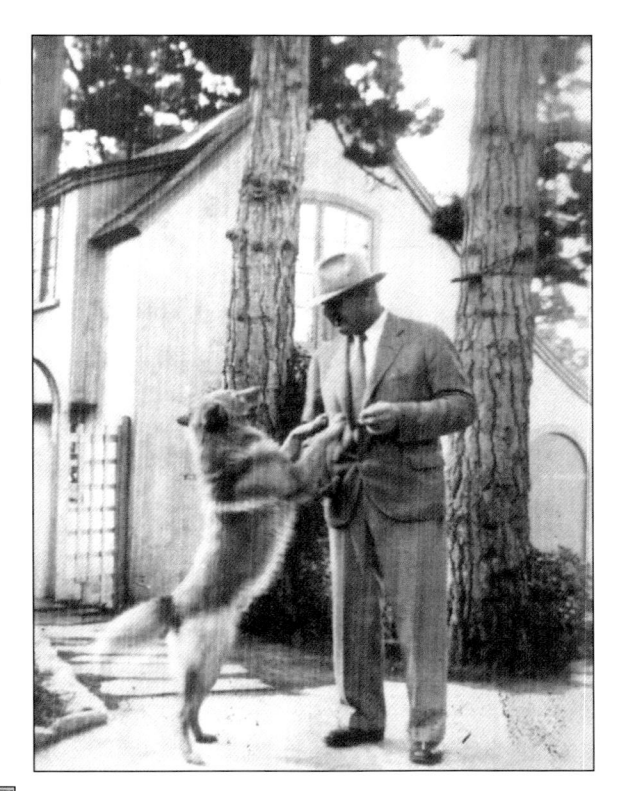

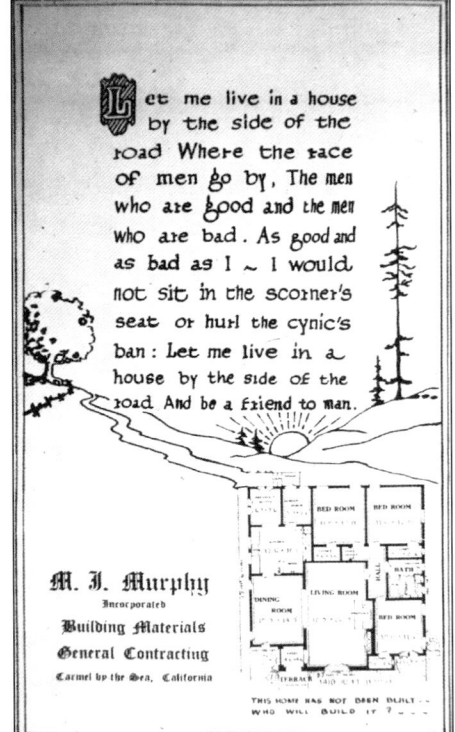

Master builder M. J. Murphy was well aware of the writing talent abounding in Carmel. About 1925, he hired local author A. Thacher Covely to prepare a promotional brochure with a literary bent for his business. Through prose and poetry, and a significant number of photos of Murphy's work, Covely extolled the virtues of Murphy's "Structures of the Period." (Photograph from author's collection.)

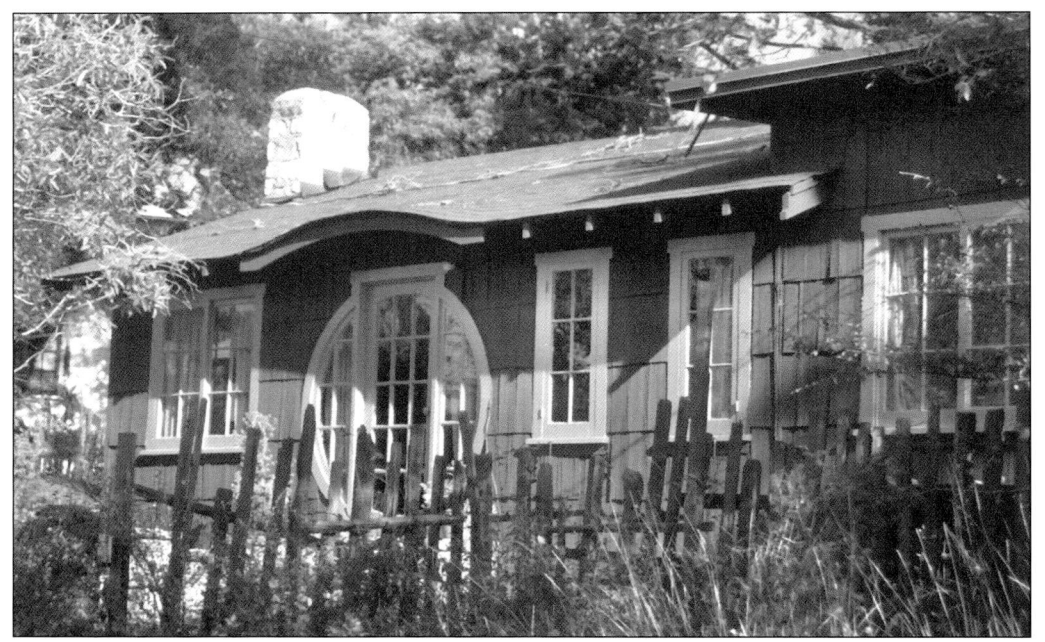

Personal expression through eclectic design has long been a Carmel tradition. Mritz De Haass, a successful Santa Monica financier, had Carmel designer Earl Percy Parkes create this Chinese-influenced bungalow with its unique moon door on Mountain View Avenue and Torres Street in 1925. Parkes came to Carmel in 1919 and designed a number of commercial and residential buildings in a variety of period styles. (Photograph by the author.)

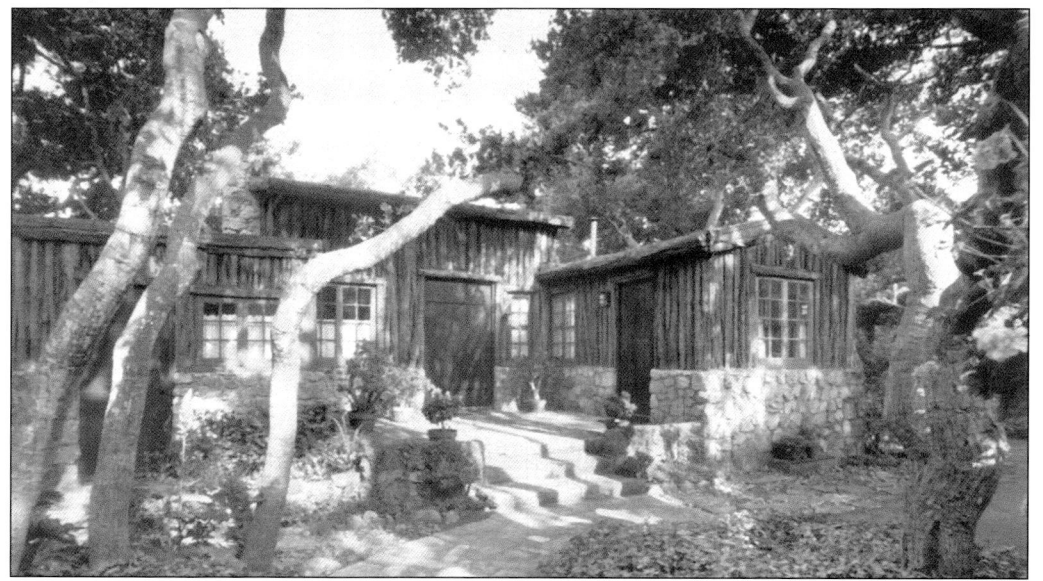

Carmel was noted as a haven for independent and creative women. J. S. Cone was responsible for the design of this rustic 1922 weekend cottage clad in redwood bark—perhaps the ultimate expression of natural materials. The 14-foot-high central living room ran the length of the building. Lee Gottfried was her contractor. (Photograph by Morley Baer; courtesy of Monterey Peninsula College.)

Perry Newberry was Carmel. A journalist, playwright, and political activist, in 1922, he was elected mayor. Allen Griffin, publisher of the *Monterey Herald* called Newberry "the greatest force Carmel has ever had for the preservation of its beauty, its artistic identity, and fine community spirit." Newberry also kept busy designing and building small houses. (Photograph courtesy of the Thomas Fordham Collection.)

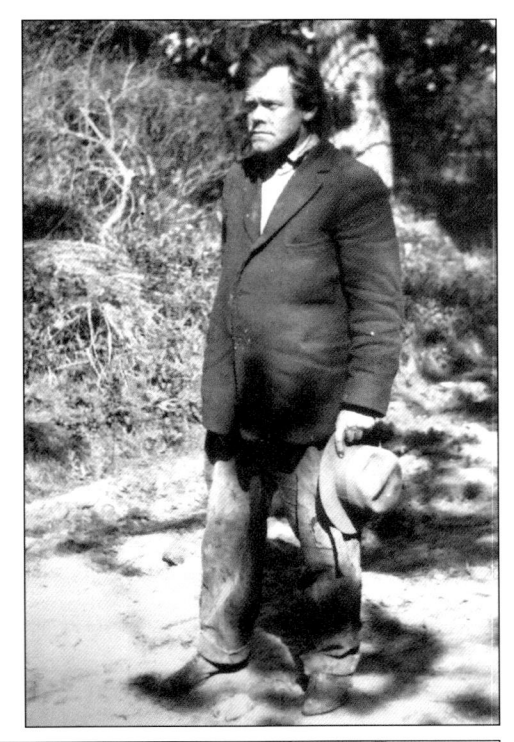

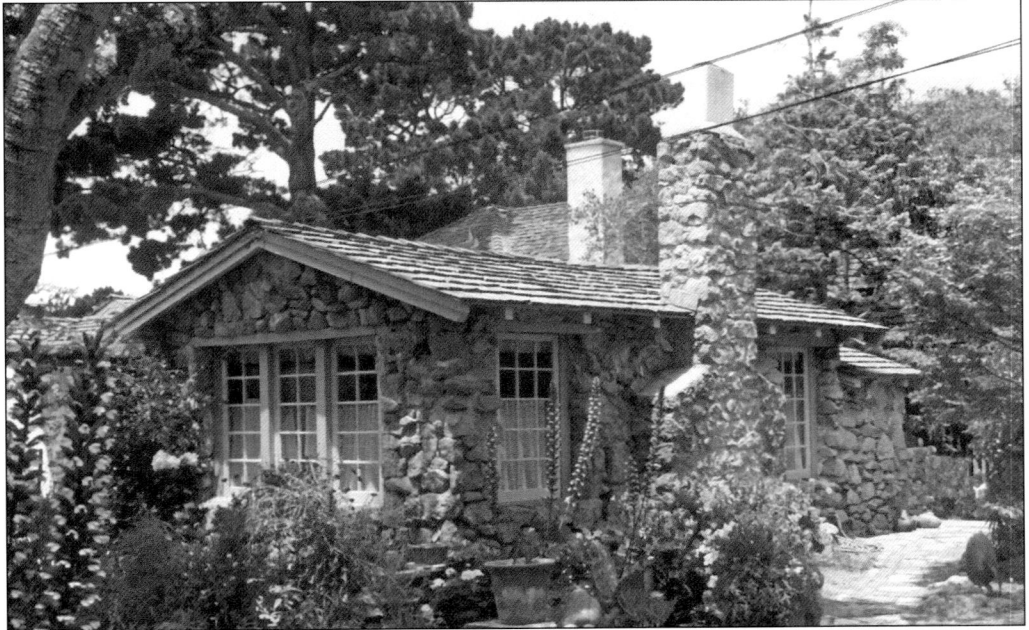

Perry Newberry favored brick or stone masonry construction for his eclectic little cottages and did the work himself. His houses tend to be U-shaped in plan. They often leaked, and their chimneys did not draw well. In spite of these shortcomings, they were unique and artistic with a distinct charm and sold well. His home on Dolores Street (seen here) was built in 1923. (Photograph by the author.)

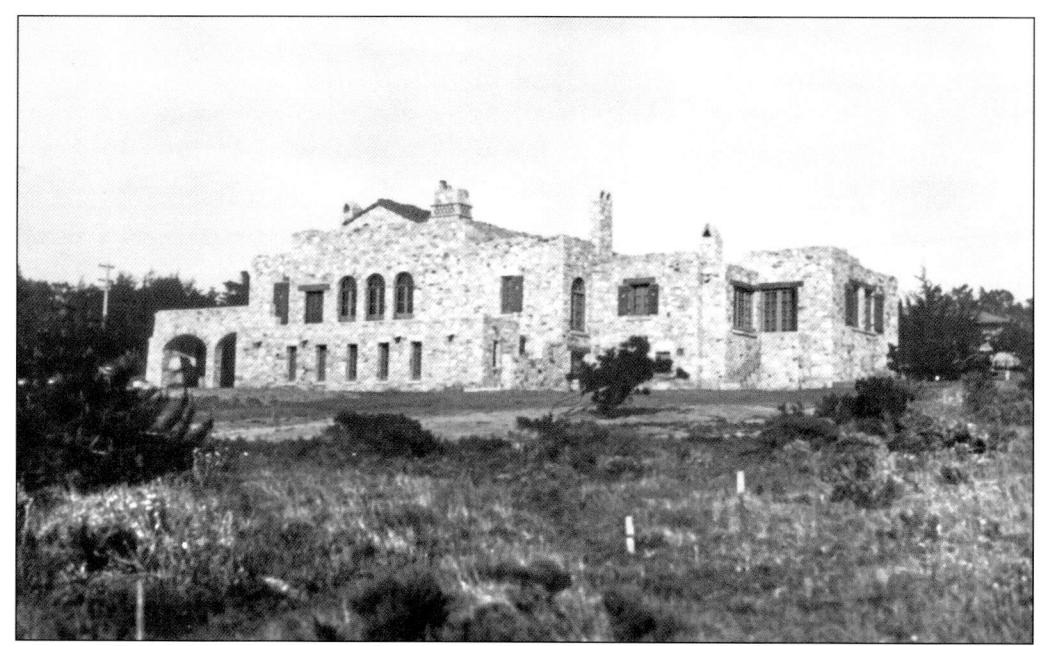

San Francisco architect George F. Ashley reintroduced the use of native Carmel stone for residential construction on the Monterey Peninsula in his 1922 Casa del Mar Azul for Paul and Marie Gordon. The design owed as much for its look to Morocco as it did to Andalusia. Lee Gottfried was the builder with local stonemason Juan Rubell. (Photograph from author's collection.)

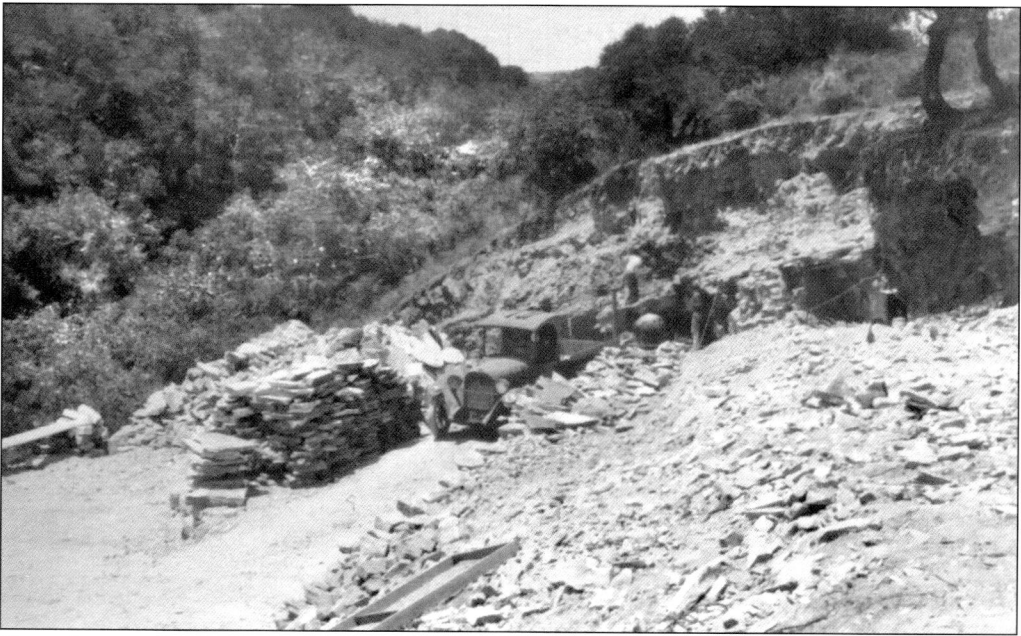

Carmel stone, or chalk rock as it is locally called, was first used in construction of the Carmel mission church in the 1790s A seabed shale, it was easily quarried and cut "green," hardening with age. Carmel stone is seen everywhere on the Monterey Peninsula—on buildings, as chimneys and retaining walls, and as walkways and patio decks. (Photograph from author's collection.)

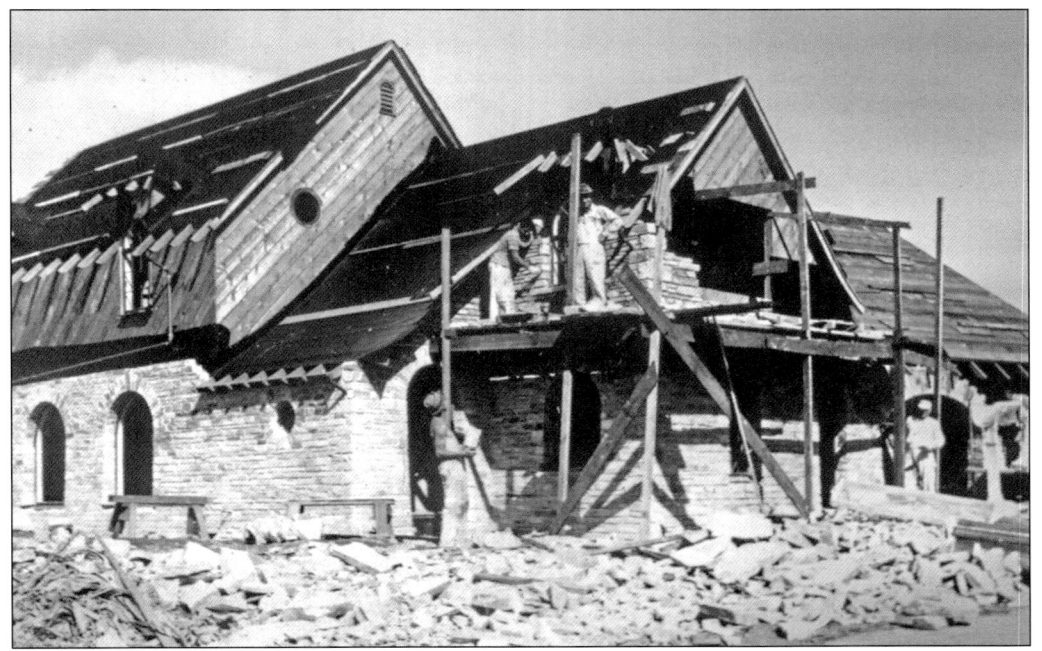

Contractor Ernest Bixler's crew faces the wood-framed T. J. Brennan House with its Carmel-stone veneer at the corner of Scenic Road and Martin Way on Carmel Point. The locally quarried shale was employed both structurally and as an exterior wall cladding on buildings of various styles—in this case, a small Tudor manor house. (Photograph courtesy of Laurel Bixler Fosness.)

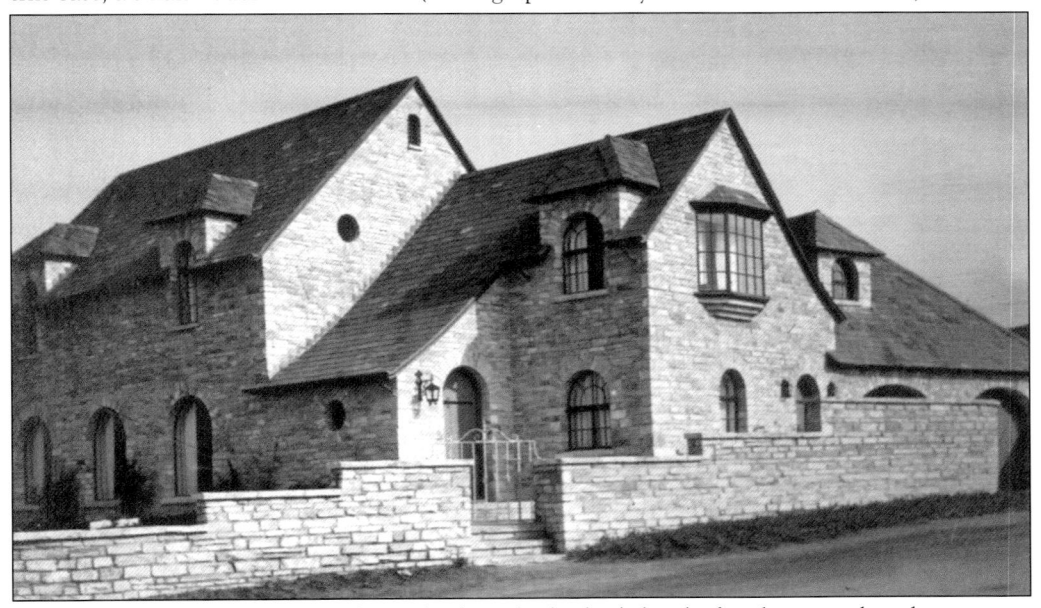

By the 1930s, local residential design had reached a high level of architectural sophistication. Designer-builder Ernest Bixler came to Carmel from Oakland in 1928. At the start of the Depression, he worked as a carpenter for $4 to $6 dollars a day, building up his practice. Bixler constructed over 80 homes in Carmel between 1929 and 1965. (Photograph courtesy of Laurel Bixler Fosness.)

CARMEL STONE....

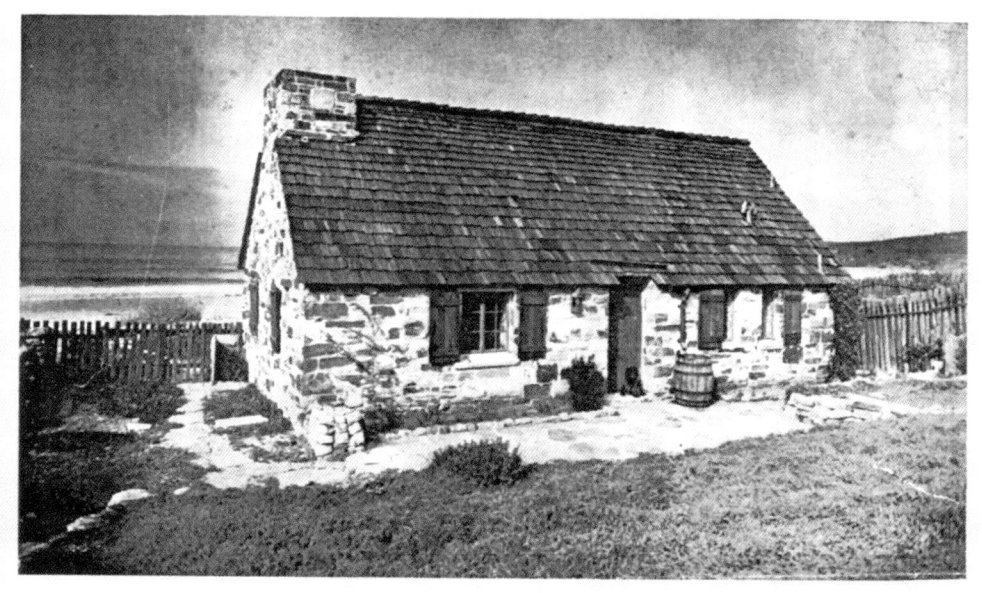

Plan 1015 *Carmel*
C. J. RYLAND, Architect

Quaint, fascinating, intriguing—any number of words might describe this Carmel stone house built right on the edge of the blue Pacific. In the background can be seen the breakers and the beach.

In the hills back of Carmel are large deposits of a chalk stone which has been aptly named "Carmel stone." A rainbow hue of colors seems woven into the stone, which is easily split into convenient sizes for building purposes. Sometimes an entire house will be built of Carmel stone; more often it will be used for a trim up to window height, with the rest of the house in wood; for a chimney, or for stepping stones and walls. Such houses as the one pictured above lend a charm all of its own to the Monterey Peninsula.

It is estimated that the above house can be built for $5000, dependent of course upon the locality in which it is built. If the house was financed through a twenty-year FHA insured loan, monthly payments would be about:

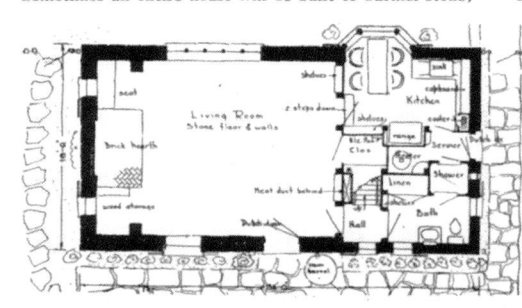

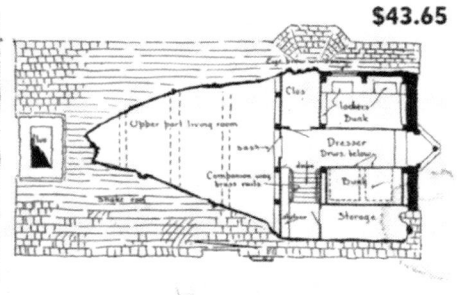

$43.65

Home for Henry S. Tusler

CALIFORNIA HOUSE AND GARDENS FOR JUNE, 1941

Beginning in the 1940s, the work of Carmel architects and designers began appearing more and more in popular and professional architectural journals. C. J. Ryland built this tiny Carmel-stone Cotswold cottage as a vacation home for Henry Tusler in 1934. (Photograph from *California House and Gardens* magazine, June 1941.)

Allen Knight was one of Carmel's beloved eccentrics. Musician and inveterate traveler, he was also a civic leader who served as a police commissioner, councilman, and later as mayor. Among his many community activities, Knight found time to design several eclectic buildings. He was also an inveterate collector of maritime history. (Photograph courtesy of Allene Knight Fremier Collection.)

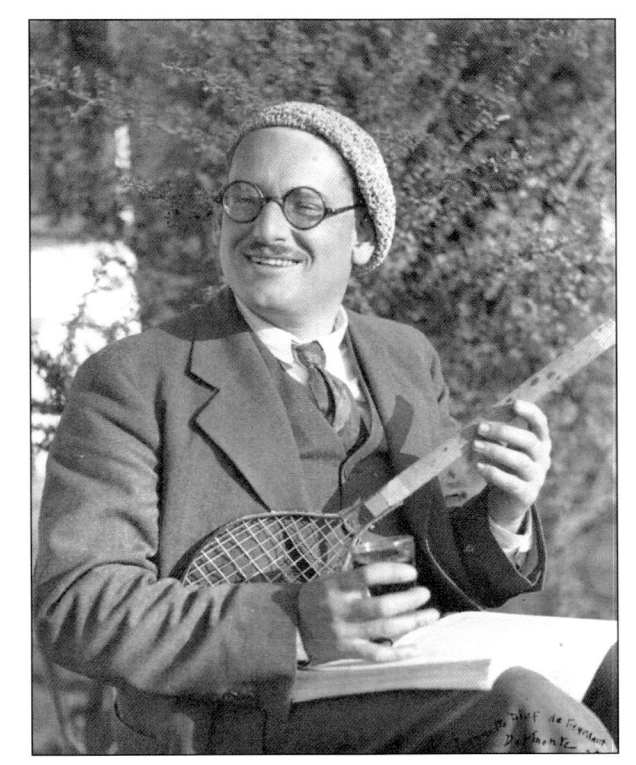

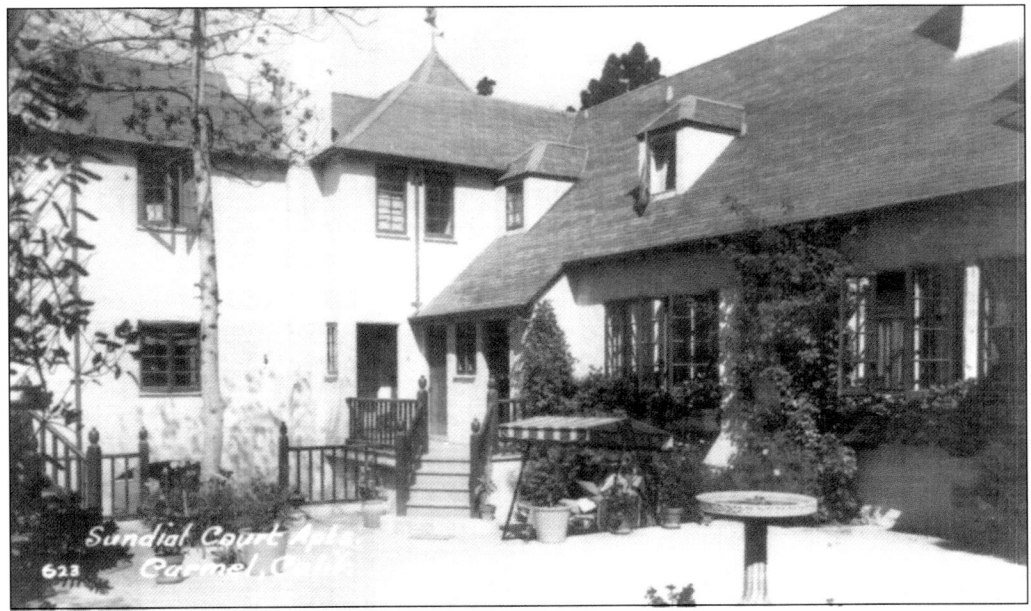

In 1929, friends Alys Miller and Mary L. Hamlin provided financial backing for a residential apartment building constructed around an open interior court. Allen Knight based the initial design on Bohemian architecture he had recently seen traveling in Czechoslovakia. San Francisco architect Albert Farr refined the design, and M. J. Murphy built it in 1930. (Photograph courtesy of Allene Knight Fremier Collection.)

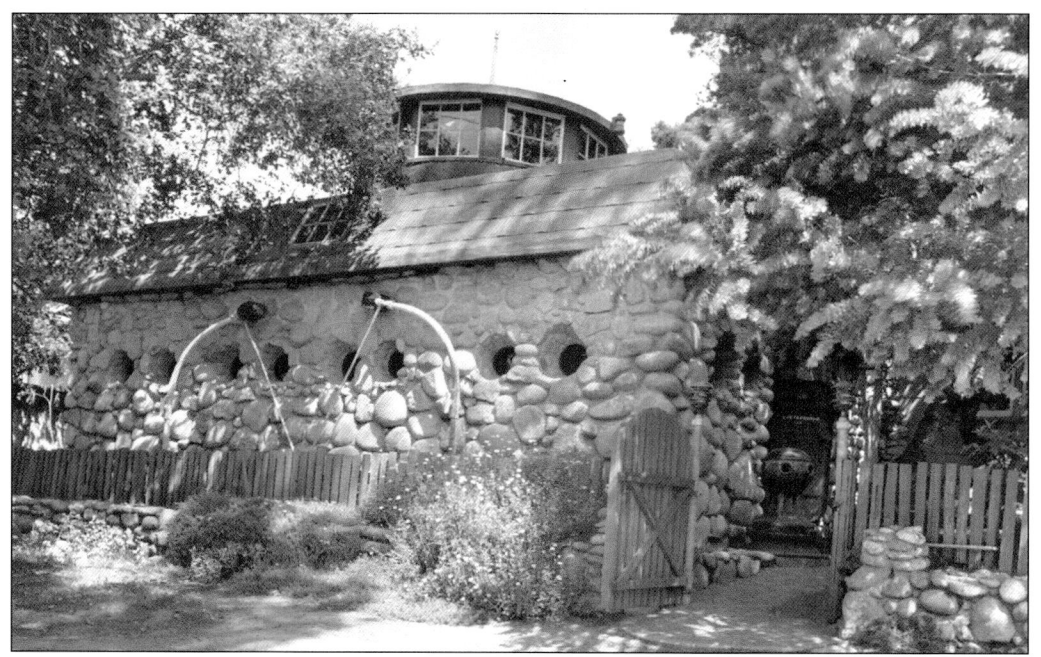

When the Sundial apartments were constructed in 1929, Allen Knight had to move his home on the building site to a new location at Guadalupe Street and Sixth Avenue. Knight had sailed before the mast as a young man and became an avid collector of all things nautical. In 1936, Knight began a three-year project, personally building a stone ship's cabin to house his maritime treasures. (Photograph by Roger Fremier; courtesy of Allene Knight Fremier Collection.)

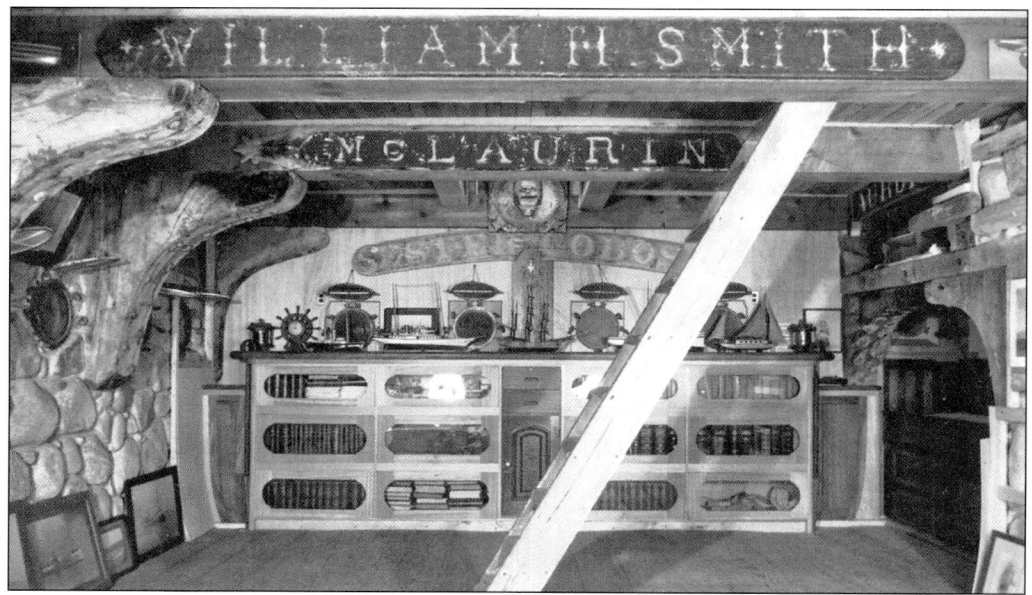

Allen Knight's collection of nautical material filled the interior of his stone ship, seen above. Eventually his artifacts and photographic archives would form the basis for the Allen Knight Maritime and History Museum, built on the Custom House Plaza of Monterey's State Historic Park in 1992. (Photograph by Roger Fremier; courtesy of Allene Knight Fremier Collection.)

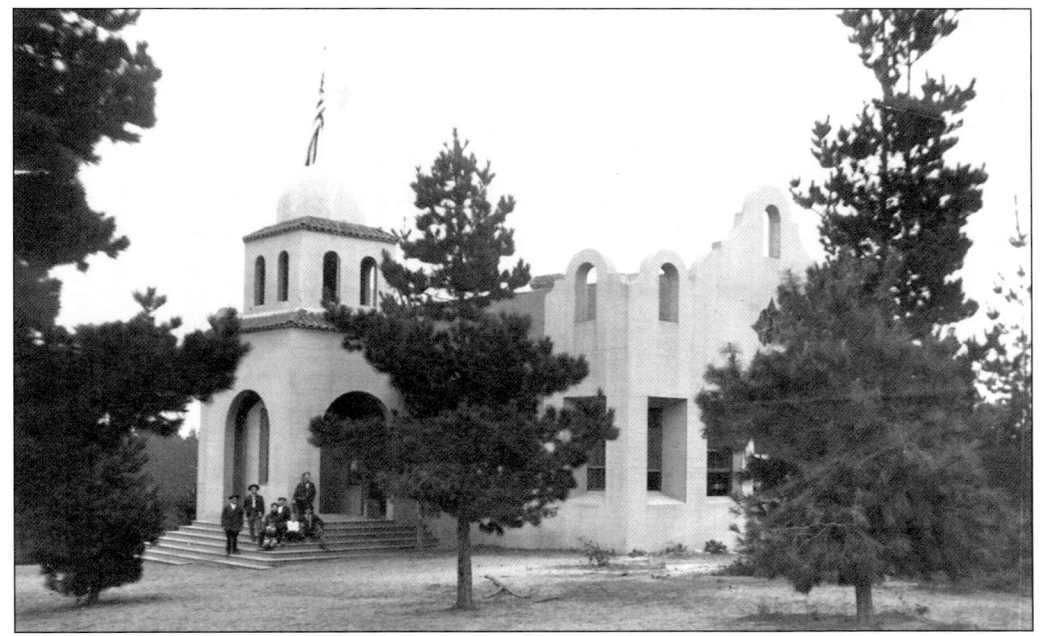

Built in 1906, Carmel's first formal schoolhouse was one of the very few examples of Mission Revival architecture in Carmel. Its arched entry with a towered dome and exaggerated curvilinear parapet walls reflected California mission forms. It even employed the odd-shaped quatrefoil window found on the Mission San Carlos chapel. (Photograph courtesy of the Harrison Memorial Library Collection.)

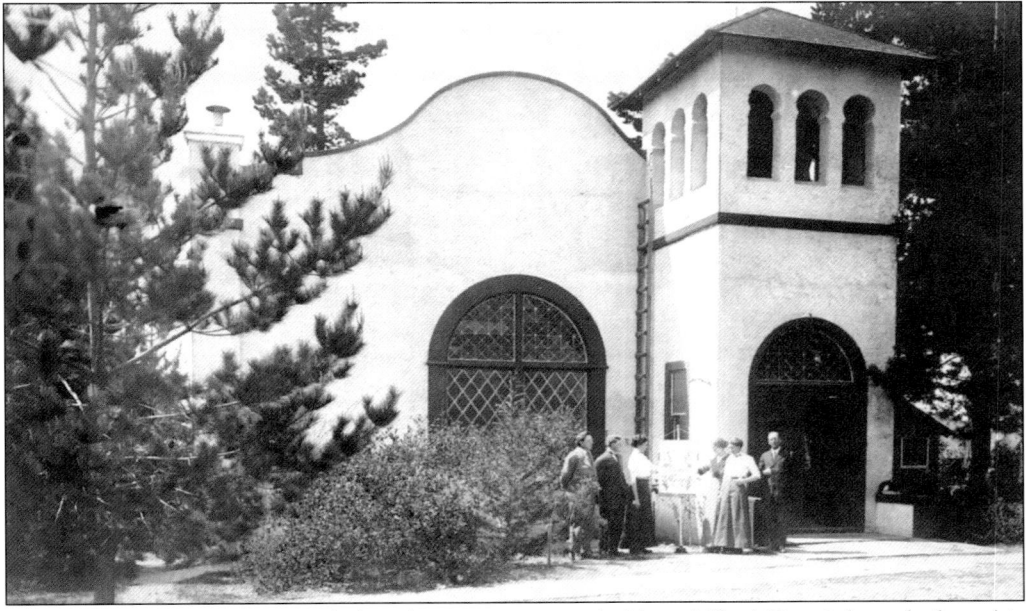

Carmel's Methodist Episcopal church meetings were held in Alfred Horn's barn before this simple, wood-framed chapel of Mission Revival design was completed in 1905. The bell tower is interesting for its use of Moorish-inspired keyhole openings. It was capped with a red tile roof. (Photograph courtesy of the Harrison Memorial Library Collection.)

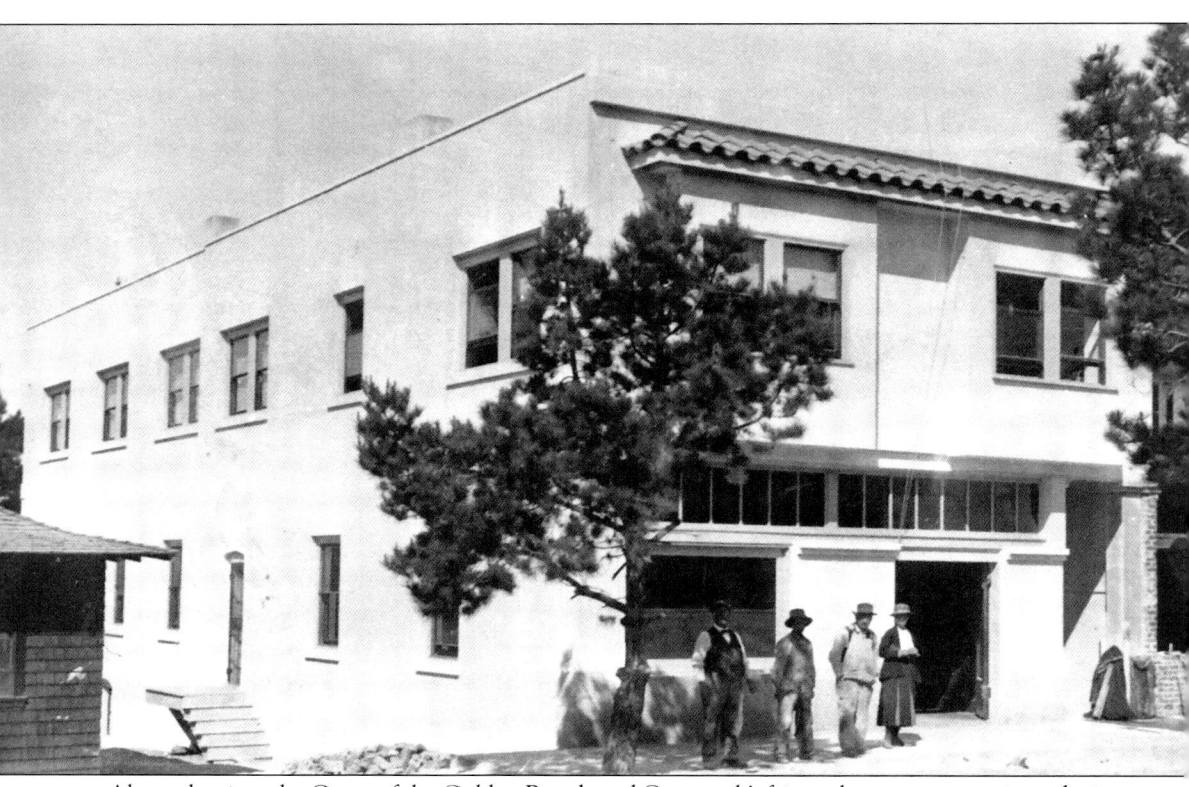

About the time the Court of the Golden Bough and Comstock's fairy-tale cottages were introducing Carmel's citizens to the aesthetic charm of medieval European building types, others were at work reviving interest in Spanish Eclectic architecture, including architect Thomas Morgan, with his new city hall and post office on Dolores Street near Seventh Avenue, seen above. (Harrison Memorial Library Collection.)

Seven

IN A MEDITERRANEAN MODE

Despite the presence of Mission San Carlos, the Mission Revival style was noticeably absent in the village save for the first Sunset School, the 1905 Methodist Episcopal church, and one or two shop fronts. However, by the mid-1920s, Spanish Eclectic was becoming the design of choice on the Monterey peninsula, especially for business blocks. Carmel entered an era of economic growth that saw Tudor shoppes vying with Spanish villas for design dominance in the business district. Even the Pine Inn was stuccoed over and roofed with mission tile in 1925. It was this eclectic mixing of medieval and Mediterranean architectural modes into a visual potpourri that continues to imbue Carmel's commercial streetscapes with their constant sense of discovery and surprise. The downtown tends to employ open space, especially as lanes and courtyards in association with building shapes, which encourages pedestrian exploration and movement. Interest and enthusiasm for things Spanish expanded over time, introducing a number of new faces and names to Carmel's building trades. When the Depression hit, much of Ocean Avenue and its tributary streets east of Dolores Street were beginning to look like the hill towns of Andalusia.

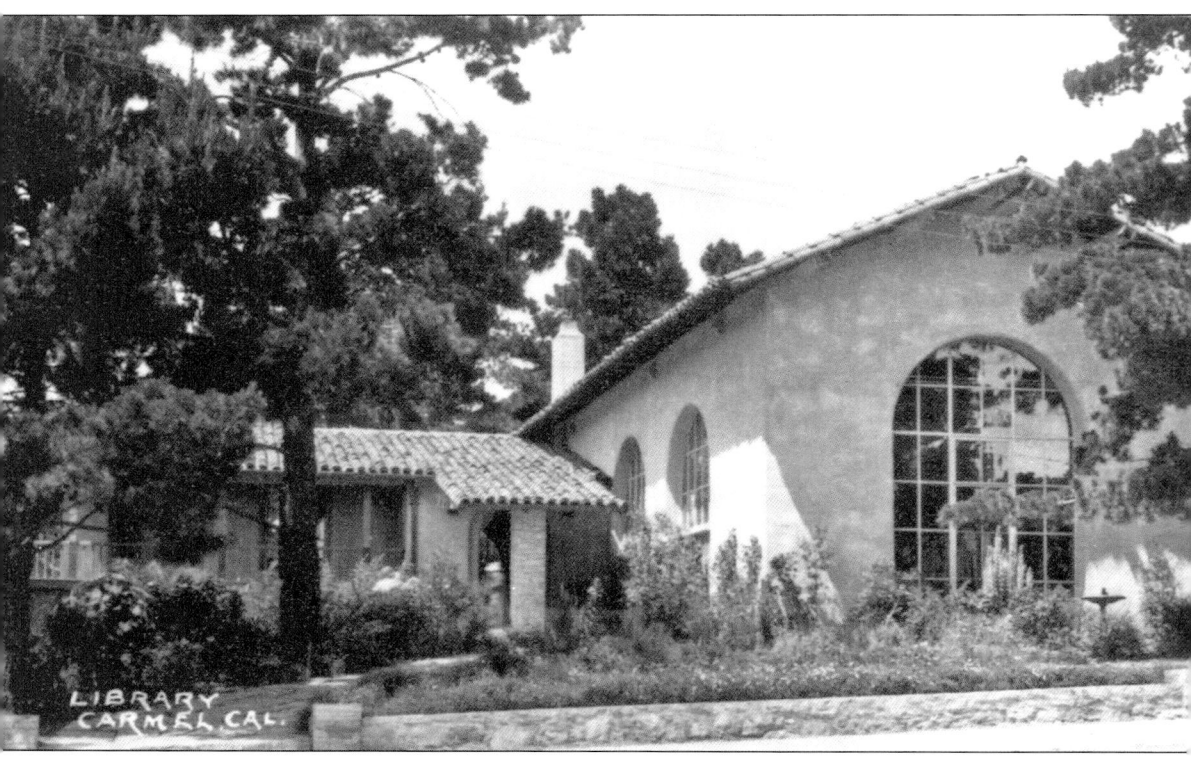

Carmel's city council held a competition for design of the Harrison Memorial Library in early 1926. There were nine entries. Plans were submitted by Hugh Comstock, M. J. Murphy, Percy Parkes, Robert Stanton, Clay Otto, Calvin Bates, W. A. Beckett, W. Hastings, and A. Natovic. None of the entries were accepted. The city council then asked noted architect Bernard Maybeck to assist in coming up with an appropriate "Spanish-type building." According to council minutes, Maybeck's role was to advise and consult with M. J. Murphy on the plans the master builder had prepared for the library. (Photograph courtesy of the Harrison Memorial Library Collection.)

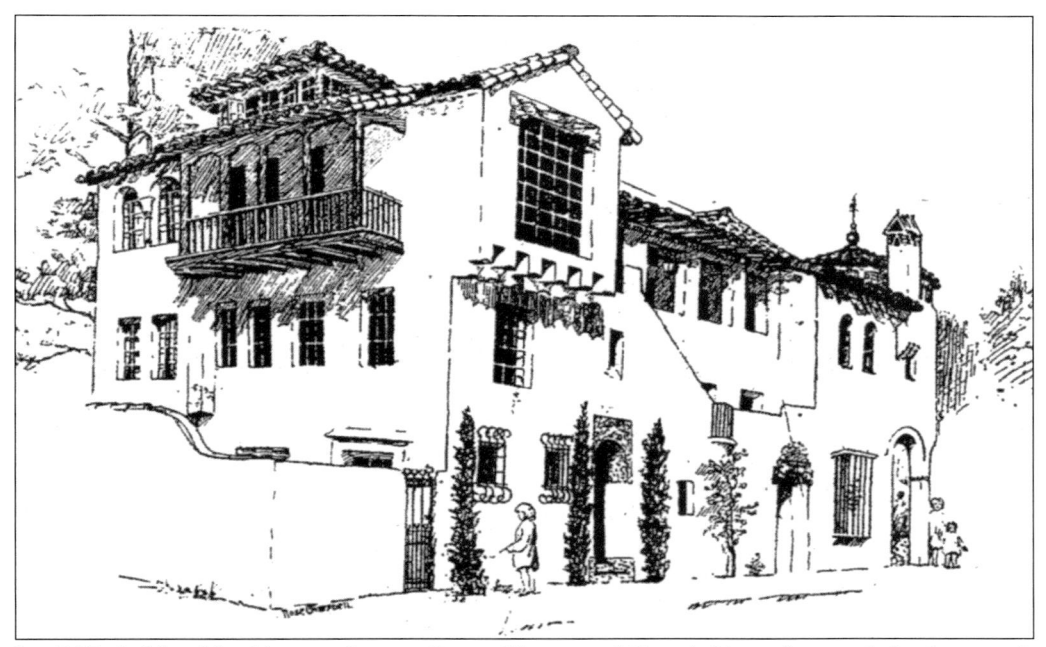

In 1927, Oakland building architects Roger Blaine and David Olsen designed the first steel-framed concrete commercial block in Carmel, the La Giralda Building at Seventh Avenue and Dolores Street. Each of the three visible elevations clearly expresses its function within an artfully orchestrated arrangement of elements from the decorative vocabulary of old Spain. (Drawing by Rose Campbell, *Carmel Pine Cone*, August 3, 1930.)

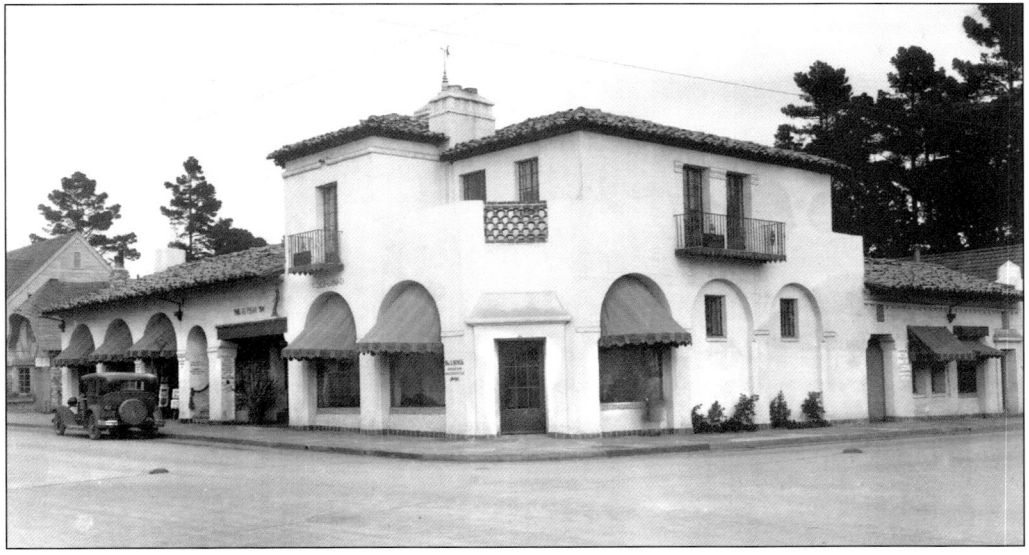

Carmel businessman L. C. Merrill had architects Blaine and Olsen design his El Paseo Building anchoring the northeast corner of Dolores Street and Seventh Avenue in 1928. Writer Perry Newberry wrote about the highly artistic complex in the October issue of the *Architect and Engineer*, "There is distinction about every detail of the building." It is the best remaining example of Spanish Eclectic design in Carmel. (Photograph courtesy of Pat Hathaway, Historic California Views.)

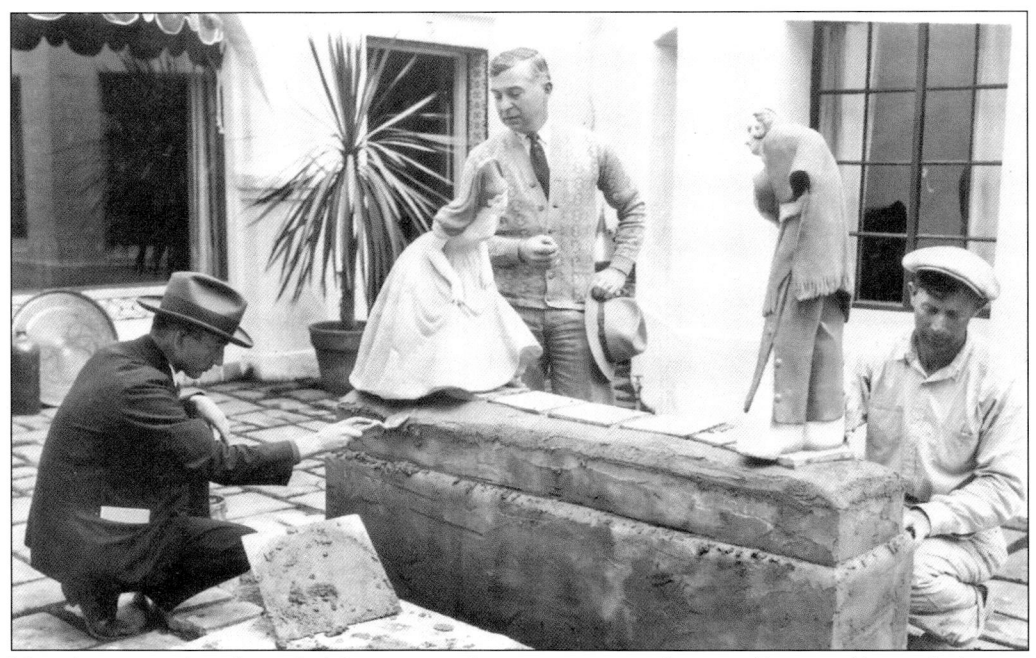

Noted artist and sculptor Jo Mora is seen here supervising the installation of his polychrome terra cotta sculptural group, titled *El Paseo*. The young Californio bowing to his señorita is the signature artwork in the courtyard of the El Paseo business block of L. C. Merrill. (Photograph courtesy of Pat Hathaway, Historic California Views.)

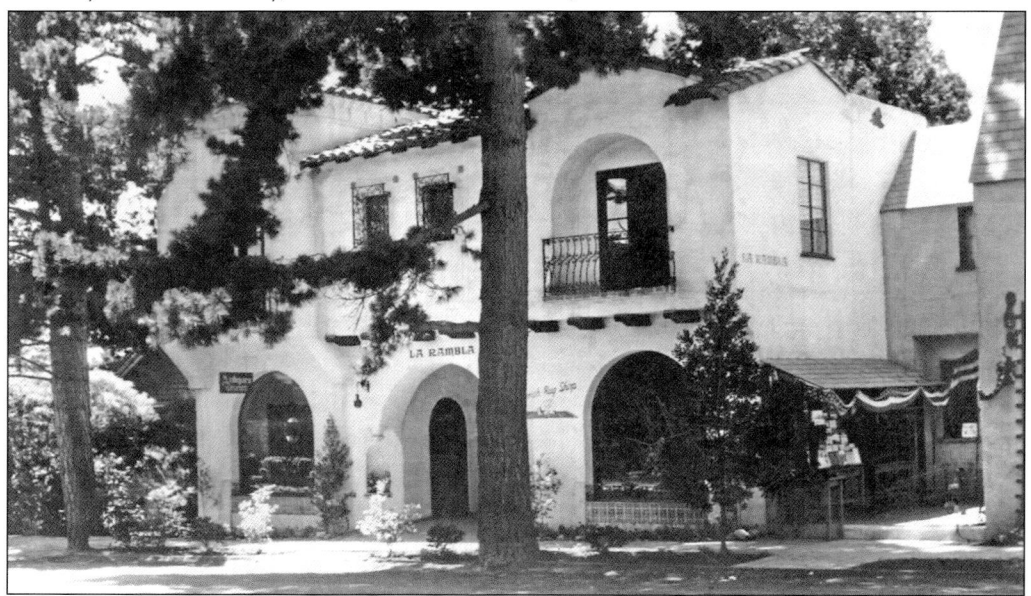

Not to be outshone by outside architects, Carmel building designer Guy O. Koepp created the La Rambla Building on Lincoln Street for Josephine Baber in 1929. A. Carlyle Stoney was the contractor. La Rambla was of stuccoed wood-frame construction with a central passage into a garden court to the west. Large arched openings characterize the facade. (Photograph courtesy of Pat Hathaway, Historic California Views.)

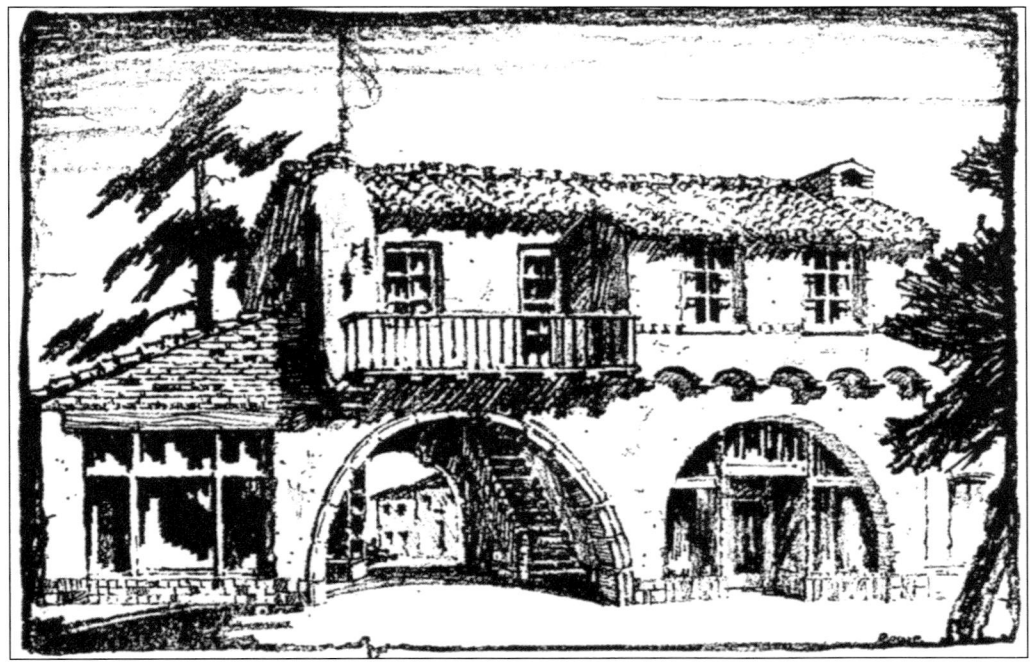

In 1930, realtor Ray DeYoe brought his version of old Mexico to Ocean Avenue when he had Fresno architects Swartz and Ryland design his mixed-use Las Tiendas Building. M. J. Murphy was his contractor. It has low-pitched side-gabled tile roofs, parabolic archways, and a wooden Monterey-style balcony. (Drawing by Ruth Rowe, *Carmel Pine Cone*, August 3, 1930.)

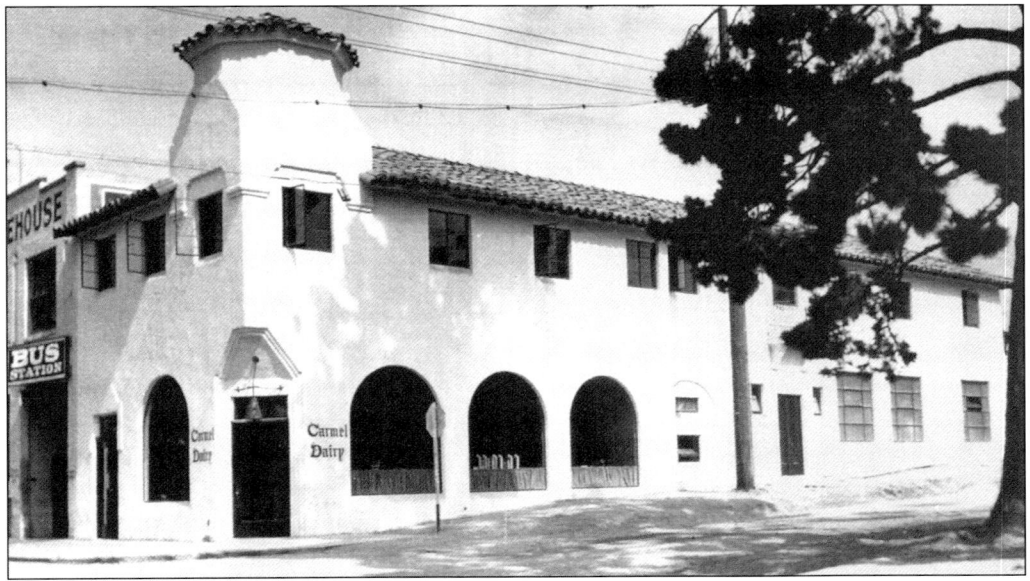

Guy O. Koepp's Carmel Dairy is an interesting expression of inventive commercial design. The stucco walls, arcaded windows, and tile roof are conventional Spanish Eclectic decorative elements. The milk-bottle shaped tower, with a tile cap, is all advertising. This building and M. J. Murphy's 1932 Doud Building, directly across Ocean Avenue, frame the entry to Carmel's downtown. (Photograph courtesy of the Harrison Memorial Library Collection.)

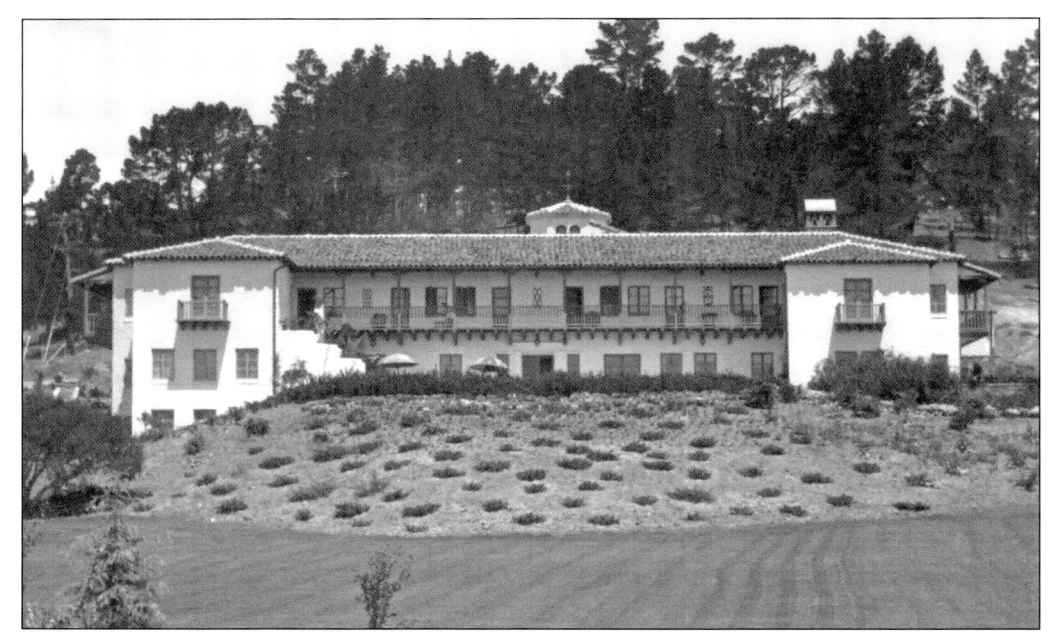

The 1930 Grace Deere Veile Clinic is an important example of the Spanish Eclectic design work of noted California architect Gardner Daily. Sited on rising ground, the unusually symmetrical facade faces south towards Carmel Valley. The research clinic studied nutritional diseases prior to becoming the Monterey Peninsula Community Hospital in 1934. (Photograph by Lewis Josselyn; courtesy of Pat Hathaway, Historic California Views.)

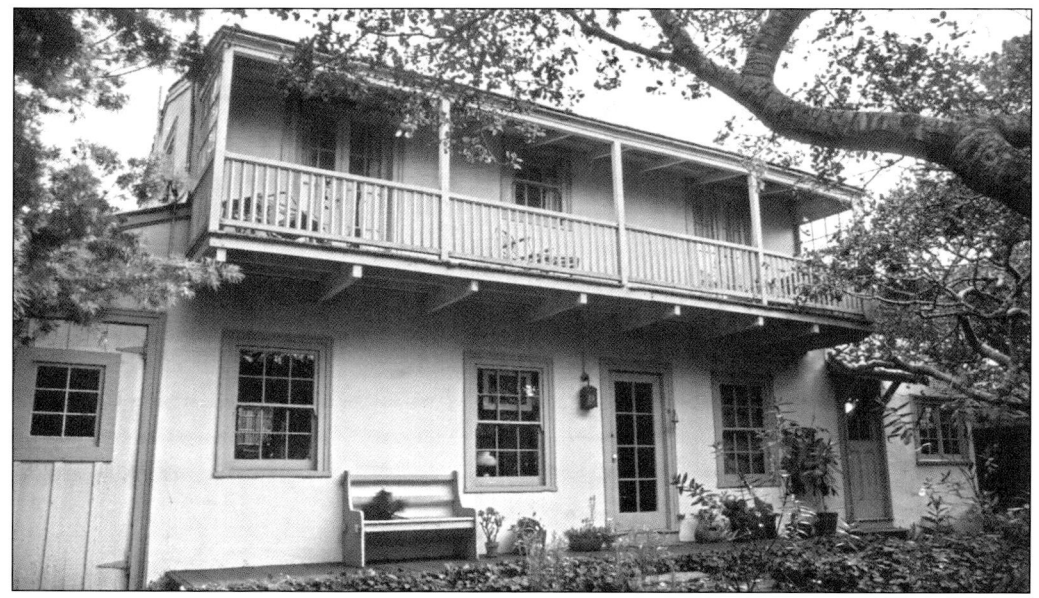

The Kluegel residence on Camino Real, designed and constructed by M. J. Murphy in 1922, is perhaps the most historically correct example of the Monterey Colonial architectural style in Carmel. The design may have been inspired by the James Stokes adobe in Monterey. The house is two stories with a wood-shingled roof overhanging the cantilevered balcony. (Photograph by the author.)

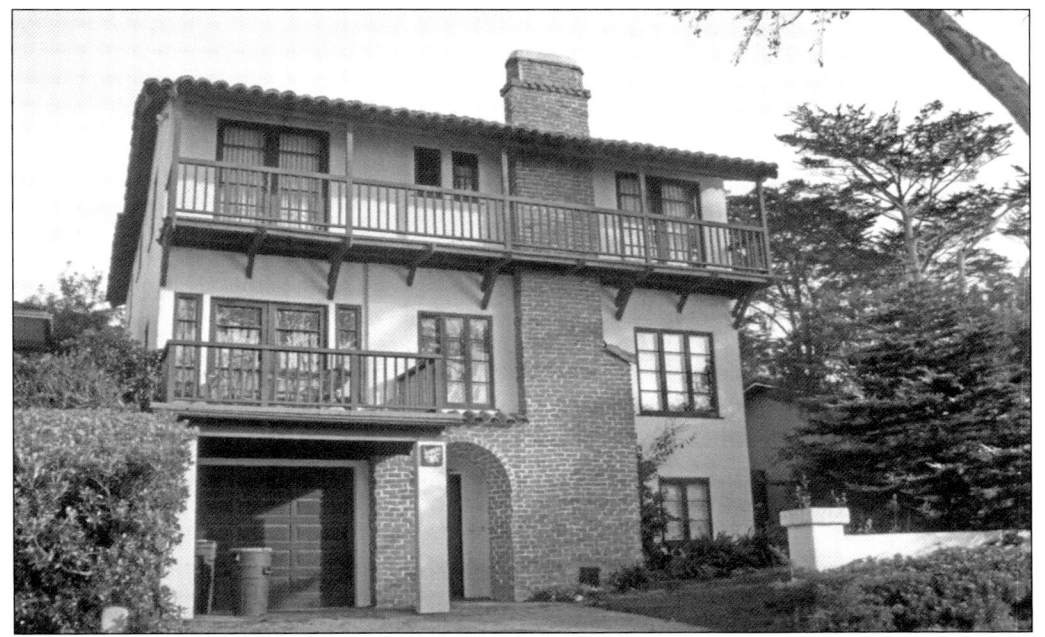

In 1930, designer Guy O. Koepp created this unique residential expression of the Monterey Colonial style on Scenic Drive. The massive exterior brick chimney, with its arched door surround, anchors the unusual residence firmly to the ground. Meese and Briggs, the construction firm from Burlingame that built the La Ribera Hotel, were the contractors for the Cox house. (Photograph by the author.)

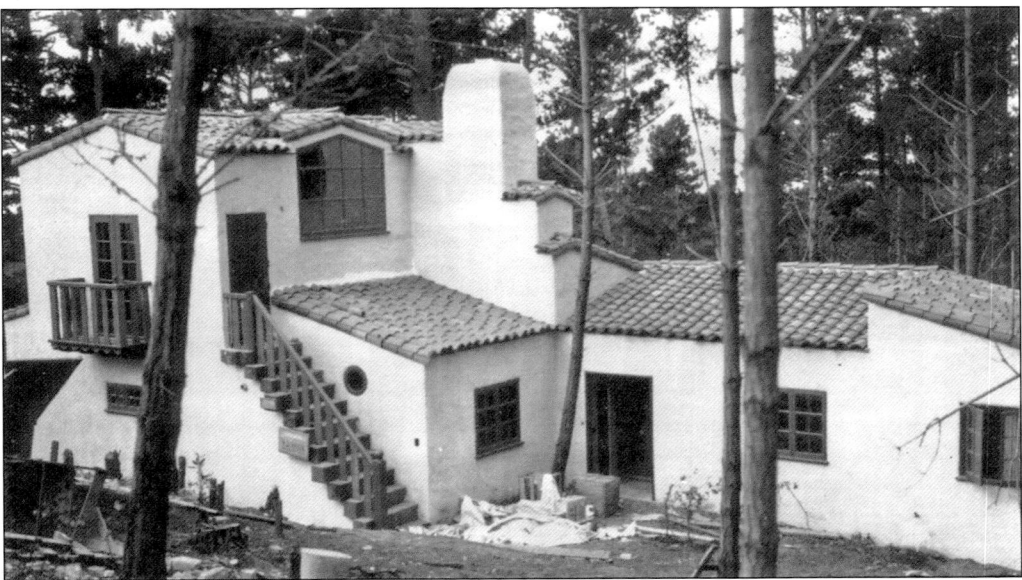

Carmel builder Walter B. Snook constructed this Spanish Eclectic residence for award-winning watercolorist Paul Whitman and his family on San Luis Avenue in Carmel Woods in 1928. Andalusian in its hill-town feeling, the studio portion of the structure is clearly defined by the large focal north window on the second floor. Whitman and his wife, Kit, managed the Carmel Institute of Art. (Photograph courtesy of Ann Whitman Chapman.)

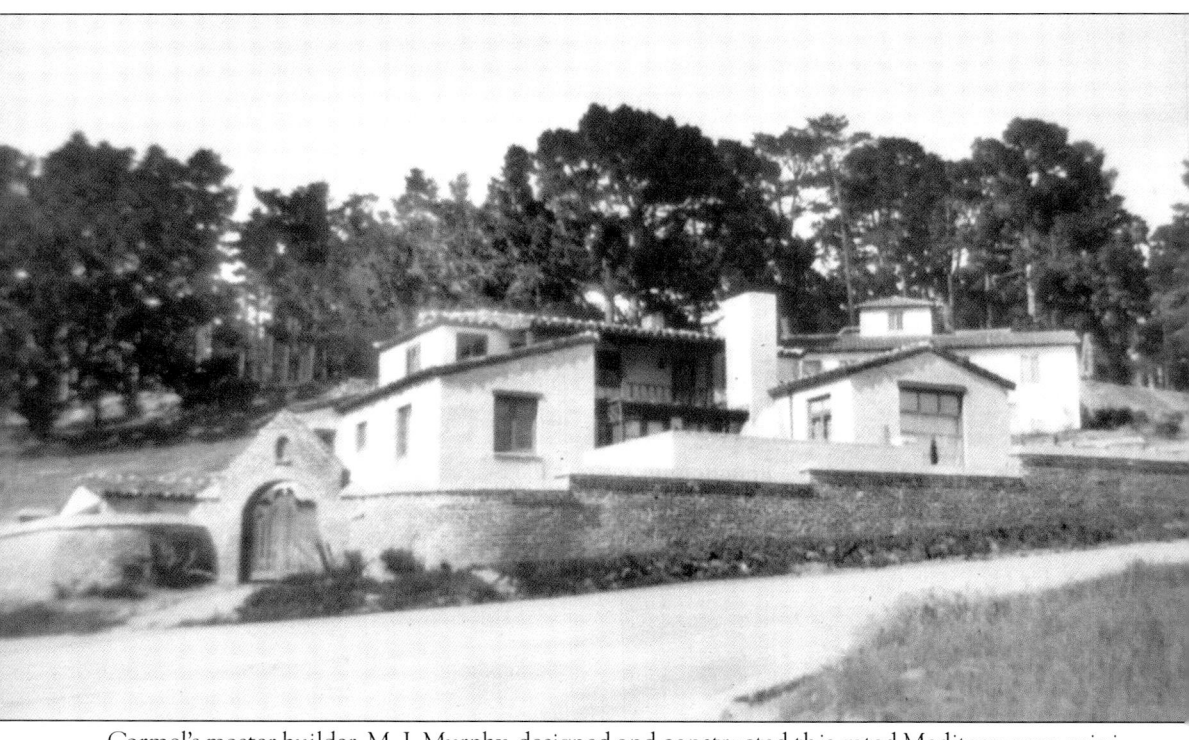

Carmel's master builder, M. J. Murphy, designed and constructed this gated Mediterranean mini-estate near Camino Del Monte in Carmel Woods for Lillian Ramillard about 1928. Its stepped building components with varying roof shapes were meant to reflect the look of ancient Spanish hill towns. The masonry work in the surrounding brick wall is some of the best for that period in Carmel. (Photograph from author's collection.)

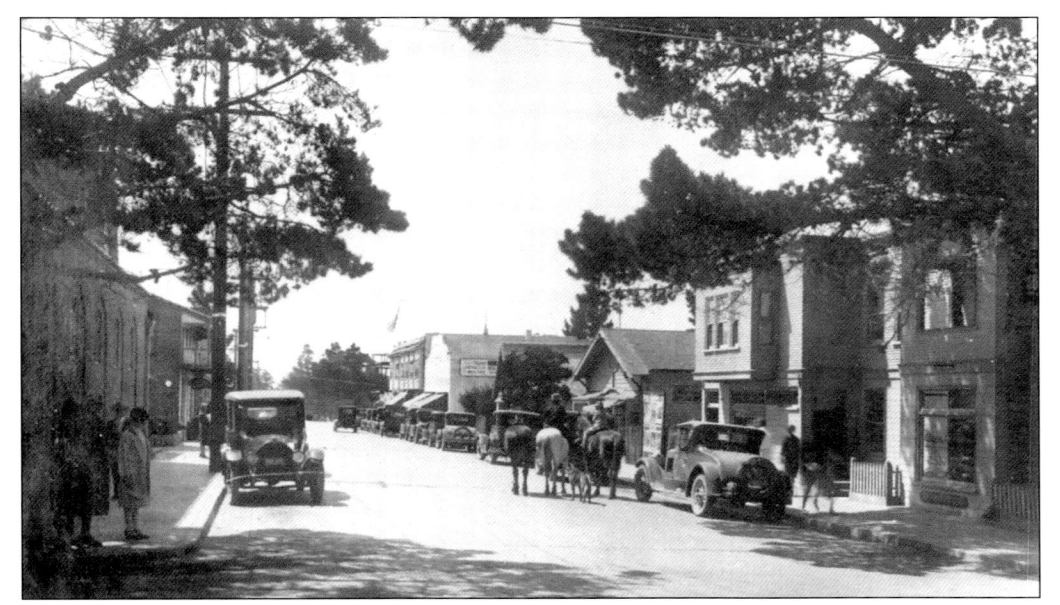

During the 1920s and 1930s, Dolores Street between Ocean Avenue and Seventh Avenue developed as a social and civic center in Carmel. This group of horsemen converse outside the Corner Cupboard in 1931. It was the only Pueblo Revival–style commercial building in the village. It was designed and constructed by Percy Parkes in 1924. Parkes designed several Pueblo Revival residences in Carmel. (Photograph courtesy of the Harrison Memorial Library Collection.)

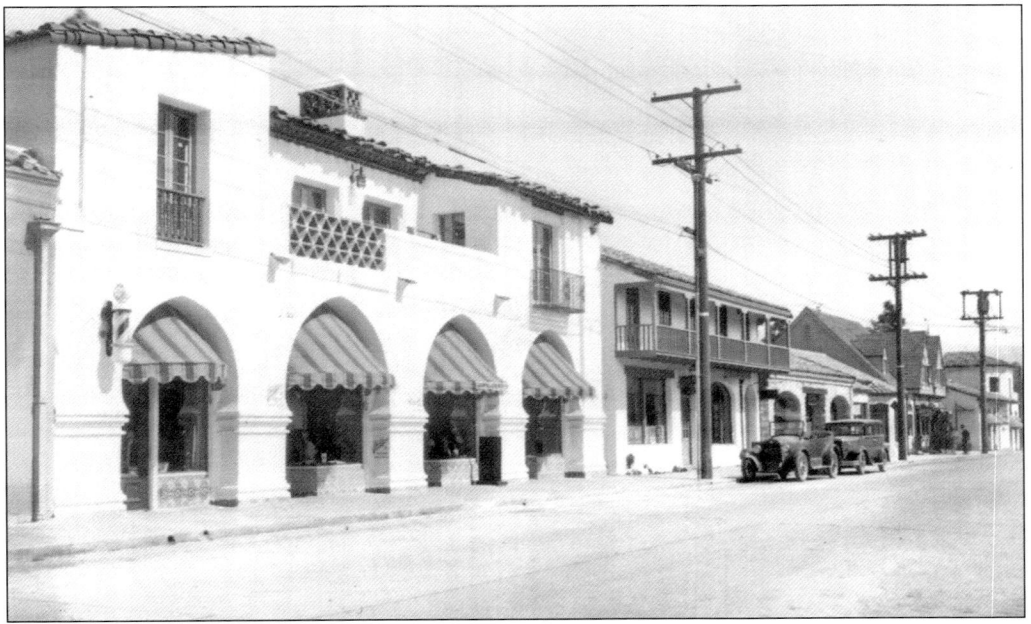

In 1929, the *Carmel Pine Cone* considered Robert Leidig's new reinforced-concrete, mixed-use building on the east side of Dolores Street near Ocean Avenue the best example of the artistry and design of Oakland architects Blaine and Olson. C. H. Lawrence was the contractor. Its Mexican-inspired arcaded bays housed commercial shops. (Photograph courtesy of the Harrison Memorial Library Collection.)

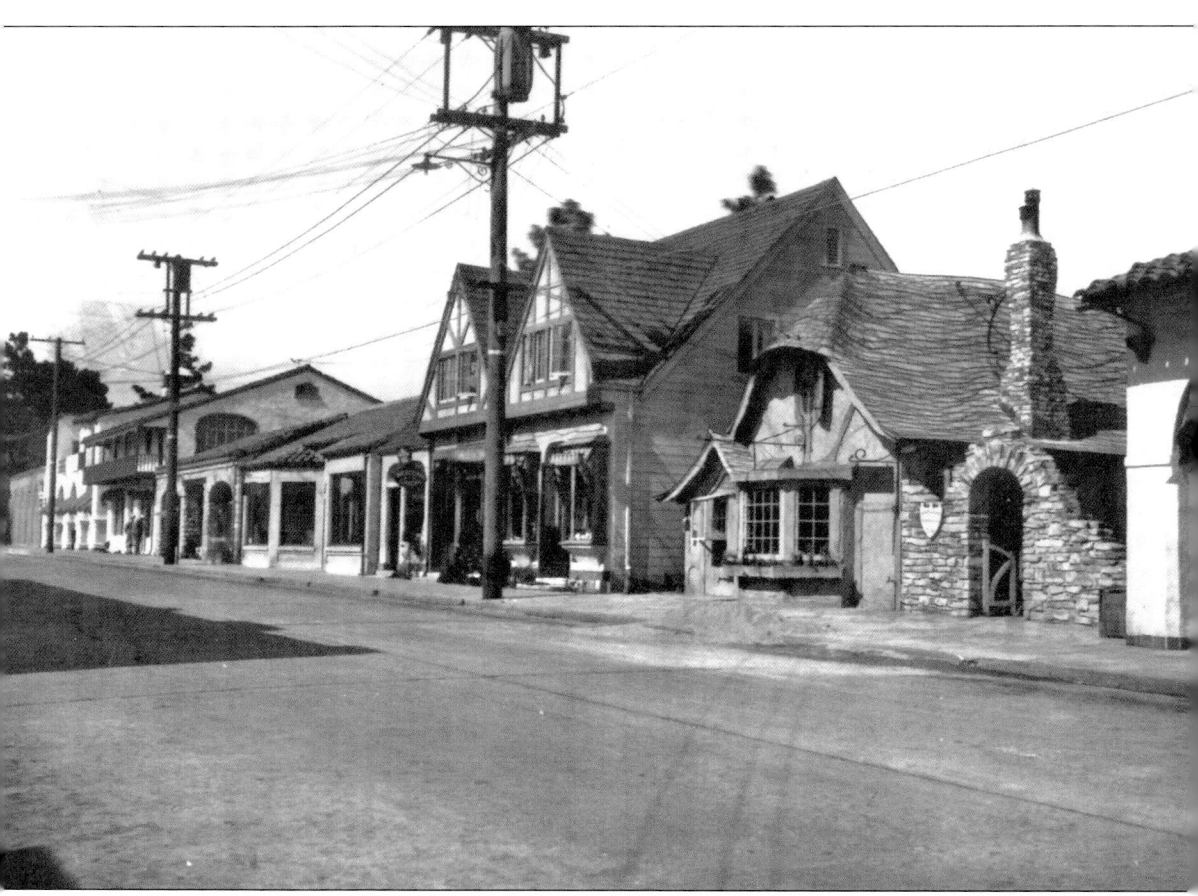

An artistic grouping of eclectic business houses, seen in 1931, runs north from the El Paseo building along the east side of Dolores Street and includes, from right to left, Hugh Comstock's Tuck Box, M. J. Murphy's half-timbered DeYoe Building, Percy Parkes's tile-roofed Vining's Meat Market, Murphy's Carmel-stone-faced W. C. Farley building, and his balconied Monterey Colonial block for Isabel Leidig. The group forms one of the most architecturally significant commercial blocks in Carmel. (Photograph courtesy of Pat Hathaway, Historic California Views.)

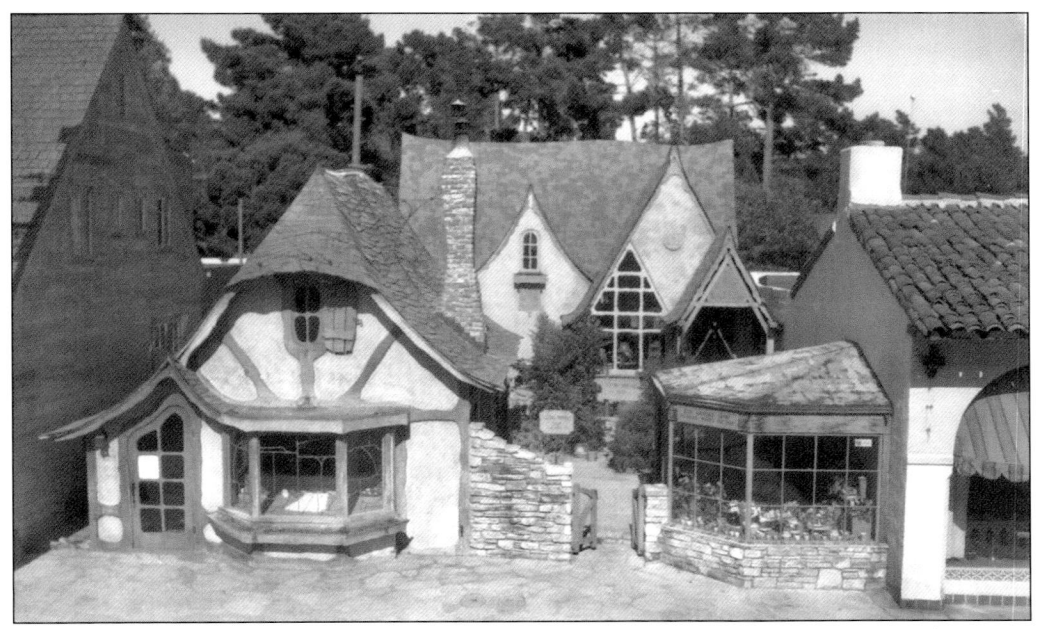

The Tuck Box was Hugh Comstock's only fairy-tale commercial building, constructed in 1926. Stanford University Art Department director Pedro J. Lemos bought the building and adjacent property to "be filled with unique, rambling shops and studios." His first addition, done by Comstock, was a simple garden shop, followed by a fairy-tale design of his own at the rear of the parcel. (Photograph courtesy of Pat Hathaway, Historic California Views.)

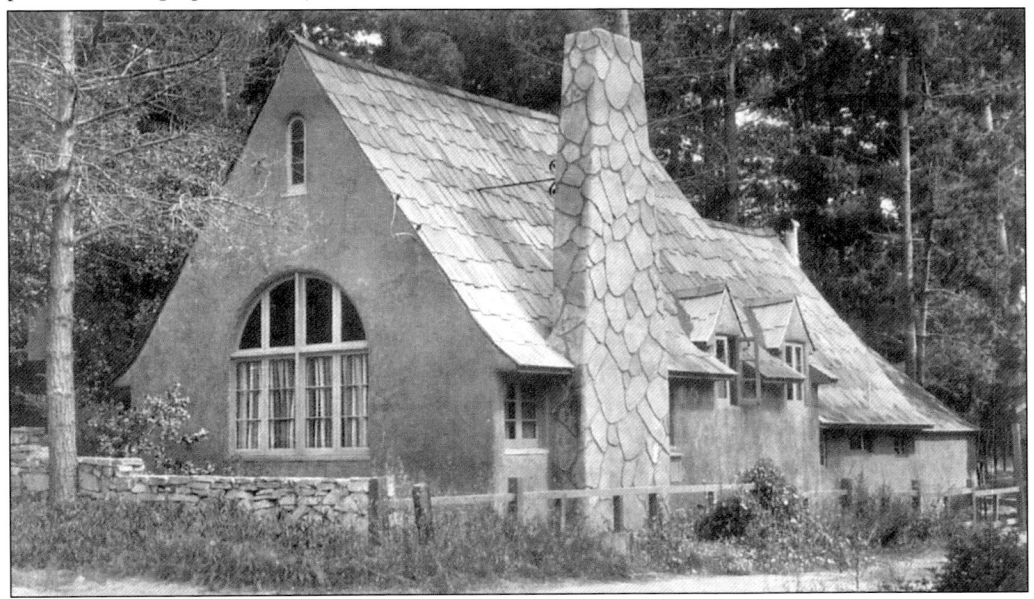

Pedro Lemos designed and had Palo Alto contractor Louis Anderson build his Carmel art studio on Seventh Avenue near Casanova Street in 1926. Lemos was a business owner and first president of the Carmel Art Association. He fervently sought to "keep Carmel natural and unveneered," realizing that economically, "the town is going to reap even bigger rewards if it retains its individuality." (Photograph courtesy of Phyllis Lyon Munsey.)

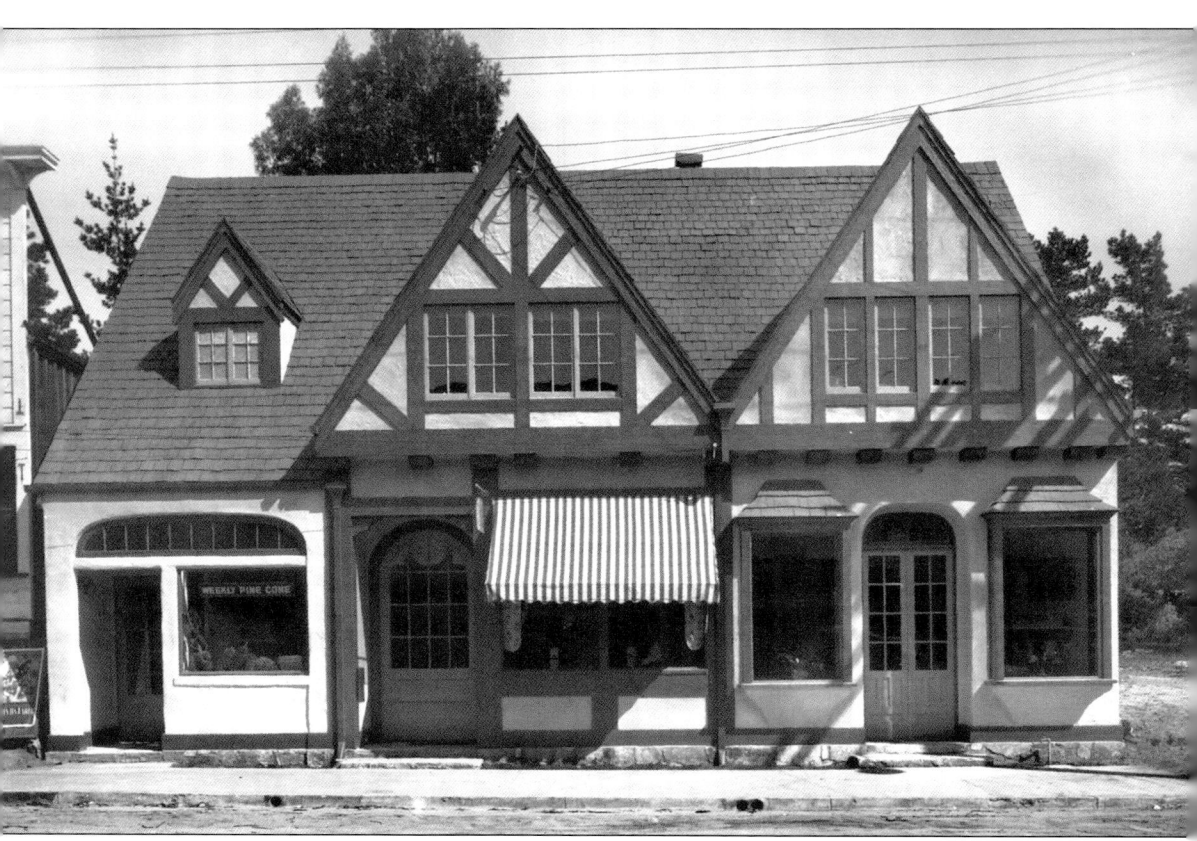

M. J. Murphy designed and built this Carmel cultural icon across from the new city hall in 1924 for realtor Ray DeYoe. It housed the *Carmel Pine Cone* and later the Denny-Watrous art gallery and theater, where early chamber recitals helped establish the Carmel Music Society and the Carmel Bach Festival. Both Richard Neutra and Rudolf Schindler lectured on modern architecture in the gallery during the 1930s. (Photograph by Lewis Josslyn; courtesy of Pat Hathaway, Historic California Views.)

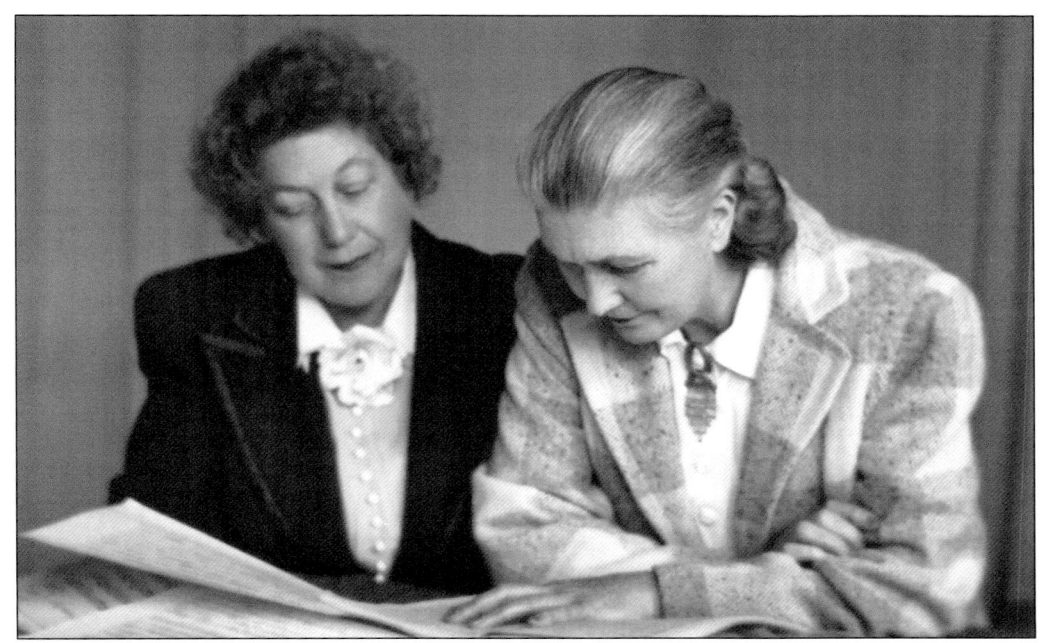

Two independent and creative women, Dene Denny (right) and Hazel Watrous, came to Carmel in 1923 on vacation and stayed on to help create the Carmel Music Society, Monterey County Symphony, and Carmel Bach Festival. They also designed and built a collection of 30 or so small residential houses, many of them in the Carmel Woods. (Photograph courtesy of the Harrison Memorial Library Collection.)

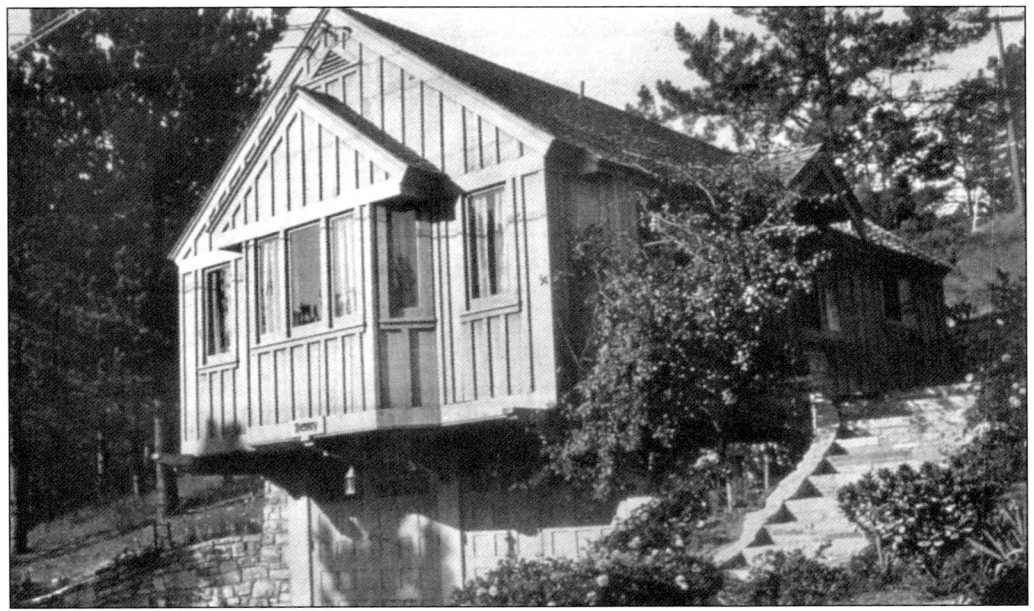

Dene Denny was a concert pianist, and Hazel Watrous was a painter, interior decorator, and stage designer. In partnership, they designed and constructed about 30 small houses, like Fremont Ballou's board-and batten cottage on Upper Trail. Ballou was a plant biologist at the Carnegie Institute's Coastal Laboratory. (Photograph courtesy of Pat Hathaway, Historic California Views.)

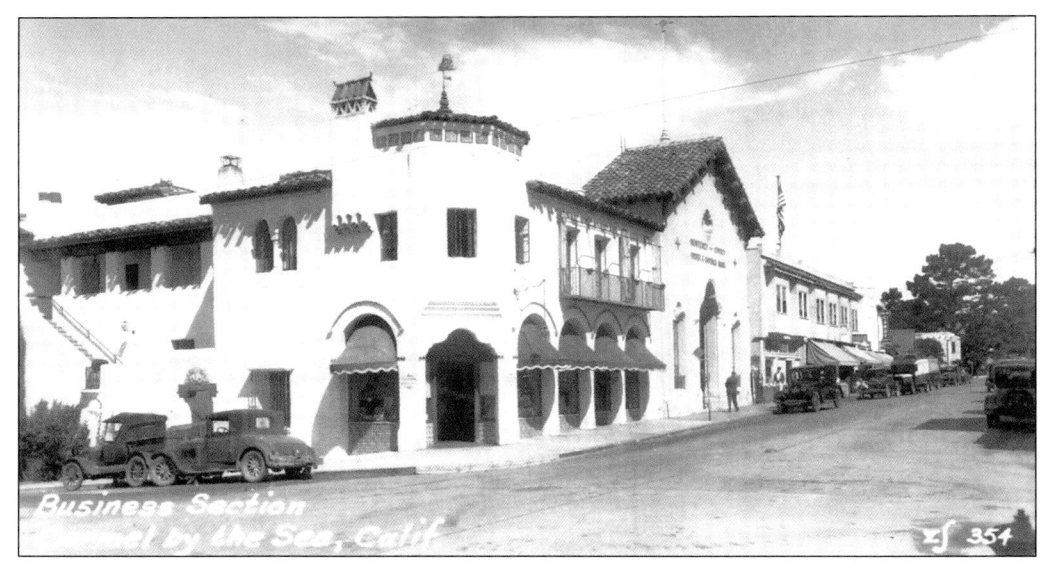

San Francisco architect H. H. Winner designed the imposing 1930 Spanish Colonial–style Monterey County Trust and Savings Bank. Its tiled gable roof, with a quatrefoil window in the apex and symmetrically composed facade, evokes an early California feeling. Hugh Comstock was the low bidder on this, his first major commercial building. (Photograph courtesy of the Harrison Memorial Library Collection.)

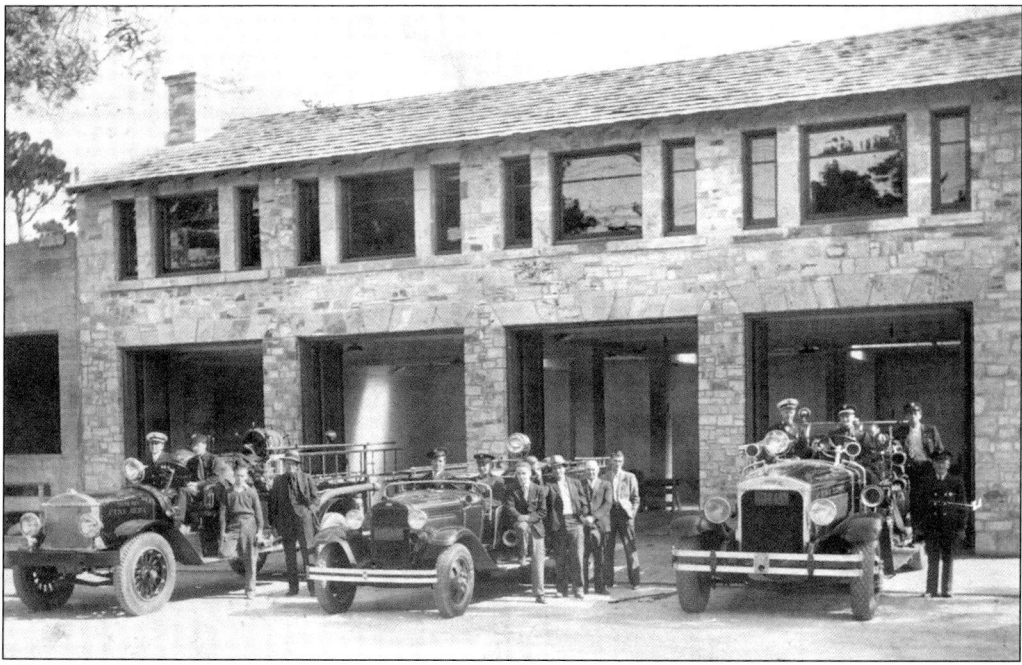

The recently rehabilitated Carmel Fire Station at Mission and Sixth Avenue was designed by architect Milton Latham in 1934. Funded in part by the Works Progress Administration, M. J. Murphy was the contractor. Stone masons Joseph Martin, Walter Barfield, and Joe Lopez laid the Carmel-stone veneer, and noted metalsmith Francis Whitaker fabricated the engine bay doors. (Photograph courtesy of the Harrison Memorial Library Collection.)

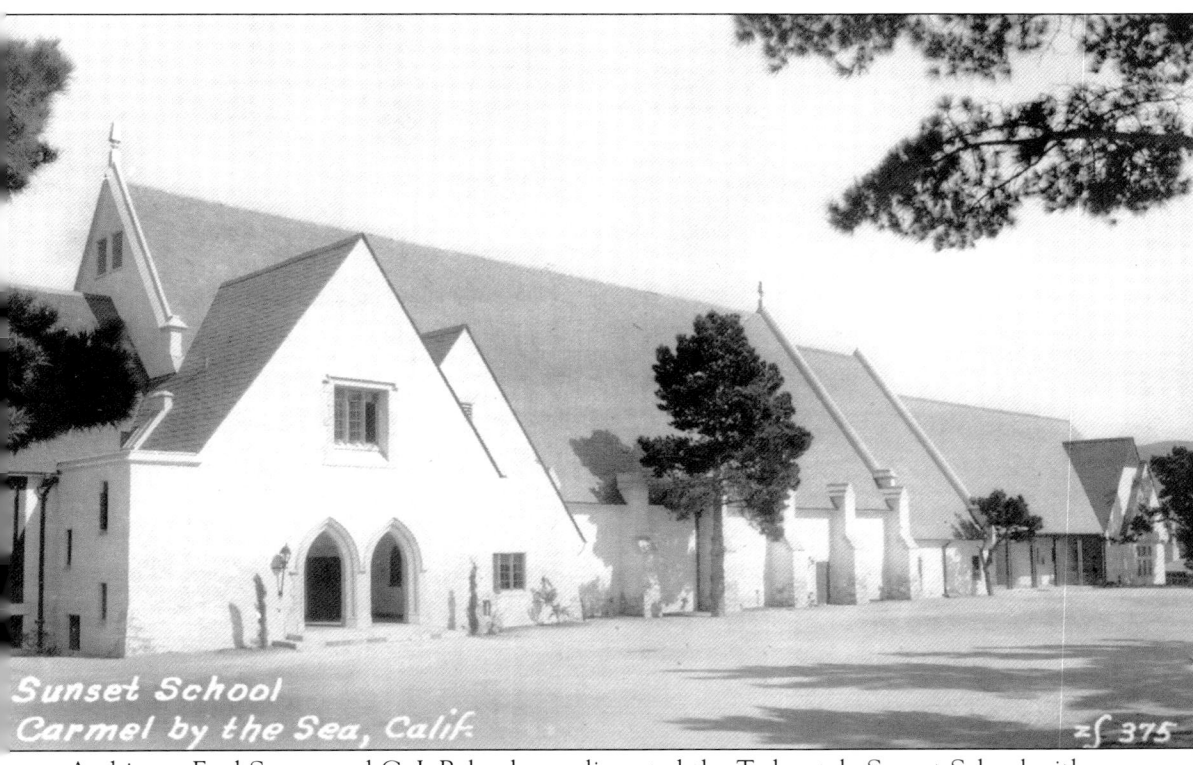

Architects Fred Swartz and C. J. Ryland complimented the Tudor-style Sunset School with an impressive auditorium in 1931. The inspiration for the design came from medieval English tithe barns, with Gothic detailing. The Sunset School Auditorium later became, and remains, Carmel's cultural center, hosting concerts by the Carmel Music Society, Bach Festival, and a wide variety of other venues. Listed in the National Register of Historic Places, the property has recently undergone a major rehabilitation. (Photograph courtesy of the Harrison Memorial Library Collection.)

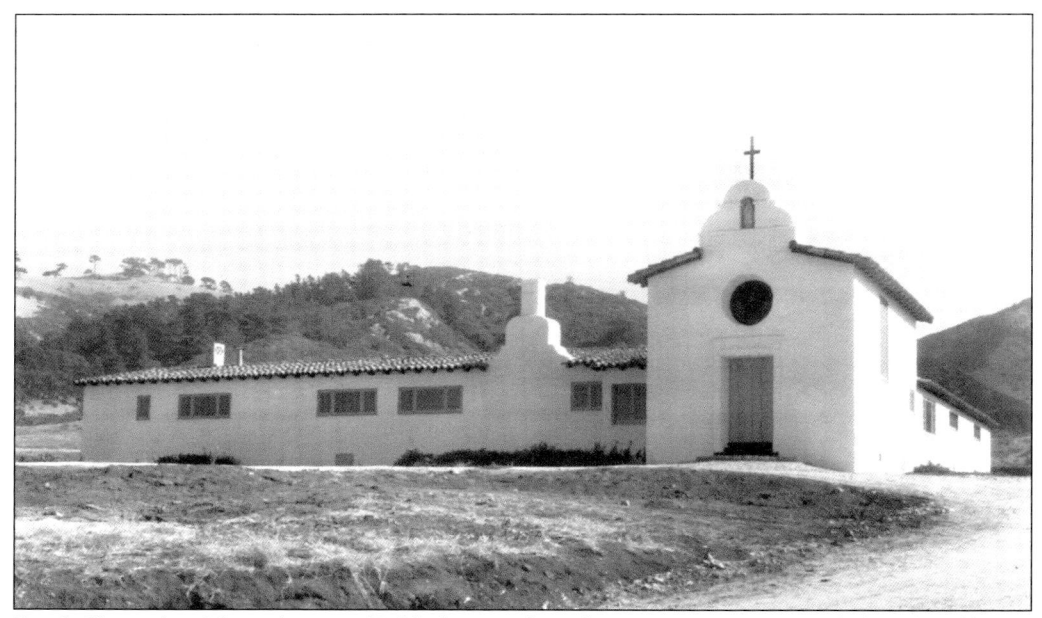

Funded by author Maria Antonia Field, this simple and austere Mission Revival chapel and living quarters were designed by artist Jo Mora for Field's friend and mentor, Sr. Mary Angelica. Sister Mary, in turn, donated the Monastery Beach property to the Carmelite Sisters of Notre Dame de Namur. (Photograph courtesy of Pat Hathaway, Historic California Views.)

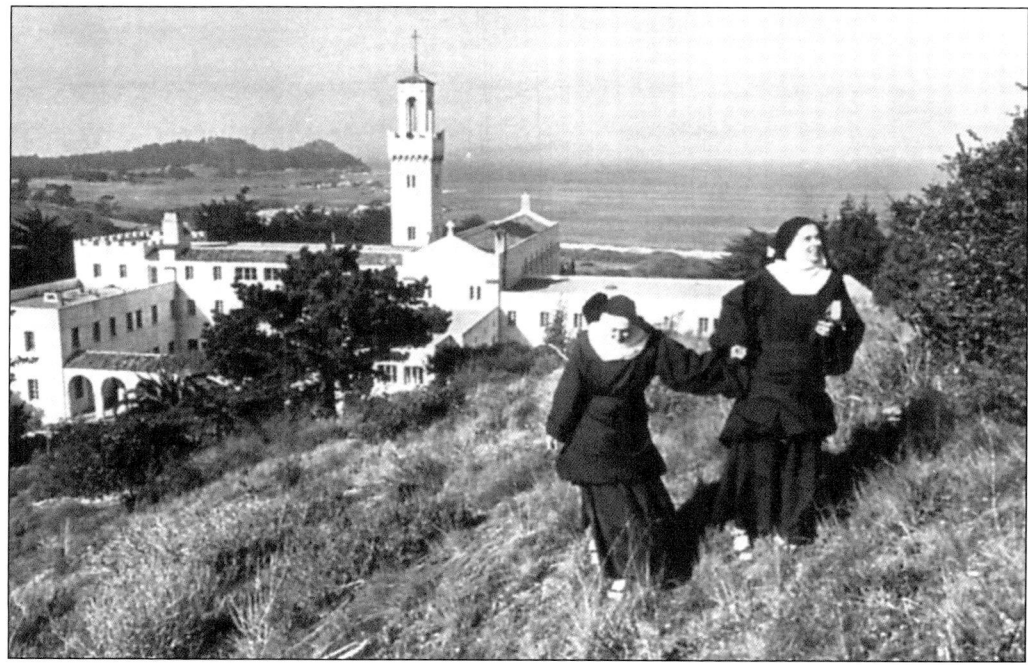

The beautiful concrete chapel of the Carmelite Sisters was designed along Spanish Romanesque lines by the Boston architectural firm of Maginnis and Walsh. The interior finishes include cut stone, marble, and terra cotta. The chapel is sited above Monastery Beach with impressive views of Point Lobos and the Pacific Ocean. (Photograph courtesy of the *San Francisco Examiner*.)

Eight

CARMEL MODERNISM

Carmel's introduction to the modern movement came appropriately through residential design in the "soft modernism" of William W. Wurster and others, including Harwell Hamilton Harris, in the mid-1930s. Master builder Hugh Comstock adopted the style in a Western ranch mode, leading him to develop his post-adobe construction method. Young modernist Jon Konigshofer was slated to superintend the construction of one of four houses to be designed by Frank Lloyd Wright on the Monterey Peninsula before World War II. Three were slated for Carmel, but only the Walker House was built. Wright's Usonian principles prevailed locally, in part through former apprentices including Mark Mills and Rowen Maiden, as well as admirers like Olaf Dahlstrand. Southern California architect Gordon Drake believed that architecture was without meaning unless it was used. The school he planned for Carmel was intended to find a way to make the purchase of good architectural design as normal as the purchase of any other service. By the time Henry Hill arrived in Carmel, he had already established himself as an architect fully capable of melding the traditions of European modernism with California's laid-back sensibility. Marcel Sedletzky was an artist whose medium was architecture. He turned geometric abstraction into habitable space replete with natural materials and great respect for the landscape setting. A number of fine modern architects and designers have worked and are still working in the Carmel area. The aesthetic threads connecting them to their predecessors include independence and creativity in working with form and materials, knowledge of the lessons of the past, curiosity about the possibilities of new or different technologies, and a profound respect for the environment.

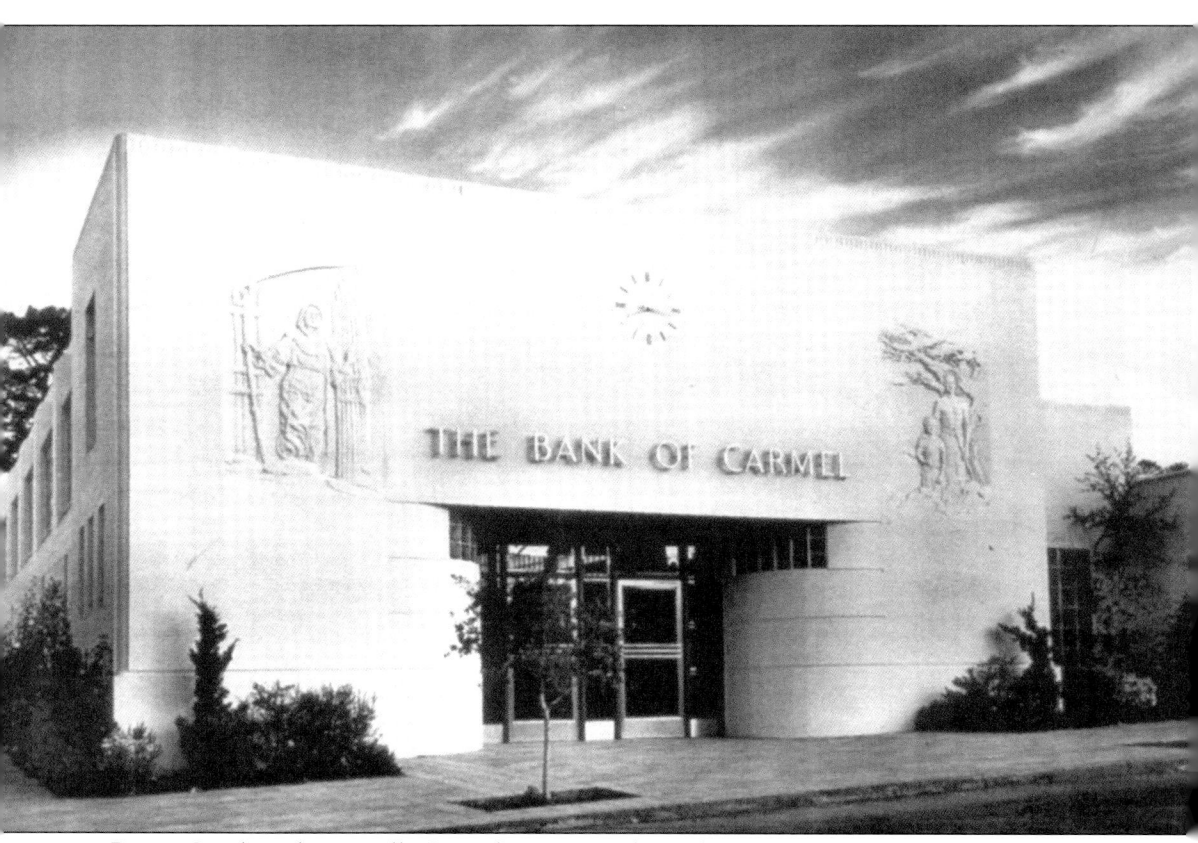

Barnet Segal was historically Carmel's most significant financier. In 1939, instead of the Spanish Colonial design that architects Swartz and Ryland prepared for the Bank of Carmel, the bank officials had them produce the art moderne building seen above. The bank's characteristic curving surfaces, glass-block windows, and speed lines define the style. The only concessions to Carmel's design traditions made by the stark concrete monolith were two wall relief sculptures by local artist Paul Whitman set into the building face. The iconic nature of the building established a precedent for displaying corporate identity through distinctive architectural expression that has been followed to the present. (Photograph courtesy of Betty Turnquist.)

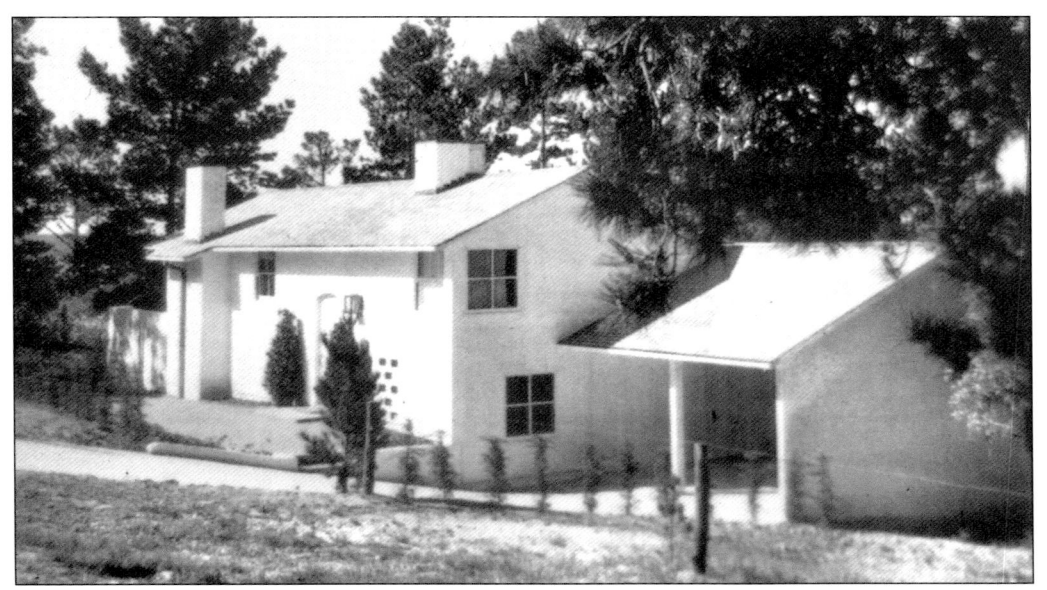

The 1933 E. C. Converse residence on Santa Fe Street was architect William W. Wurster's first residential design in Carmel. Its clean, simple lines and carefully positioned fenestration barely reveal the architect's hand in its creation. However, its highly practical and equally personal split-level open interior plan became a trademark of Wurster's future work. It won an AIA Honor Award in 1936. (Photograph courtesy of Fred Keeble, AIA.)

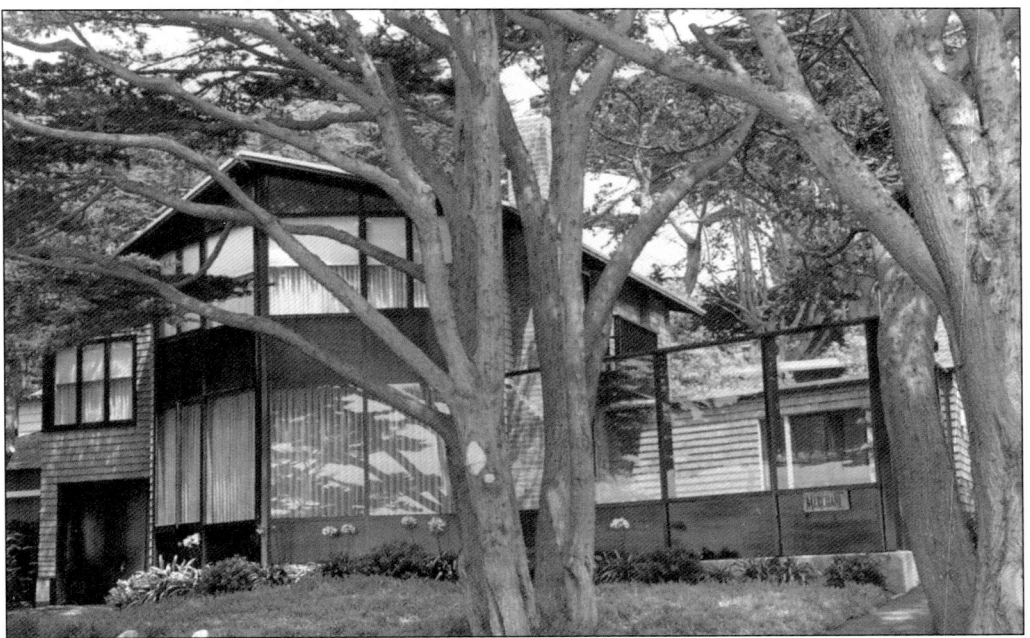

William Wurster's architectural firm created this two-story, wood-shingled Second Bay Area–style residence on Scenic Road in 1962 for Dr. Albert K. Merchant. Its angled facade with large plate-glass windows faces Carmel Beach. Its open plan is enhanced by the use of Wurster's laminated, prefabricated "Arch-Rib" ceiling trusses that span the rooms. (Photograph courtesy of the Monterey Public Library, California History Room Archives.)

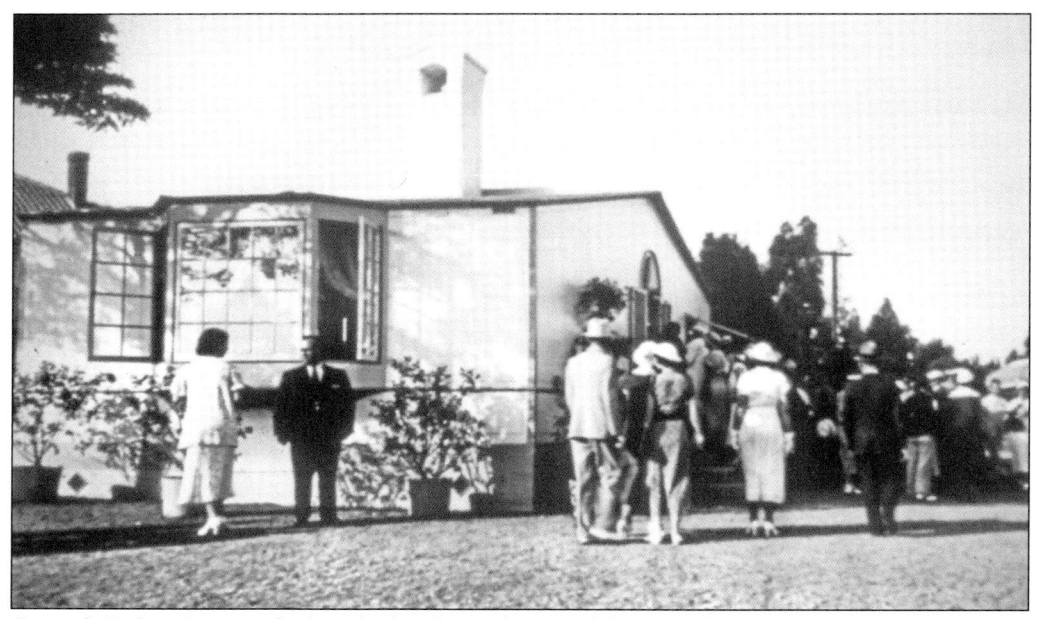

Carmel's Robert Stanton had worked with Southern California architect Wallace Neff in the early 1930s, developing a modern, low-cost, prefabricated, factory-built modular housing unit. It was named the Honeymoon Cottage by film star Mary Pickford. The first model home is seen above in Los Angeles. The project proved expensive, and few houses were constructed. (Photograph courtesy of the Robert Stanton.)

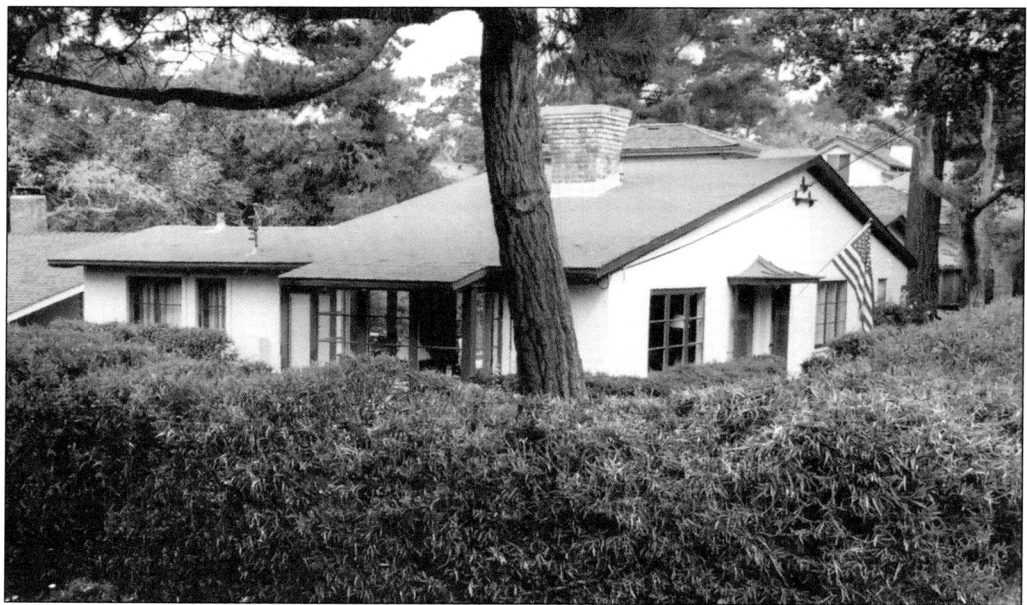

Robert Stanton employed the Honeymoon Cottage design for three houses on the Monterey Peninsula in the late 1930s. Two were built in Carmel. Almost postmodern in expression, the residence, located at Dolores Street and Eleventh Avenue, is still in the family of former Stanford philosophy professor Dr. Sinclair Kerby-Miller and is listed in the California Register of Historic Resources. (Photograph courtesy of John Kerby-Miller.)

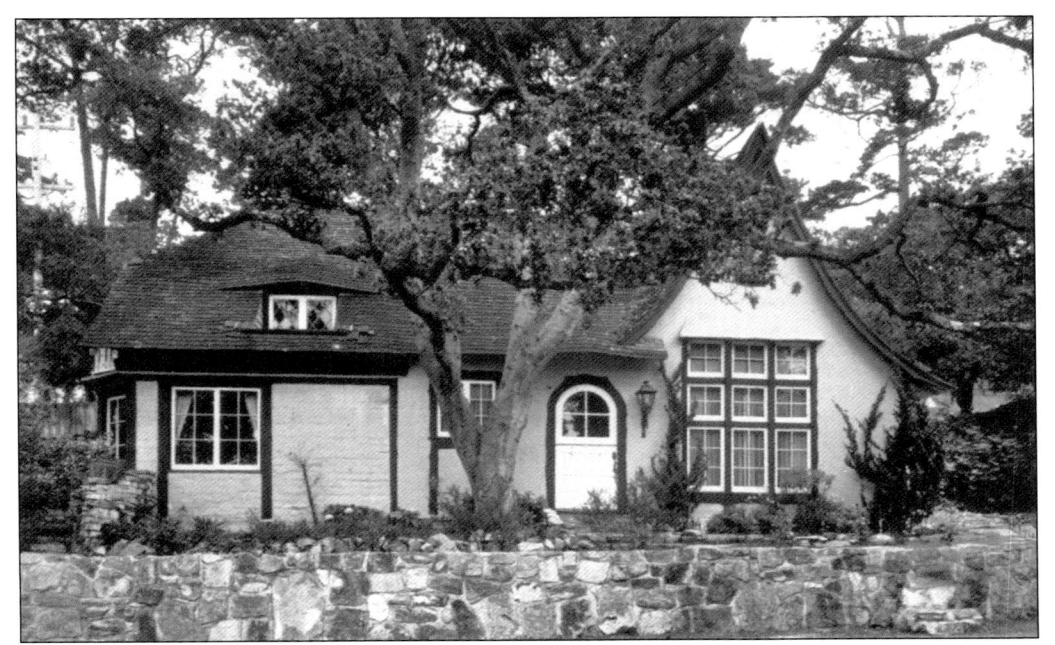

In the mid-1930s, Hugh Comstock built an addition to his home (left of the oak tree) employing an inexpensive new method of construction from available local building materials. He used modified timber framing in-filled with waterproof adobe bricks. He called the system post-adobe, introducing his own variation of the ranch-house style to the Monterey Peninsula. (Photograph by Morley Baer; courtesy of Monterey Peninsula College.)

Housing construction grew at a rapid rate in the Carmel area following World War II. In 1948, Hugh Comstock published a how-to booklet on post-adobe construction that saw a considerable expansion of the building type throughout the Monterey area. The publication also addressed a steel-frame adobe building method and showed examples of flat-roofed models. (Photograph from the author's collection.)

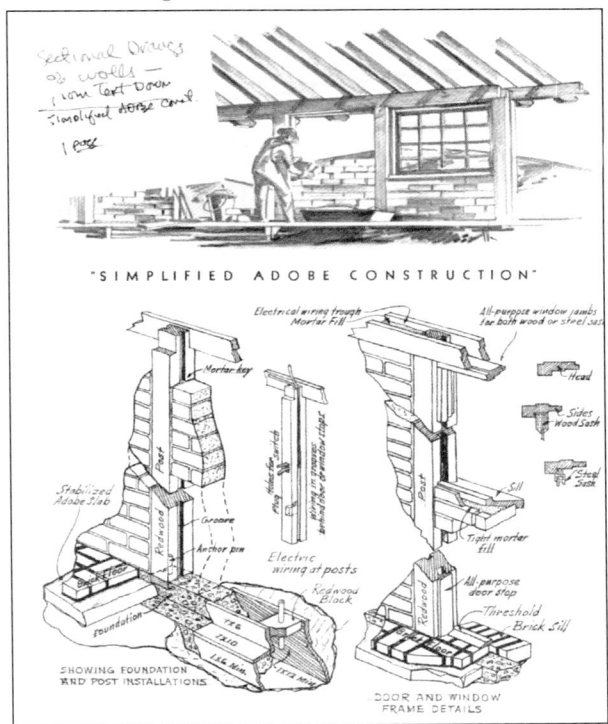

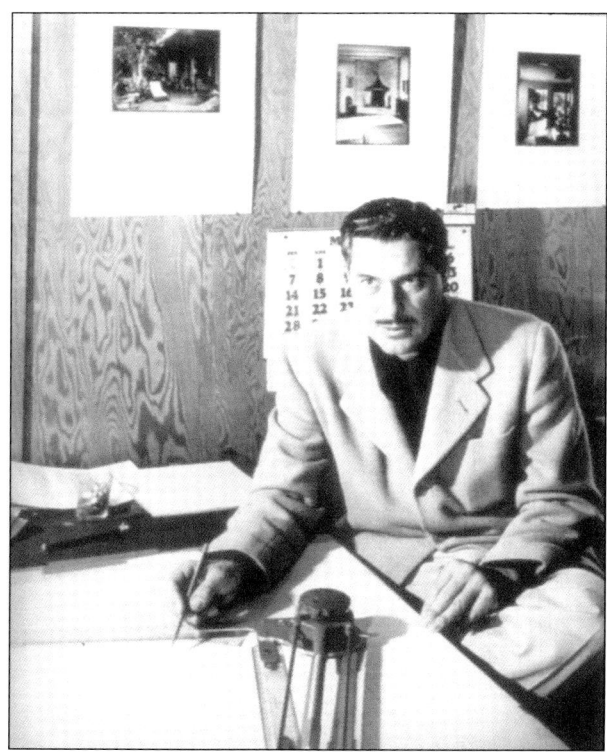

Noted building designer Jon Konigshofer first worked in Carmel as a draftsman for M. J. Murphy in 1937. He went into private practice a year later and is credited with designing over 200 buildings on the Monterey Peninsula. Working with realtor Elizabeth M. White, Konigshofer designed Sand and Sea in 1941, the first modernist subdivision in Carmel. (Photograph courtesy of Jon Konigshofer.)

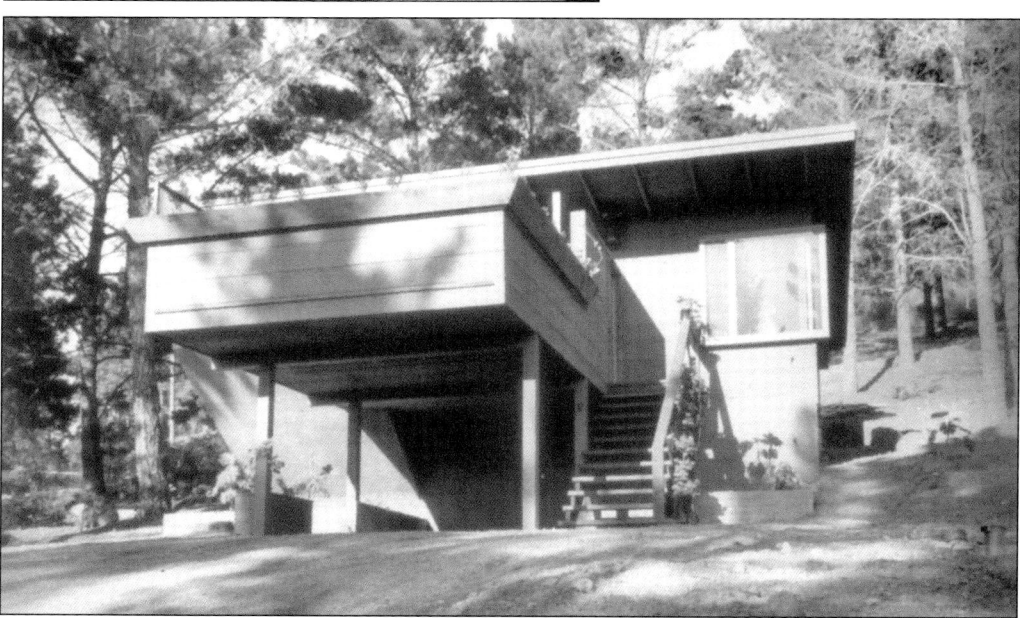

Jon Konigshofer copyrighted the design for his signature Hillside House in the early 1950s and rented plans with strict provisions to protect his designs from "tract house duplication." His small residences could be constructed and furnished for under $10,000. Hillside lots were inexpensive at the time and often afforded the best views as well as greater privacy. (Photograph courtesy of Jon Konigshofer.)

Architect Robert Jones came to Carmel in 1936 to work for Robert Stanton, who he had known at UC Berkeley. He began designing house plans for contractors on his own in 1939. By the end of World War II, Jones's office was almost as large as Stanton's. Jones's employees included a number of individuals who would go on to become significant architects in the region. (Photograph by Morley Baer; courtesy of Monterey Peninsula College.)

Architect Robert Jones framed this commercial property on Sixth Avenue near Lincoln Street to read as if its roof was being lifted off the building envelope. Jones's 1950 design for the Monterey Peninsula Airport was the modernist icon for that era, earning praise from Frank Lloyd Wright and a major design award from the Smithsonian Institution. (Photograph by Morley Baer; courtesy of Monterey Peninsula College.)

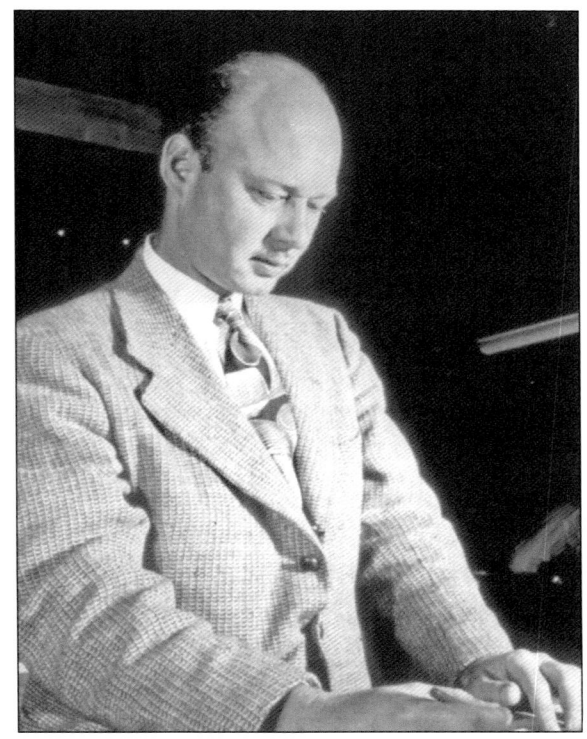

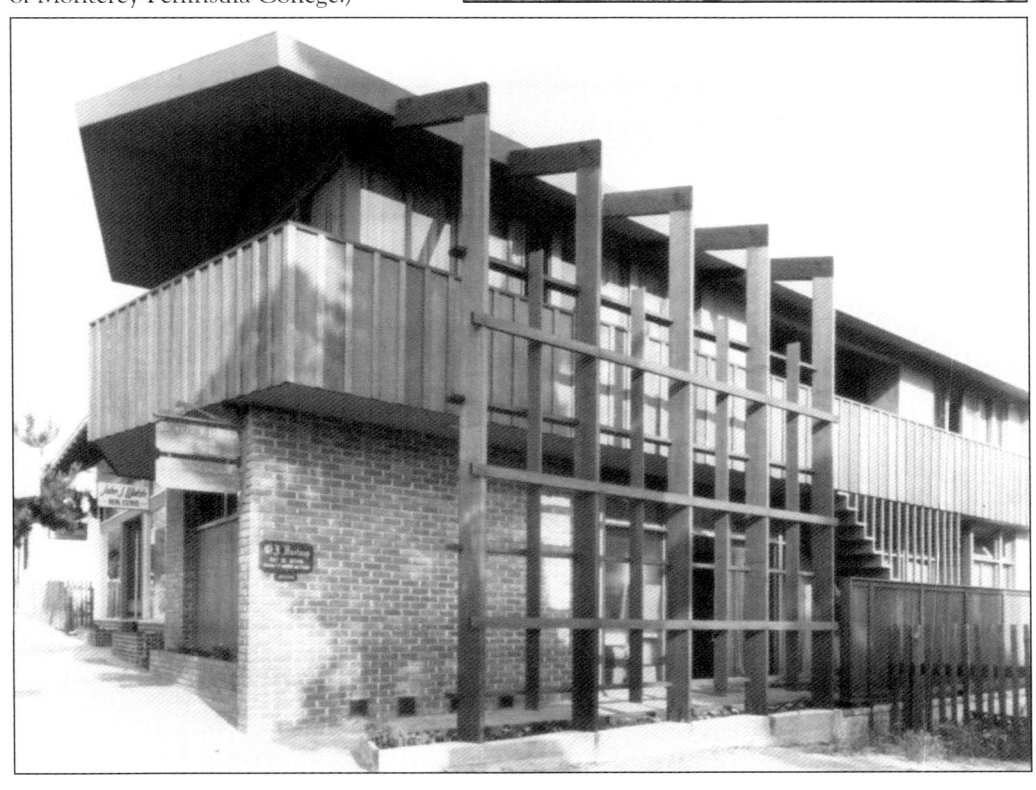

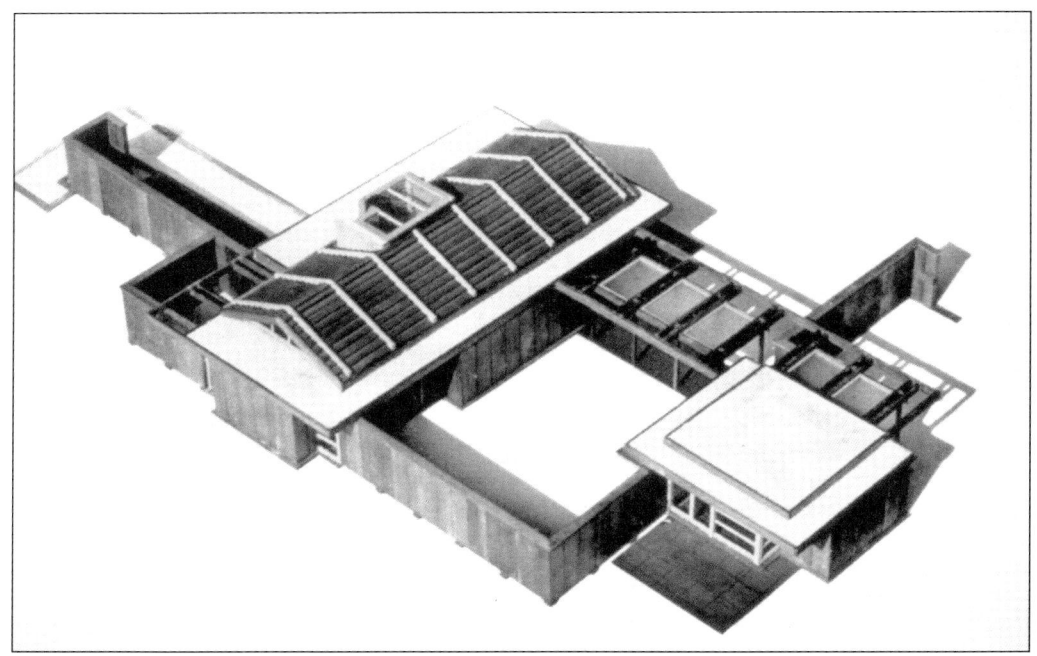

Gordon Drake was an exceptional young architect from Southern California whose post–World War II residential designs emphasized indoor-outdoor continuity and modular construction. In 1948, he came to Carmel to establish a comprehensive school of design through his working architectural office. The model for the office/school complex is seen above. (Photograph courtesy of Reinhold Publishing Corporation, New York.)

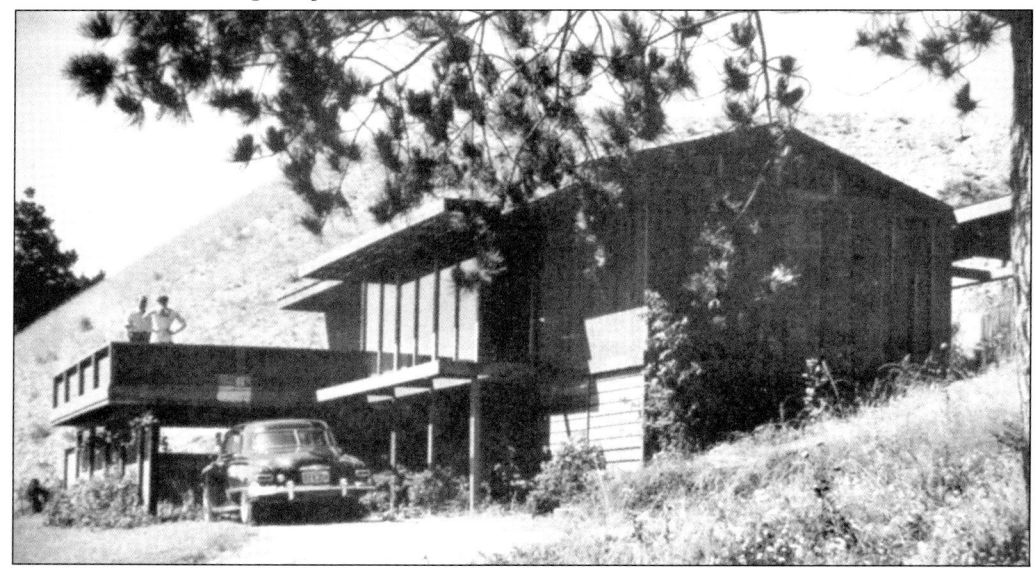

Gordon Drake built a small speculative house on Flanders Way in 1949. He employed three diagonally stepped modular units in the hillside design. They included a sun deck, a main living area, and a kitchen/bath unit. The supporting structural system was left exposed. The architect died in a skiing accident in 1952, before his design-school dream could be realized. (Photograph by Morley Baer; courtesy of Monterey Peninsula College.)

Albert Henry Hill and Jack Kruse met in the office of Eric Mendelsohn, setting up their own firm in 1948. Hill was the creative force in the office, and Kruse handled the engineering. Hill designed a striking vacation home on Lopez in Carmel in 1961. Kruse and another associate liked it so much that they purchased two adjoining lots and had Hill design homes for them. (Site plan courtesy of Heather Hill.)

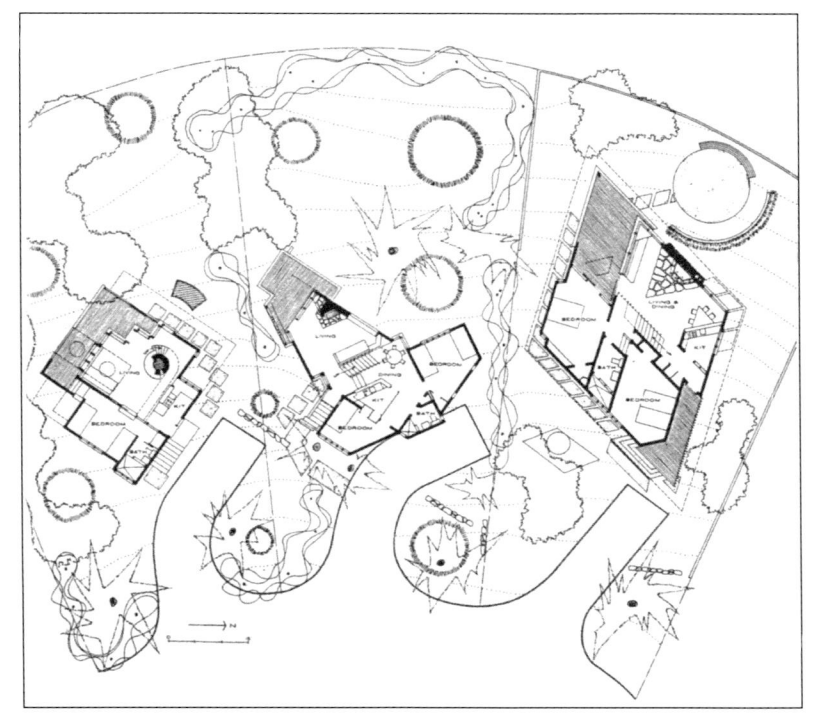

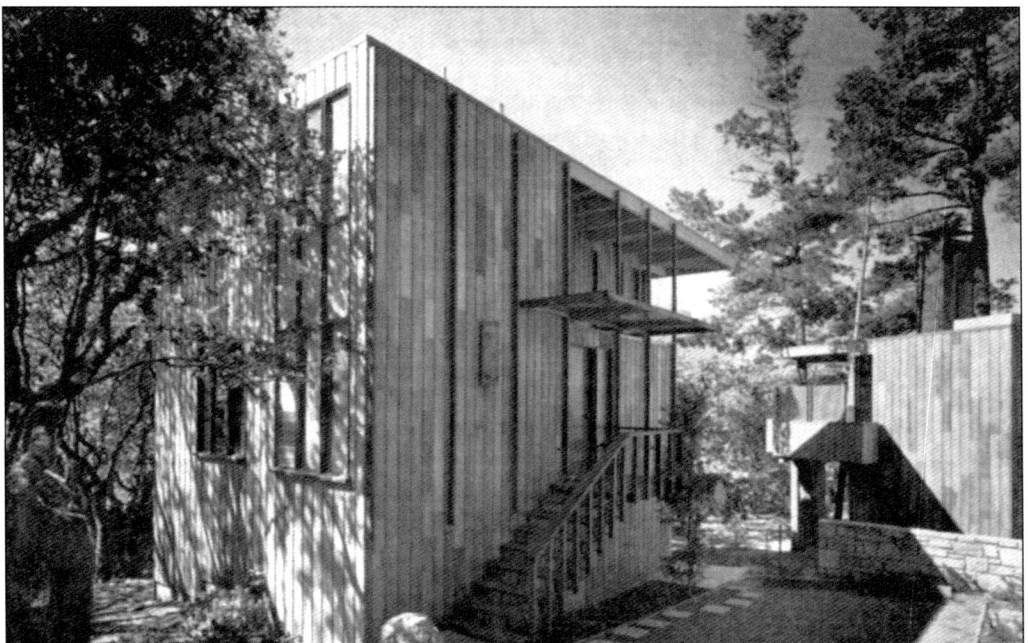

Following the principles of Bay Area Regionalist tradition, Henry Hill gave first consideration to preserving the natural setting of his somewhat pie-shaped, downward-sloping lot. By raising his house above ground level, views of Carmel Point and Point Lobos could be obtained. He emphasized the verticality of the building with natural cedar siding. Its cubic shape derives from its orientation on the lot. (Photograph courtesy of Heather Hill.)

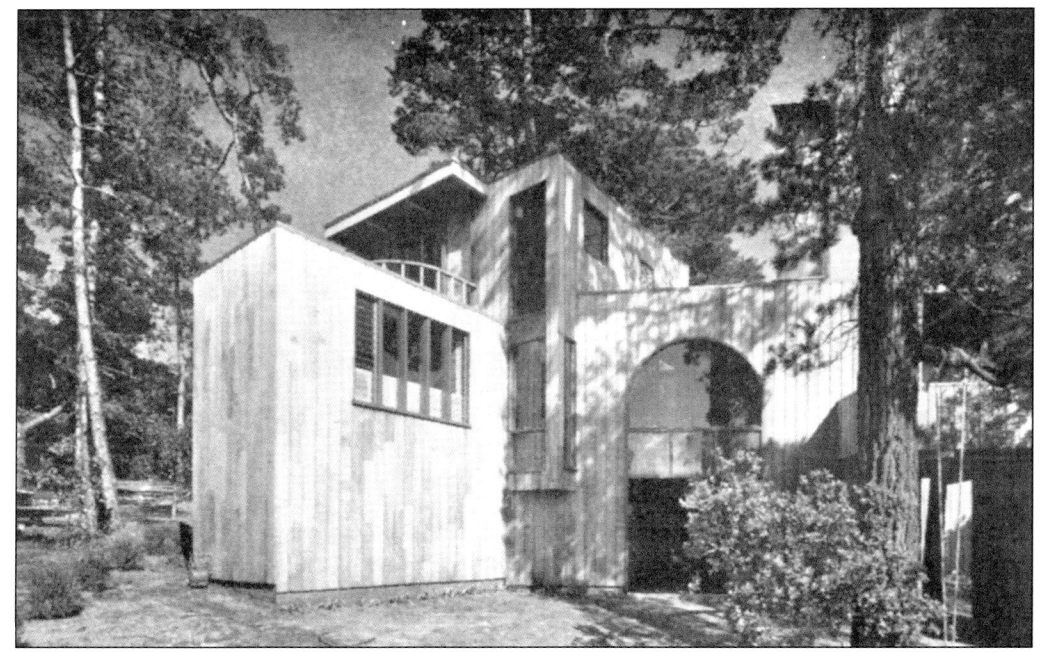

The 1962 Kruse house is the connecting element for the three residential designs on Lopez and the most visually abstract, combining the tall cubic volumes of the Hill house with the angular plan of the Cosmas house to the north. Issues driving the design were lot shape and topography, available ocean views, and privacy. (Photograph courtesy of Veverka Architects, San Francisco.)

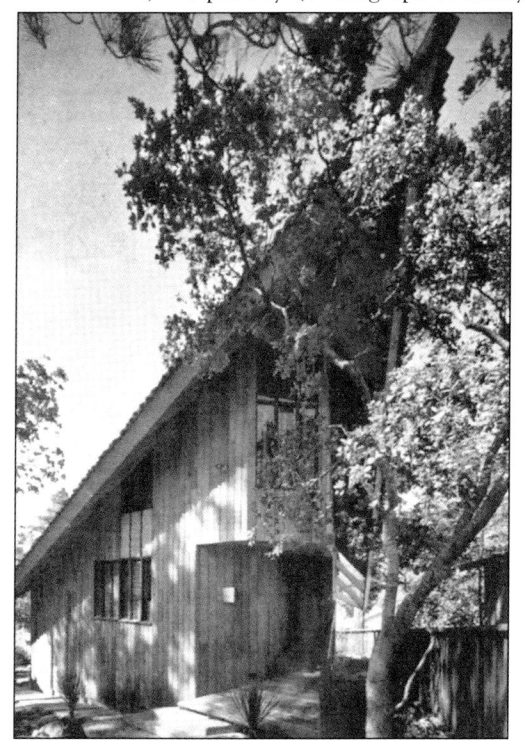

Henry Hill looked to Frank Lloyd Wright for the massive, folded, square-roof surface that contains the 1962 Cosmas house. The 30/60 degree grid for the angular plan corresponds to the axis of the major viewsheds. Hill lived permanently in Carmel after 1971, designing a number of homes locally, and served on the planning commission. (Photograph courtesy of Heather Hill.)

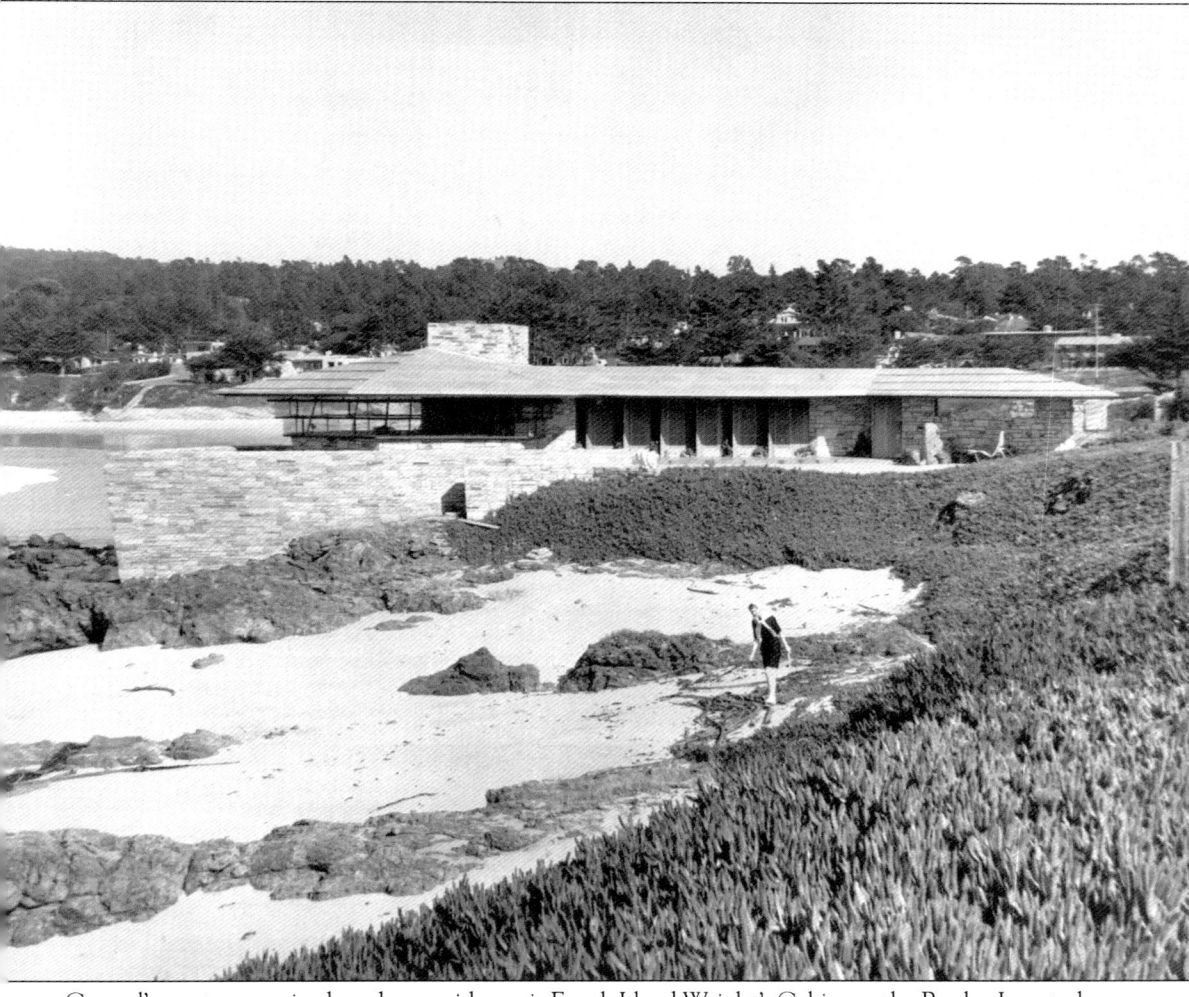

Carmel's most recognized modern residence is Frank Lloyd Wright's Cabin on the Rocks. Located on Carmel Point, it has the appearance of a ship whose Carmel-stone prow is cutting the waves. The stepped glazing of the windows allows for easy drainage and contains small sliding vents for air circulation. Miles Bain was the contractor. Wright designed it in 1951 for Della Walker, who asked the master builder to create a house "as enduring as the rocks but as transparent and charming as the waves." She got her wish. (Photograph by Steve Gann; courtesy Monterey Peninsula College.)

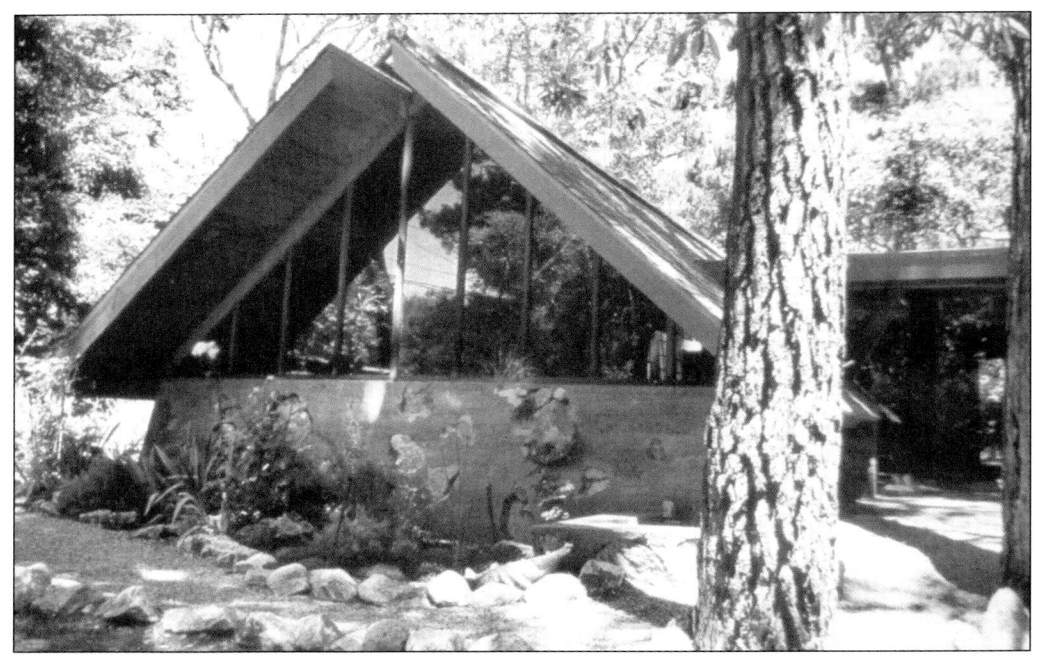

Architect Mark Mills's parents occupied this speculative house he designed for Mrs. Clinton Walker at Mission Street and Thirteenth Avenue. Mills's imaginative design skill at successfully integrating such an abstract plan comfortably into its landscape setting is in keeping with the Carmel tradition of architectural innovation by independent designer-builders. (Photograph by Morley Baer; courtesy of Monterey Peninsula College.)

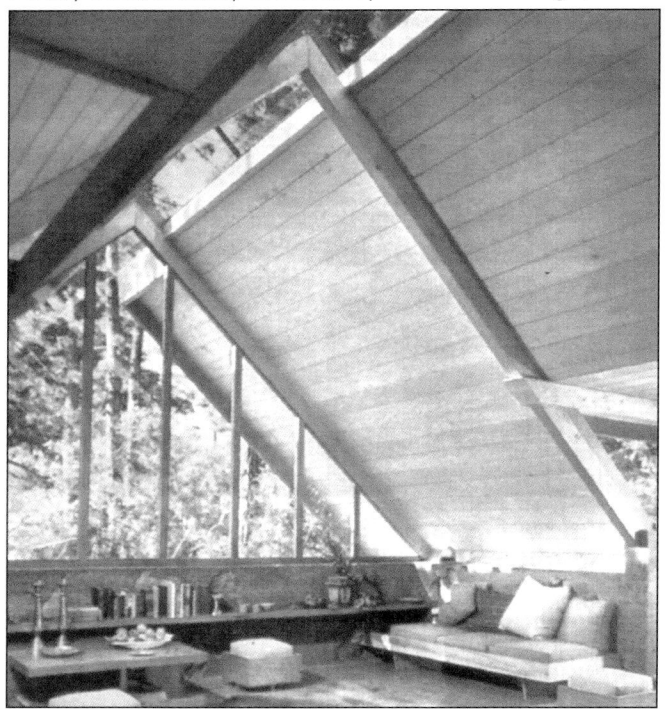

Mark Mills split and glazed the ridgeline of this small house to allow natural sunlight into its interior. In the mid-1950s, Margaret and Nathaniel Owings (of Skidmore, Owings, and Merrill) visited the residence and were impressed by the treatment of the A-frame roof and skylight, which with Mark Mills's help they incorporated into the design of their Big Sur home, Wild Bird. (Photograph courtesy of John Saar.)

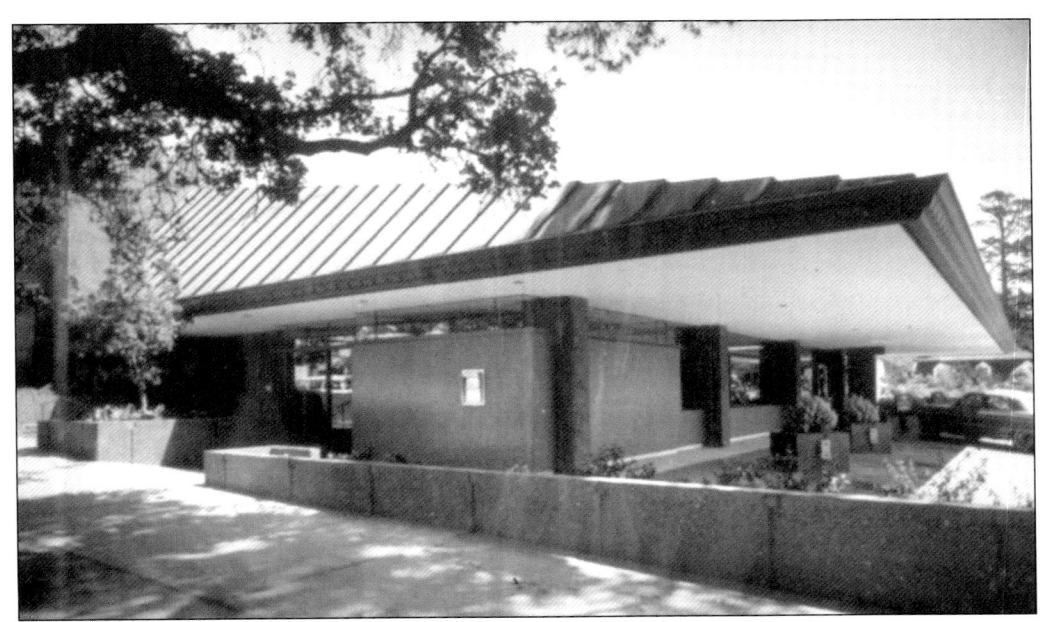

Architect Olaf Dahlstrand was influenced by Frank Lloyd Wright's organic design. The massive roof system of his 1964 bank building, anchored into a textured monolithic concrete wall, has wide overhanging eaves that float above the bank's glazed exterior skin. Dahlstrand, like many Carmel architects and builders, served both on the planning commission and city council. (Photograph by Morley Baer; courtesy of Monterey Peninsula College.)

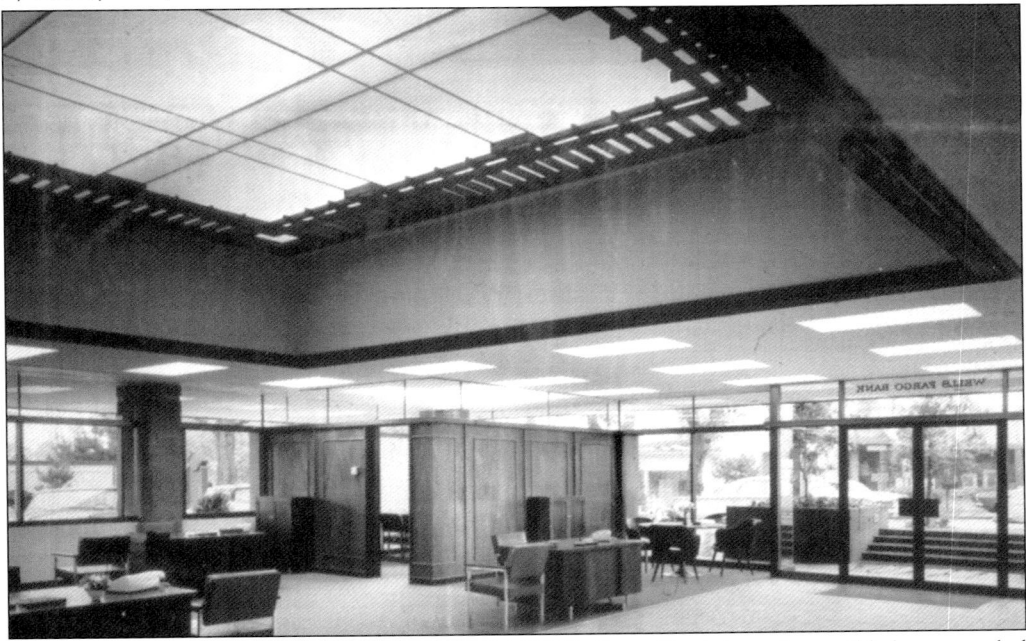

The open interior space of Olaf Dahlstrand's 1964 Wells Fargo Bank is made possible by concealed cantilevered trusses springing from the monolithic north wall. The delicate wood tracery and recessed lighting of the textured earth-toned ceiling is reminiscent of elements found in Wright's prairie houses. (Photograph by Morley Baer; courtesy of Monterey Peninsula College.)

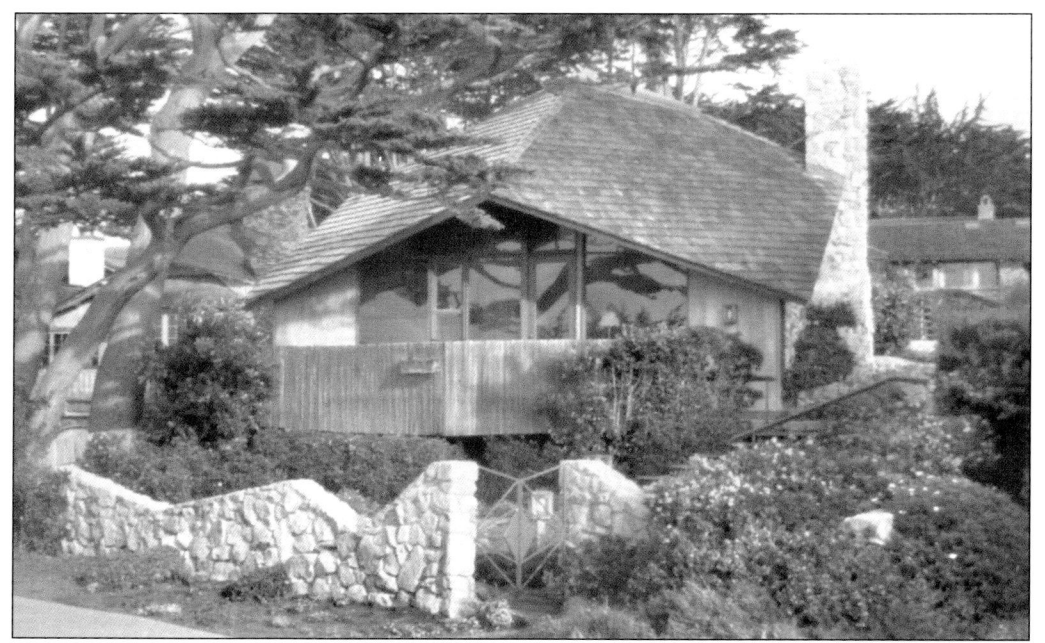

In 1964, architect Marcel Sedletsky's client asked for a Tudor cottage for her Scenic Road parcel. What she got was a sculptural exercise in geometry. It hugs the ground and is housed within gray cedar siding with a folded wood-shake roof system. Sedletsky's work, according to his biographer Bill Staggs, "was a blend of Le Corbusier's forceful modernism and Frank Lloyd Wright's organic fusion of housing form with place." (Photograph by the author.)

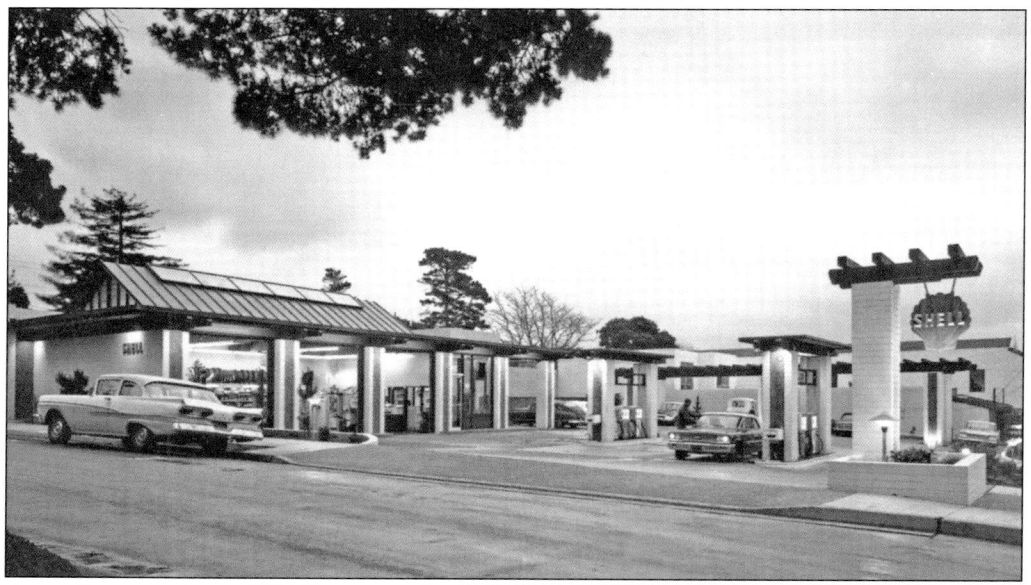

According to architect Will Shaw, in order to be a good building, it must show concern for artistic integrity, have sympathy for its environment—whether natural or urban—and have structural expressiveness showing the function and effect of the building. All these elements are present in his award-winning 1964 Shell gas station at San Carlos Street and Fifth Avenue. (Photograph by Morley Baer; courtesy of Shaw Architecture Planning, Inc.)

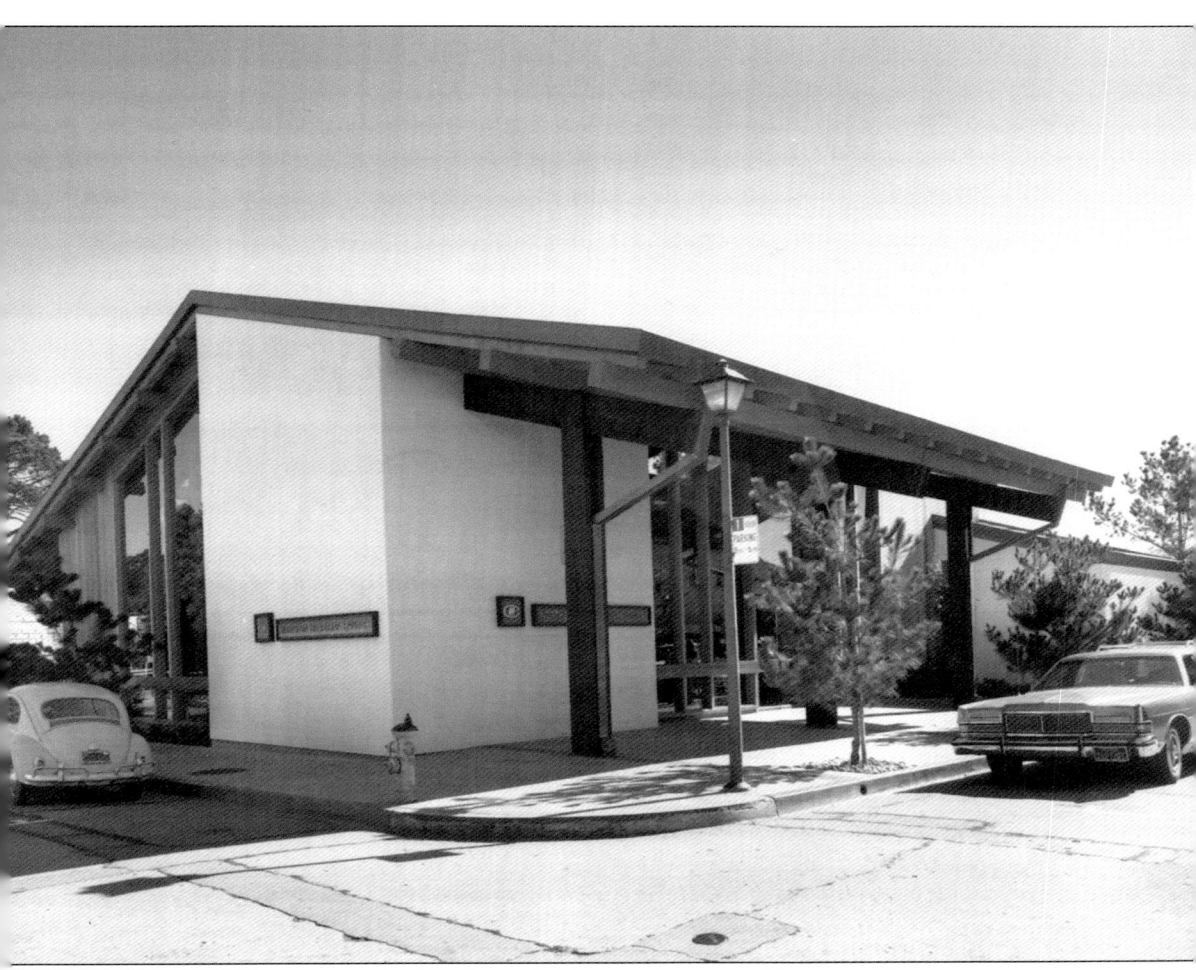

The corporate expression of the Northern California Savings and Loan building is an excellent example of Second Bay Area Regionalist design by Walter Burde with Will Shaw. It exhibits the use of natural materials, exposed roof framing, dramatic structural innovation, and the simple open plan characteristic of the style. Burde's work combines tradition and the elements of industry seeking to unite formal, technical, and social ideas. (Photograph by Morley Baer; courtesy of Shaw Architecture Planning, Inc.)

DISCOVER THOUSANDS OF LOCAL HISTORY BOOKS FEATURING MILLIONS OF VINTAGE IMAGES

Arcadia Publishing, the leading local history publisher in the United States, is committed to making history accessible and meaningful through publishing books that celebrate and preserve the heritage of America's people and places.

Find more books like this at
www.arcadiapublishing.com

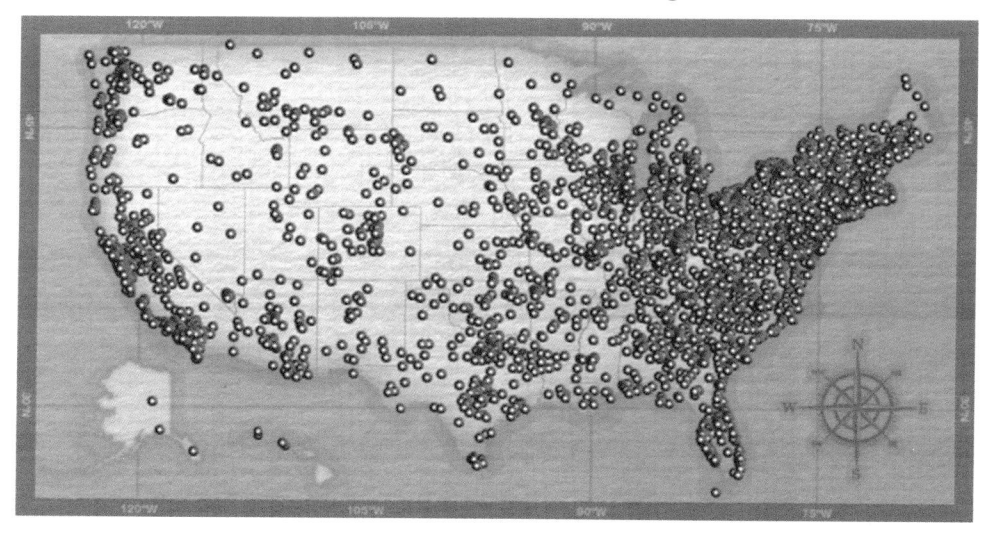

Search for your hometown history, your old stomping grounds, and even your favorite sports team.

Consistent with our mission to preserve history on a local level, this book was printed in South Carolina on American-made paper and manufactured entirely in the United States. Products carrying the accredited Forest Stewardship Council (FSC) label are printed on 100 percent FSC-certified paper.

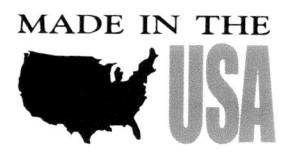

MADE IN THE USA